Office Workers' Survival Handbook

A guide to fighting health hazards in the office

If you have any comments, disagreements, corrections or descriptions of actions around any aspect of health and office work, we would be interested in hearing about them. In this way we hope to put groups of office workers fighting similar problems in contact with each other.
Please write to *Women and Work Hazards Group*, BSSRS, 9 Poland Street, London W1.

Acknowledgements

Thank you to all those who read the drafts, helped me with difficult bits and raised the funds to publish this book. I am especially grateful to Evelyn Barker, Alan Dalton, Gail Chester, Debbie Glass, Mike Hughes, Greg Lucas, Tony Fletcher, Charlie Clutterbuck, Charmian Kenner, Clare Dennis, David Albury, Jude Connor, Pete Marsden, Greg Cohn, Seb Schmoller, Rosaleen Shiels and Malcolm Tomkins. Thanks also to all members of the Women and Work Hazards Group and to the many office workers who talked to me about their experiences. Most of their names have had to be changed in the text to protect them where necessary. Many thanks to everyone who donated funds to help produce this book and for financial sponsorship from:

    APEX Blackheath TUPS
    ASTMS 992 Branch
    ASTMS Division 5
    Birmingham Hazards Group
    CPSA London Broad Left
    Leeds Trades Union, Community and Information Centre
    Northern Ireland Public Service Alliance
    Politics of Health Group
    Women and Work Hazards Group

This book was researched and written by Marianne Craig.
Typesetting by Rosemary Ahmed, Printacolour(TU), 101 Praed Street, London W2.
Front cover design and layout by Evelyn Barker, 232 Mare Street, London E8 (01-986 5861).
Printed by the Russell Press, 45 Gamble Street, Nottingham (0602 784505)
Distributed by Trade Union Book Service, 265 Seven Sisters Road, London N4.
Published by BSSRS Publications Ltd, 9 Poland Street, London W1 (01-437 2728).
Contents copyright © February 1981
ISBN 0 9502541 5 0

Contents

*Fiona McNally, author of a book about office workers, tells of
her experience as a temp in a credit company:*
*'...With minimal understanding of the filing system, and no idea
whatsoever of the nature or functioning of the company, I
struggled to muster the process of filing into bays. This bleak
situation was not helped by the fact that the filing system
contained many anomalies which led to a great deal of mis-
filing and consequently made the task even more difficult.
Physically the work was very tiring since it involved reaching up
to very high shelves and crouching very low in order to reach the
bottom ones. Had I not been very tall it could have been much
worse, for many girls had to make use of the solitary stool in
order to file in the top shelves. Sitting on the floor proved to be
one of the least tedious ways of performing the job, though at
great peril to one's tights, and on one occasion resulted in my
having to have a number of large splinters removed from my
bottom by a nurse. It would be hard to overstate the dreadful
conditions of the work — dirt, splinters, laddered tights, aching
backs and feet — all were part and parcel of this tedious
occupation. On top of all this, there was not even the
customary satisfaction of getting through the work because not
only was there no end to the backlog of filing, but in addition
it was impossible to file a great deal of it on account of the chaos
and disorder in the bays.'* (Women for Hire, *A Study of the
Female Office Worker,* London 1979, p. 163)

*When you get home you feel tired and tense and irritable. All the
girls here complain about headaches and waking up in the
morning with puffy eyes. Sometimes when you're working you
get very dizzy and have to have a break. A friend of mine went to
have her eyes tested because the headaches were getting so bad.
The optician said she had long vision so it's very bad for her to be
working so near the screen (it's about 18 inches away). He said
she'd have to wear glasses if she went on working under these
conditions. He'd been getting people in practically every day
from working with these things. (Leeds Trade Union and
Community Resource Centre* Interview 1978)

Introduction

Look around your office. Do people look well? Or do you all feel tired at the end of the day, exhausted at the end of the week? Do you get headaches, sore throats, upset stomachs, rashes, backache? It's probably your job that's doing it. If we take the definition of health used by the World Health Organisation, how many office workers can say they are healthy:

> 'Health is a state of complete physical, mental and social well-being, not merely an absence of disease and infirmity.'

If you work in an office you know it's not the easy life of tea breaks and chats that many people believe. Offices are often tiring and stressful places to work, and have their health hazards — physical, chemical and emotional. In any office you're likely to find some of the following: inadequate seating, space or lighting, dust and fumes, bad ventilation, fire hazards, noisy machinery, trailing wires. Many workplaces are small and gloomy, often overcrowded and airless, particularly if it's a converted attic or basement as so many offices are. Yet modern offices blocks bring problems too. They usually have uniform, constant lighting, accompanied by air conditioning throughout the year — perpetually artificial conditions. The office 'machine age' has also created new hazards: chemical fumes, electrical and mechanical risks, stress from working at the pace of a machine, eyestrain from 'screen-gazing'. As thousands of office workers now have to work at night to keep the machines running, there are also the health problems of shiftwork — digestive disorders, ulcers, exhaustion. Office work is changing fast with the introduction of new technology and stress is on the increase, with the fear of the unknown and the fear of unemployment.

Do you and your colleagues have complaints like these about your working conditions? What is being done about them? How could things be improved?

This book aims to help you look at your office through new eyes, pinpoint what is wrong, and decide what to do about it. It is written for *everyone* who is concerned about their working environment, not just for those who are trade union safety representatives. It is mainly addressed to women office workers because they are the vast majority. But it goes without saying that health hazards affect men who work in offices too.

Hazardous conditions are found in all types of workplace. It has been estimated that each year in Britain 2000 people are killed in accidents at work or die from injuries received there, 1,000 more die of recognised industrial diseases, a million people are injured or off work with industrial disease for more than three days, and ten million people need first aid for injuries at work.* The total effect on our health is an unknown, since so many long-term effects go unrecognised.

Offices on the whole may be cleaner and safer than factories, and the occupational accidents and disease perhaps less dramatic, *but that does not mean they should be taken less seriously.* While the hazards of office work may not kill you on the spot, they do cause serious problems if you have to face them day after day. The Alfred Marks Employment Bureau did a survey in 1974 which they called 'Machine Age Girls' and found that 46 per cent of those who replied suffered from headaches, 38 per cent suffered backache, 33 per cent suffered eyestrain and 15 per cent wrist strain.

Information about the many health hazards afflicting office workers is collected together in this book for the first time. Up till now these have usually been ignored or dismissed as trivial. Because they have not been taken seriously, what little has been written has focused on the more dramatic accidents and injuries. But what about the accumulated effect of working in a stressful environment, with many hidden hazards that can gradually break down your health? Much more research is needed on the long-term effects of office processes and substances. What, for example, is the effect on body and mind of operating a photocopying machine for eight hours a day, forty hours a week? The medical and scientific professions and the manufacturers have a lot to answer for on the low priority they give to occupational ill-health and its prevention.

This book emphasises repeatedly that you have a *right* to a safe and healthy job. But more than that, you have a right to work in a stress-free job, where there is flexibility and where you have control over what you are doing. You have a right to work in comfort with good facilities such as canteens, rest rooms and nurseries. In an age when they have sent men to the moon, there is no acceptable reason why these basic rights should not be ours.

In our society companies pay for safety out of their profits, while government offices aim always to keep costs to a minimum. People are fired, services are cut back, and workers' health is put bottom of the list so that, we are told, 'the economy' can be made well again. We have a system where profit is always put before health. Some people try to argue that 'we are all in this together'. This is not so. There is a *conflict of interest* between you and your employer over health and safety, just as there is over wages. That is why workers always have to fight for better conditions, to wheel and deal, to struggle and negotiate. The better organised you are, the more you'll win.

* From *The Hazards of Work* by Patrick Kinnersly

And this book is about getting better organised. You can use it as both a practical and a political tool. You could read it right through, as a catalogue of hazards with examples of how people have fought against them, but it is also a reference book to guide you through a particular problem — there is a subject index at the end. Every chapter focuses on the tools available — legal, practical and organisational — to help you fight health hazards, and the final chapter is on strategy, a step-by-step example of how to go about it. Another practical guide is contained in the checklists at the end of every chapter, which anyone can use to check how safe or unsafe their office is. Appendix 1 contains a sample questionnaire to help you carry out a simple health survey in your office, to find out what symptoms people are suffering from. This is a good way to begin doing something about health hazards at work.

Becoming better organised is not just a practical task, it is also about deciding on your own standards, and thinking about how things came to be as they are — and how you would like them to be. For this, the chapters on the history of office work and on how to organise should be particularly useful, as well as information elsewhere on new technology, together with the boxes and illustrations scattered throughout the text. This is not the sort of health and safety manual that tells you to avoid tripping over the telephone wires for that approach is based on the belief that accidents and health hazards are results of individual carelessness, to be solved by individual workers taking greater care. On the contrary, this book sets out to show that the cause of most health hazards is the economic system and management practices that control how your offices are designed and run. So the only way to cut back these hazards is for office workers to organise themselves and take control over their own working environment.

Throughout, this book emphasises how interconnected are all aspects of our lives, how your social class and your sex affect your state of health as much as what job you do...which is itself determined by your social class and sex. Writing this book came out of that interaction of personal experience with politics which is so vital in bringing change. I have been an office worker for five years, in Britain and abroad, a socialist and a feminist for ten years, and now work for a Community Health Council — in an office! I am a member of the Women and Work Hazards Group, which is affiliated to the British Society for Social Responsibility in Science. The members of the BSSRS are committed to a radical reassessment of the role of science and technology in society, at work and wherever health is at risk.

Office work is dangerous to your health, but where you can trace the cause of ill-health and organise against it, it can be prevented.

Marianne Craig
London, December 1980

Office Work

1 Stress

Do you get headaches and 'bad nerves'? Do you get a lot of indigestion or stomach ache? Do you sometimes feel irritable or depressed? Do you find it hard to relax in your time off because you're stiff and tense? The pressures on you at work and at home are probably the cause. Everyone's body reacts differently to pressure and everyone has his or her breaking points. While some stress is normal to life, if stress is repeated or prolonged the body becomes worn out and illnesses can result: ulcers, high blood pressure, heart diseases, nervous breakdown.

A great deal of time and money has been spent on research into the stress suffered by executives and managers — yet one researcher concluded that an executive's risk of coronary heart disease is related to over-indulgence in food, tobacco and alcohol and lack of exercise.[1] By contrast, very little research has been undertaken into the effect of pressure on people *working* in offices, services, catering and factories. What evidence there is suggests that stress is more common among working people than in the boardroom.

In 1977 the National Institute for Safety and Health (a US government department) examined the health records of 22,000 workers in 130 occupations. They found the 12 most stressful jobs to be:

1 *labourer*
2 *secretary*
3 *inspector*
4 *clinical laboratory technician*
5 *office manager*
6 *foreman*
7 *manager/administrator*
8 *waitress/waiter*
9 *machine operator*
10 *farm owner*
11 *mine operator*
12 *painter (not artist)*

*These are in order; secretary was found to be the second most stressful job of all. (*National Safety News, *USA, Jan 1979)*

In a massive study of 270,000 employees of a large American corporation, researchers found that the incidence of first disabling coronary heart disease was 2½ times greater among skilled manual workers than among executive grades. The rate *increased* as you went down the occupational grades.[2] The US National Heart, Lung and Blood Institute, found that women in clerical jobs suffer twice the incidence rate of heart disease of all other working women, including housewives.[3]

Countless office staff work in huge bureaucracies, which have been described as 'honeycombs of depression'. The work you're doing can make you sick: work under pressure of time, to keep up with production quotas or deadlines, work that 'drives you crazy' because it's so boring. All these and more produce stress and anxiety. Office workers frequently keep tablets in their desks to get through the days, or take frequent days off. They then go to their doctor, where the problem is treated as a personal one, in isolation. The doctor probably won't ask about your job. He or she certainly won't ask about the symptoms suffered by your co-workers. Yet *many* people in the same job will also be suffering from the strains. Stress has *social* causes and can therefore be prevented. It's not 'just one of those things'. So often doctors simply dole out tranquillisers. They're too busy to try to seek the causes. All too frequently the early symptoms of stress — nervousness, headaches, irritability, and so on are written off as 'female problems', 'menopause' or 'your imagination'. Beware especially of company doctors, who may suggest that you're 'malingering'. (Company doctors are often not primarily interested in your health: one anti-union publication commissioned by a management organisation and entitled *White Collar Restiveness: A Growing Challenge* suggested that a counselling service is a good way of finding out what employees are thinking. It pointed out that 'doctors and nurses constitute an unusually good source of information about the ebb and flow of dissatisfaction')[4]

When suffering stress symptoms, some people feel there is something wrong with them as a person, so they feel guilty and inadequate, rather than seeing that their distress is a genuine response to intolerable conditions. Stress is the result of pressure on your mind, which can end in health breakdown. Such pressures are numerous and complex. Your job may be boring and repetitive and you may feel stultified by it, or may be too demanding because your department is under-staffed and you simply can't cope. Your boss might be sexually harassing you but you're afraid to leave because you may not get another job.

Stress at work can't be divorced from personal life. Perhaps you've never got a minute to relax at lunchtime because you've got to get the shopping. Or you can't concentrate on your job because you're worried about illness in the family. Allowances

now for the other 40 hours!

are rarely made on the job for such pressures. You may feel you have little control over what happens at work; this feeling builds up and can make you feel you have no control over your own *life*. This is the crux of stress.

Causes of stress

Physical pressures

Bad lighting, poor ventilation, overcrowding and noise can all lead to stress. Bad catering facilities and crowded transport to and from work add to the problem. If you're having to sit at a visual display unit or stand all day filing you'll probably be aching by five o'clock. Repetitive movement and lack of physical exercise result in muscle fatigue — which in turn can be stressful. If you are anxious about your job you are probably not sleeping well, which will also add to mental fatigue. Physical and mental fatigue interact on each other to increase stress.

Pressures caused by the organisation of work and management practice

Anyone who has worked at a job which was some combination of tedious, boring, socially useless, over-regimented, and under the supervision of an oppressive person or for the profit of someone else, can attest to the stresses of work. If you find your job repetitive and boring, an insult to your intelligence, it's no accident. Some 'work study' people, some 'time and motion man' — or maybe they were called O & M (organisation and management) — will have been called in by your employer to 'rationalise' your office. *They made it more boring* and they probably got rid of a few jobs along the way. Most people as a result are working in jobs that are well below their potential. All this rationalisation comes from 'scientific management'. The aim is higher productivity from the office worker

> 'From the beginning, office managers held that all forms of clerical work, not just routine or repetitive ones, could be standardised and "rationalised". For this purpose they undertook elaborate studies of even those occupations which involved little routine, scores of different operations each day, and the exercise of judgement. The essential feature of this effort was to make the clerical worker of whatever sort account for the entire working day. Its effect was to make the work of every office employee, no matter how experienced, the subject of management interference. In this way, management began to assert in the office its hitherto unused or sporadically exercised right of control over the labour process.'[5]

Take keypunching, for example. Your hands are occupied, your eyes are occupied, you can't move your body, you can't talk. Many data processing centres and typing pools are nothing more

11

than clerical factories, and the twentieth century clerk has become a cog in a huge machine. The way office work is now organised means that mental labour has been reduced, the necessity for thought and creativity progressively eliminated. The jobs themselves have been carefully divided into numerous simple tasks. They have been deliberately deskilled, because for employers, repetitive work is more productive and therefore more profitable.

H. Cemach, an O & M man, wrote a book called *Work Study in the Office* in the 1950s, when all this was pioneer stuff. He said:

> 'One of the aims of O & M is eliminating "know-how" as a necessary component of clerical work. It leads to higher output, disappearance of difficulties previously connected with the holidays or sickness of "the experts". No more "indispensable" clerks with high nuisance value.'[6]

What was wanted was well-controlled, passive workers who didn't have to think; leave that to management. Never mind if the office jobs we're left with cause misery and stress because they are so unfulfilling and so pressured.

John, a clerical employee in a major American insurance company, describes the pressures of his job:

> 'When you work at a place like this, it's really a sweatshop! I was a claims examiner and there were about a hundred of us. Each of us had a minimum of five hundred claims a day. That's faster than one claim a minute. And you have to check the person's eligibility, the doctor's eligibility, the disease, the diagnosis, doing all these things and checking the adding. And they were usually pushing you to do six hundred, seven hundred, a thousand, twelve hundred a day. They were incredible. Some people just sat there like machines because they were so intimidated, and wouldn't pick their heads up from their desks from eight in the morning until four-thirty at night.'

Work overload like this is stressful. One study was done in the United States of 12 women invoice clerks who were put on to piecework, where they could attain a maximum of four hundred invoices an hour, which gave a bonus of over eighty dollars for two days' work. Productivity was measured in terms of invoices per hour, with deductions for clerical errors. On piecework the output rose by 114 per cent. The adrenalin in their urine rose by 40 per cent — adrenalin is secreted in the body when highly stressed. Work has been measured to eliminate 'wasted time'. Speed-up increases production, efficiency and profits — and causes stress. These methods are usually accompanied by increased automation, machines that can do the job of five women, or six, or seven; visual display units; collators; photocopiers, and the host of other new technologies based on microprocessors. While some have eliminated boring jobs, these machines have generally made office work *more* unsatisfying. Typists, coders, telephone operators, keypunch operators, reprographic assistants, and word process operators are amongst the people subjected to monotonous tasks often paced and controlled by a machine, demanding concentration but little creativity. Feelings of being spied upon by layers of supervisors, both people and machinery, also add to the pressures of the job. *Business Systems and Equipment,* in an article entitled 'Safety and security in the office' in their April 1979 issue, discuss surveillance techniques:

> 'Some copiers (R-X, 3M, for example) can be supplied with security devices to prevent misuse, and there are a number of computer-controlled systems for monitoring telephone calls…The Swiss Borer System combines high level access control with a full flexible working hours system. All flexible working hours systems provide some measure of security of access.'

According to one French white-collar union report to the World Health Organisation, 40 per cent of office workers suffered mental and nervous disorders in automated offices in the early 1960s.[8] How much higher is the figure now?

Ironically, having taken skill and satisfaction out of much of clerical work, a number of management schools are now flourishing in the business of job satisfaction: how to make the job more meaningful. Birchall and Hammon, in an article entitled 'Can clerical work be made more interesting?' published in *Management Services* in February 1978, say that as a result of changes over the past ten to twenty years, 'white-collar jobs possess the features of assembly line work'. This has led to 'assembly line blues' in some offices, they inform us. One United Biscuits job satisfaction experiment in a factory failed because 'team work' was made difficult with the noise and pressure of work…! These 'progressive thinkers' seem to fail to grasp the fact that work is inherently meaningless, alienating and stressful if it is paced by a machine, if the worker has no control over how it is carried out, *and* if the workers have no interest in the product.

However, responsibility does come with some clerical jobs, such as supervisors, bank workers, housing officers, but often these jobs don't allow the power to make decisions. Clerks in the Civil Service, particularly in unemployment benefit offices, are a good example of this process. The individual office worker is powerless in dealing with many of the complaints, yet feels responsible and has to take much of the brunt. Deirdre Hoyle, working for Hackney housing department in London, said that counter clerks working in some local authorities had to be upgraded to get them to do the job. 'It's so rotten, many counter clerks ask to be transferred or leave, it's so stressful.' Lack of recognition of your worth and lack of trust add to feelings of being trapped.

Managers have more control over their work (and other people's). They are not confined to one place, don't have to clock in and out, and are not so constrained by 'superiors'. They have responsibilities and can participate in more decisions which affect themselves and others. All these, it is claimed, result in stress for the poor boss, but it is the *absence* of control and responsibility which is fundamentally at the root of the problem for many office workers suffering from stress. While there is clearly some stress in managerial work there's an awful lot of nonsense talked about 'executive stress'. Office and manual workers have a much, much bigger problem. It's safer at the top.

> 'The myth of executive stress presents a picture of senior personnel as lonely individuals making lonely decisions. This is the now familiar the-buck-stops-here version of the executive as hero image, who, at great personal cost, combines self-sacrifice with high levels of expertise.'[9]

Rest, breaks and flexitime

An absence of rest breaks is a real killer. Your job may have been organised in such a way that you have predetermined lunch breaks and tea breaks — if you're lucky. Many office workers still don't have 'official' tea or coffee breaks. They make a cup of coffee or get one from a machine or trolley, bring it back to their desks and carry on working.

> 'The Offices and Shops Act doesn't legislate for tea breaks, and it should. They should be a *right* rather than subject to grace and favour.' (*Bob Tanner,* BIFU rep, Barclays Bank)

Clocking in, under the guise of flexitime, is a factory floor method now common in offices.

> 'There used to be a much more relaxed atmosphere in the office. Some days you'd be busy, but others there was time to chat and take your time with a job. Now it's rush, rush, rush. When there's a lot to do the supervisor will make everyone stay late…and when it's a quiet day she'll say "Right, girls, why don't you leave a bit early today — take some time off." When they're there, they're always under pressure.' (*Gail Foot, CPSA staff rep*, DHSS un-employment benefits office)

While flexitime has obvious benefits for workers, it makes people work longer hours during busy periods without overtime pay. It can also lead people to work flat out without breaks so they can leave earlier. Often for women this means they are getting home in time for kids, and their work continues — with no rest breaks.

They can find themselves with a large debt of hours to make up. In effect, flexitime usually meets management's needs more than those of workers.

Before agreeing to move to a flexitime system, look at what it will mean. How does it compare with the system you have at the moment? What will you gain and lose? Will the 'core time' (obligatory working time) mean you can never have a day off? Will it affect union meetings? The final decision about introduction of flexitime should be taken by those who will be affected by it when they've had a chance to discuss what it will mean for them in practice.

TASS recommends that their members avoid flexitime arrangements where possible. They argue that flexitime undermines benefits such as the right to time off for personal matters, and they say:

> 'The increased output based on more concentrated labour during working hours tends to increase unemployment or reduce employment potential.'[10]

Overtime

Working long hours leads to fatigue, accidents and general stress. It also leads to unemployment and a lowering of basic rates of pay. A few unions don't tolerate overtime working for their members under any conditions, for example, the National Union of Journalists. In some places workers have negotiated time off in lieu (known as TOIL) agreements, where they take off time for unsocial hours worked. Here is an example of such an agreement taken from the NUJ Book Branch model claim which has been successfully negotiated in several book publishing offices:

1   *The hours of work shall be 7 hours per day and 35 hours per week.*
2   *The company agrees that employees shall not be expected to work outside these hours except in exceptional circumstances to be agreed with the Union.*
3   *Overtime working will not be used as a means artificially to depress staffing levels in any area of the company.*
4   *All overtime working is optional.*
5   *Overtime shall be construed as work done by members who are asked by management to work additional hours beyond the flexibility of their normal working hours. Such overtime is to be compensated for by time off in lieu, 1½ times the time worked as overtime on weekdays outside normal office hours, and twice the time worked at weekends or public holidays. Management undertakes to ensure that this time off in lieu can be taken by the member within eight weeks of the overtime being worked. Reasonable notice shall be given of the member's intention to take time off.*

15

6   *If a member is to be required to work overtime, her or she must be informed beforehand by the manager concerned, and the matter discussed.*

7   *The FOC (shop steward) must be given sufficient notice of the possibility of any department being asked to work overtime consistently over an extended period. The FOC will then be free to seek the views of his/her members to determine whether this constitutes a breach of Clause 3 (above).*

8   *Any member working overtime past 7 pm will be entitled to claim £1.50 meal allowance and his/her taxi fare home or to the appropriate rail terminus, whichever is the nearer.*

9   *Members will not be compelled to produce material which by their normal work schedule would be due during their holidays.*

Shiftwork

Shiftwork is being increased for office workers, for example, where they are required to staff computers, as in the Lloyds Bank computer centre on London's South Bank, which is staffed almost twenty-four hours a day. But receptionists and switchboard operators also commonly do night and shift work, often with inadequate catering facilities. A Russian study of data process centre operators working the three shift, eight-hour system, found a falling off in vigilance and memory during the second two shifts and recommended special work and rest arrangements, and a change of work during the day shift to relieve monotony.[11]

Shiftwork is damaging to your health and physiological well-being. Basically there is a conflict between the daily pattern of activity required by shiftwork and the normal daily activity cycle of your body, as well as that followed by your family, friends and the rest of the community. Health effects result directly from the disturbance of bodily rhythms involved in eating, sleeping and so on. Others are due to the disruption of social and home life.[12]

> 'The problem of "jet lag" suffered by globe-trotting executives is a popular press feature. Yet many industrial workers on rotating shifts suffer in the same way without getting sympathetic news coverage. Now it looks as though "shift lag" could become a white-collar illness.' (*ASTMS Finance News*, Summer 1978)

Nightwork in particular upsets the natural rhythm of the body and causes stress. Yet often the only justification for nightwork is economic; expensive machinery and buildings are kept working constantly. No account is taken of the social and medical costs. An International Labour Office report states:

> 'Nightwork should be banned whenever its practice is motivated solely by the financial considerations of making costly equipment pay for itself.'[13]

Sweden has banned all nightwork except for 'socially necessary' labour or where the employer can prove exceptional circumstances. If your employer is trying to introduce shiftwork and you are concerned about the health effects, try to make sure a meeting is called of all the people affected, so that you can work out what it will mean for you. It might be worth preparing a leaflet beforehand where you explain some of the health hazards and stressful effects of 'unsocial hours' shifts.* You should also consider whether it will reduce jobs and make it impossible for some people to work (e.g. shifts might interfere with childcare arrangements). If there are shift bonuses, what will you be 'selling' in exchange? Extra money won't be much use if there's no time to enjoy it. How will shift working affect union organisation?

Economic causes of stress

Working people suffer particularly from economic stress in this society. Firstly, each person suffers because he or she has to manage as an individual. But also they suffer because the standard of living of all working people is being consistently attacked by government policy. While cutbacks in public expenditure are harming people in obvious ways (such as cuts in the ambulance service), cuts are also compounding our suffering in more insidious ways: fewer meals on wheels, less daycare facilities, worse public transport. Declining services compounds people's stress. For workers in public services stress is also increased. There is more pressure on each individual, more insecurity and fear of redundancy for those left with a job.

Being paid a low wage is stressful in two ways. Firstly, if you're not getting enough to make ends meet it puts a great strain on you. But, in addition, a low wage in our society means someone in power doesn't think you're worth more. Women in particular are grossly underpaid at work, and are also under terrific pressure because they are usually doing a second job at home unpaid. Thirty per cent of working women are now the sole earner in their household. Most working women come home after a day's work and go on to cook a meal and do housework. Some women spend many hours a week on housework *on top of* paid work outside.

> 'The most recent survey done in Britain in 1971 showed that the average number of hours spent on housework is a staggering 77 per week — much more than most paid jobs. This means that a working woman with a full-time job is doing *more than two jobs* in terms of hours.[14]

While these social pressures may be obvious to most of us as causes of stress, there is a management school of thought that

* See BSSRS broadsheet *Shiftwork.*

17

believes women are more predisposed to be tired and irritable, emotional or nervous. One article on the occupational health of switchboard operators recommends weeding out the 'weak ones' who can't cope:

> 'Pre-employment medical examinations should include ear, nose and throat examination; after this a psychological study is necessary to determine certain traits necessary for the job. The candidate should be tested by standard psychometric, intelligence and personality tests to obtain a complete picture of her psychological and mental development. An interview is also desirable to explore any private, domestic or social difficulties that may impair the candidate's fitness for the job.'[15]

> 'In Britain consumption of tranquillisers and anti-depressants has doubled in the last ten years. In the early 1970s research showed that over three-quarters of users of anti-anxiety drugs were women.' (*News Release,* Summer 1979, p.8)

The pressures on working mothers are enormous. Feeling guilty because you're not an ideal stay-at-home mum...get the breakfasts, get the shopping done, go to the launderette, fetch the kids from school, do the ironing, clean the house. A carefully worked out timetable can be upset and life thrown into chaos when your lunch hour is switched or you're required to do overtime without notice. Of course overtime may not be mandatory, but 'flexibility' is one of the qualities you're rated for and supervisors usually keep records on you.

But these problems must never be used as excuses to force women back to the home. A woman *should not have to cope* with the stress of two jobs. The alternative of isolation and frustration as a lonely housewife is no solution. There is massive evidence to show that most women want to go out to work. This is every woman's right. Studies show high rates of depression among housewives.[16]

Stress on women outside work is a huge problem. Pressures from children and men to be at their beck and call, to be smiling and attractive, stay young looking; to avoid sexual harassment and violence in the street and in the home. Homes for battered women, rape crisis centres, women's centres, have sprung up in the last ten years as a response to such pressures on women. Men lose out too by such a system. Although they are *not* mostly the 'sole breadwinner' in the family, the economic pressures and responsibilities on men to play such a part are great. What is needed is much more flexibility in work, and fewer hours, so that either or both parents can take an active part in childcare. More and better nursery facilities, as well as equal job opportunities, pay and training for women would contribute to improving women's situation and reducing female — and male — stress (for more on nurseries see p. 97).

Sexism at work

Degrading treatment and discrimination against women on the basis of their sex is known as sexism. It is especially noticeable in office work, which is by far the largest employer of women in Western society. In this female ghetto, the split is noticeable between male executives and female operatives, women being restricted to dead-end work with little scope for promotion. This division of labour is especially obvious if we look at the job of secretary — the 'office wife'. Like housework, much office work is invisible to male (husband/boss) eyes, yet the smooth running of the house/office would collapse without it. Even though she writes her boss's letters, takes decisions for him in his absence, and organises all his movements, books his tickets for journeys, and so on, she is not acknowledged as taking any responsibility, and is not paid accordingly. Although a secretary sells her labour like a factory worker, what she is also selling is her behaviour — stereotyped as female. One magazine article with tips for secretaries suggests that their handbags should contain anything the boss might need: clothes brush, black thread, Alka-Selzer. Most books say that the boss should be shielded from the consequences of his own mistakes and that the secretary must take the blame. A few go so far as to suggest she should even pretend to *him* that it was her fault.[17] Apparently, his ego is more important than his grasp of the truth!

The social structure in the office — the sexual hierarchy — is unquestionably a source of stress for many women. Sexual discrimination, sexual harassment, sexist insults are played out daily in offices. Secretaries, filing clerks, telephonists, temps, typists — all are expected to pander to the whims of 'the dictators'.

Sexual harassment   The scope of sexual harassment is staggering. It ranges from propositions and sexual innuendo to rape. It is, as Anna Raeburn said in *Cosmopolitan* 'a new, formal title for an age-old predicament, the boss-man with anything from a lascivious line of chat, to wandering hands, to explicit demands for sex as a reward for giving you, the woman, work.' (*Cosmopolitan,* August 1980)

Our male dominated society encourages — often to the point of requiring — women to present themselves as sexual objects in order to get certain jobs. Male sexual aggression against women is rationalised as expressions of men's 'naturally' more active sex drive.

Until comparatively recently, women have rarely complained. Isabel Hilton in the *Sunday Times* reviewed the evidence:

'A woman complaining of unwanted attentions is likely to find herself the object of suspicion. The suggestion that she had 'asked for it' or at best been naive in allowing herself to be placed in a compromising position, was enough to deter most complaints. The fact that men tend to be the bosses and women the subordinates and that men tended to regard it as quite normal to make passes at their (or somebody else's) secretary, made women feel their complaint was likely to rebound.' (*Sunday Times,* 4 May 1980)

Frequently women are forced to choose between sexual harassment and lack of promotion, low pay or job loss. Women who stay on without responding to male advances can be confronted with a powerful array of penalties: demotions, reassignments of shifts, hours or location of work; refusal of overtime, impossible performance standards and negative job evaluations. The other side to the problem is the discrimination which results against older women or women who don't fit the stereotype of attractive female. The strain of both the original harassment and the penalties for not complying can have severe physical and mental effects on women. These range from minor pain to major illness, physical damage in the case of rape or nervous breakdowns.

Anna Raeburn:

'And in many of us there is an awful weary patience with the whole damned thing. I mean, it's just men isn't it? They always play these depressing little games. Is it worth kicking up a fuss about it? The whole thing's just a power trip after all. I mean, your boss gropes you and you knee him in the crotch and you'll find yourself out of a job anyway. Your colleagues may admire you but that won't pay the rent… Yet you and I must both acknowledge that only women can change the way things are for women, and as they become an increasing part of the workforce they must assume more responsibility for the conditions in which they are prepared to work.'

Since the late 1970's, major US government departments have issued guidelines to managements on what sexual harassment is (really!) and how to deal with it.

In 1979 clerical workers at Boston University won an agreement with a clause forbidding sexual harassment. And in 1980 the US Equal Employment Opportunities Commission published regulations forbidding sexual harassment at work. Employers have to pay compensating damages to employees who have been sexually harassed and are liable to court action if they refuse. These progressive laws were the direct result of the publicity and activities of American women's groups.

Ellen Shub

The Canadian Union of Public Employees defines sexual harassment as 'any repeated and unwanted sexual comment, look, suggestion or physical contact that a woman finds objectionable and offensive…it can range from unwanted suggestions or attempted rape or rape. Physically it can include pinching, grabbing, hugging, patting, leering, brushing against and touching…'

In April 1980 Victoria Stevans, an 18 year old clerk typist brought a successful action for unfair dismissal at Birmingham Industrial Tribunal. She told the tribunal that her boss persistently made unwanted advances, but when she complained to his co-director she was sacked. She brought the case, she said, not for the compensation but to clear her name and *'for the sake of office girls everywhere'.* On the other hand when three women in London's Brent local government office complained about their boss's advances, they were suspended pending investigation. The whole thing was very messy with the boss being in the same trade union (NALGO) which thus represented both parties. The investigation was a long drawn out process and wore the women down. Although they got lots of support from other NALGO members they eventually let it drop and accepted jobs elsewhere. If one man's word equals the voice of three women, more women are urgently needed to join the battle! The question here is, should an employer take responsibility under the Health and Safety at Work Act for employees, regarding assault? If management is aware of the problem because their staff have alerted them to it,

21

do they have a legal duty to do something about it? Section 2 of the Act puts a general duty on employers to ensure the health, safety and welfare of their employees.

In the final chapter of her book *Sexual Shakedown,* Lin Farley gives some hints on fighting sexual harassment at work: 'Be smart...take time to analyse the situation. Build your case, get documentation. Put it in writing. Get memos. Try to develop a case showing the way it is affecting your job evaluations and performance. Don't just behave as if the man automatically has the upper hand.' But get support from your sisters too! By discussing the problem with the other women at work you'll get support and ideas and you'll probably find you have a shared problem. Women's stamina, energy and courage in the battles against rape and for free abortion and contraception have made recent history. It looks as if the struggles against sexual harassment in the workplace are forming part of women's history now, too.

The worst thing about clerical work is that for too many women there is no alternative. They have been prepared for the job from birth, and while at school a girl will be channelled into taking typing and secretarial skills and may look forward to a glamorous job as a private secretary, which is far from glamorous anyway. Temps require a special mention at this point. While many women in offices have ways of coping with their situation by developing friendships and supporting each other, the temp is isolated. According to a temps agency report in 1975, temps are now on average working mothers in their thirties unable or unwilling to do a permanent job. Many are forced into a situation where they are grossly exploited by agencies who pay them peanuts and collect fat fees for their trouble. There are no benefits and no insurance coverage. If you're off sick or you can't get work, you're not paid, and you can't get social security. Note that in France, agencies are obliged by law to pay temps compensation for unemployment.
The day-to-day pressures of the work itself, or work and home and the overlap between the two, emotional problems, financial problems, sexism — these are some of the factors that explain the headaches, irritability and depression that plague office workers.

How the body is affected by stress

Whether the cause of stress is noise or a critical supervisor, the body readies its defence mechanisms with a discharge of adrenalin and an increase in heart rate, blood pressure and digestive juices. That system enables us to run or fight if under attack, but if the body is constantly churning in a state of readiness, vital organs begin to show signs of wear and the result is stress.

Stress comes in many guises; physical and mental (see box). Sometimes symptoms *don't* appear and chronic stress can lead directly to disease.

It has been proved experimentally that under excessive pressure of work, telephonists may lose co-ordination of movement and a general state of mental fatigue may ensue. Some disturbances can be observed clinically, eg headaches, dizziness and instability of temperament with a complex of insecurity and weariness followed by excitement and anxiety. (International Labour Office, Encyclopaedia of Occupational Health and Safety, *p.1377)*

Fatigue is a response to stress extending over a period of time. When your body is fatigued it means that a great deal of stress has been placed on your muscles. The primary reaction is a powerful urge to stop doing those actions which promote further fatigue, in other words, to stop work. This is what happens when you're exposed to high levels of noise or if you must carry out repetitive movements for an extended period. Fatigue is a sensation which is supposed to be a protection for the body, just as hunger or thirst are. It is supposed to warn the body that activity should cease or change. Chronic fatigue is often characterised by both physical and behavioural changes — symptoms of stress.

Mental stress, brain-fag, brain strain, mental fatigue, mental exhaustion, neurosis: all are names given to the consequences of pressure — of overload on the body. Wider consequences of stress include seeking release through alcohol, drugs, suicide. Some go into mental institutions, visit psychiatrists, smoke repeatedly, visit the doctor, take time off work. All these are ways of coping.

What can be done about stress?

Some people find sports such as swimming or relaxation exercises such as yoga help them. While it is important to look after your body — get plenty of rest and eat good, nutritious food — these are only curative measures. How can you *prevent* stress occurring? What are the most stressful parts of your job? How can it be improved?

One way to attack stress is to *do something* to prevent it. Doing something about a problem makes us feel more in control of our lives — lack of control is itself an underlying cause of stress at work. Clerical workers are often worn down over the years by their jobs and their employers and feel that nothing will ever change, nothing can be done. This isn't so. If you push and win even a small victory, this can reveal the *potential* power that all office workers have in their work if they choose to exercise it.

One thing you can do is to put round a short health survey to assess the levels of stress that people are experiencing. You will then have some concrete information as a starting point. Eddie Read, a Southampton bus driver and NUR representative, did such a survey among his members who drove one-person-operated buses. He asked people to list their symptoms and what they thought were the causes. He also asked what effects stress was having on their domestic and social lives. Finally, Eddie asked what improvements in the job they suggested. He got 150 replies out of 200 with evidence of high levels of stress being suffered. The data from the questionnaires was used to bargain for better conditions. He said:

> 'Some degree of success was very quickly obtained on two of the problems. Outside caterers have taken over the running of the canteen, and the management agreed to re-organise the one-man rota...Surveys of this nature should be done first on a regional basis within the bus industry, followed on a national level.'[18]

Things to go for to alleviate stressful working conditions include shorter hours, more breaks, longer holidays, good catering facilities and rest rooms, well designed furniture. Flexibility is important too, for example, a free choice of work breaks and a say in how the job is done. Remember too that a comfortable environment is important here: trying conditions of heat, cold, dust, fumes noise and bad lighting are stressful and contribute to health breakdown. Sexual harassment as a cause of stress needs to be combatted by women fighting back.

NALGO is setting up a working party on sex and power relations in the office and co-opting a representative from a rape crisis centre. You could start a women's support group at your place of work (see p. 182).

Clearly, we also need stronger laws. Several states in the USA have awarded compensation to workers suffering from occupationally-related stress, and Section 12 of Norway's Work Environment Act should serve as a model for this country. It contains several important requirements:

> 'Employees shall be afforded opportunities for personal development and the maintenance and development of their skills. Monotonous, repetitive, and machine or assembly work that does not permit alternation of pace shall be avoided. Jobs shall be designed to allow some possibility for variation, for contact with other workers... and production requirements and performance.'

A decrease in stress occurs where there is greater satisfaction on the job. Work could be very different: instead of day-to-day tedium and meaningless tasks, work could be intrinsically rewarding. But — and it is a big but — this isn't going to happen until people start refusing to do the jobs that are draining them and ruining their health, both mental and physical.

'There are some things in business I like, but I refuse to be just another bolt in the machine.' (Temp secretary quoted in Jean Tepperman's *Not Servants, Not Machines: Office Workers Speak Out*)

Footnotes

1 Morris, J.N. et al, 'Coronary heart disease and physical activity of work: coronary heart disease in different occupations' in *The Lancet,* 1953, pp.1053-1057.

2 See Fletcher, B. et al, 'Exploding the myth of executive stress' in *Personnel Management,* May 1979.

3 Haynes, S.G. and Feinleib, M. 'Women, work and coronary heart disease, prospective findings from the Framingham Heart Study' in *American Journal of Public Health,* 70, February 1980, pp.133-141.

4 Industrial Relations Councils Inc. in *Industrial Relations Monograph,* No. 22, 1963, cited in Tepperman, J., *Not Servants, Not Machines: Office Workers Speak Out,* Boston, 1976, p.141.

5 Braverman, H., *Labor and Monopoly Capital,* New York and London, 1974, p.309.

6 Cemach, H., *Work Study in the Office,* Surrey, 1958, p.146.

7 Murrell, H., *Work Stress and Mental Strain,* Medical Research Council and Department of Employment, undated, pp.25-26.

8 International Labour Office, *Effects of Mechanisation and Automation in Offices,* Geneva, 1959, p.96.

9 Fletcher, B., 'Stress, illness and social class' in *Occupational Health,* September 1975, pp.405-411.

10 *Industrial Relations Reviews and Reports,* January 1973.

11 Kononenko, A.A., 'Research in vigilance and short-time memory of data processing centre operators working the three-shift eight-hour system' in *Gig. i Sanitarija,* No. 8, August 1975, pp.102-4.

12 BSSRS Work Hazards Group, *Shiftwork Health Hazards,* London, 1977.

13 Carpentier, J. and Cazamian, P., *Nightwork,* International Labour Organization, Geneva, 1977.

14 From Hughes, U., *Working Women's Handbook,* Pluto Press, London (forthcoming)

15 Guianze, E.R., 'Switchboard operators' in International Labour Office, *Encyclopaedia of Occupational Health and Safety,* Geneva, 1972, p.1377.

16 Brown G. and Harris T., *The Social Origins of Depression,* London 1978.

17 Benet, M.K., *Secretary: Enquiry into the Female Ghetto,* London, 1972, p.98.

18 *Hazards Bulletin,* No.5, December 1976, p.9.

CHECK LIST
Stress

Some of the known *causes of stress are given in this checklist. Your office may have other causes of stress not listed.*

bad lighting
poor ventilation
overcrowding
noise
vibration
too hot
too cold
flexitime
overtime
shiftwork
VDUs
photocopiers
typing
bad chairs
low wages

boring work
too much work
too little work
no tea breaks
tea break too short
lunch break too short
poor canteen facilities
no canteen facilities
increased production
bad relations with supervisor
sexism in the office
job insecurity
no job control
job isolation
no nursery provision

Solutions to stress in the office

Good trade union organisation
Good workplace women's groups
Better control of office organisation and managers
Consultation *and* agreement on:

new equipment
work rotas
shiftwork (if any)
hours of work
conditions of work

nursery provision
canteen facilities
wages
work patterns

Many solutions are the reverse of anything you may have ticked off in the first list. Circulating this checklist will be a start towards a solution.

Can you or your members think of other ways of reducing stress at work?
Ask them through a questionnaire (see Appendix) if appropriate.
This will strengthen your case considerably when meeting management.

2 Office Environment

2 Noise

Noise can damage hearing and cause stress. Some offices, with ventilation whirring, the heating system vibrating, the fluorescent lighting humming, typewriters clattering and phones ringing, can be nerve-wracking. If your job demands concentration and skill, such noise can be the last straw.

Deafness

Exposure to noise over a long period may result in the destruction of nerve cells in the inner ear, and a loss of hearing which is permanent and incurable.

> 'Any hearing loss caused by noise will be added on to whatever you are going to suffer anyway as you get older. Even a small loss now will make you hard of hearing much sooner.
> Hearing damage doesn't just make sounds softer, it cuts them out and it distorts them. This can make life a misery, with you thinking people are muttering while they claim you're not listening. Deafness is isolating and ruins your home life as well as your health.' (P. Kinnersley, *The Hazards of Work,* p.49)

Another effect of noise which starts off temporary but can become permanent is tinnitus, or buzzing in the ears. If you are suffering this then you have been or are exposed to too much noise. Once permanent it can keep you awake at nights — you would never enjoy those moments of peace and quiet again.

Stress

Excessive noise affects your communication, sense of touch, clarity of vision, balance and co-ordination. It contributes to fatigue, loss of sleep, headaches and irritability. Exposure to noise is a source of physiological stress, causing rise in blood pressure and increased heart rate. It can be stressful *even if the noise level is low,* as it interferes with communication and your ability to concentrate. Studies have shown that office workers exposed to intense and even moderate noise have an increased incidence of circulatory, digestive, neurological and psychiatric problems.[1] A study of university staff with sedentary occupations found that after three days of systematic exposure to typewriter noise and aircraft noise, the staff complained of tiredness and irritability. The authors suggest the effect of the noise was a 'mild type of anxiety-depression syndrome'.[2]

Office noise

In an Alfred Marks Bureau survey, 24 per cent of office workers felt the noise in their offices was excessive.

One insurance company typist said of her work:

> 'It's like — especially for a machine that was designed to be typed on all day long — driving a big truck. It's very hard and it's very noisy. I can't hear anything when people talk to me. Everybody thinks their hearing is impaired.'
> (J. Tepperman, *Not Servants, Not Machines: Office Workers Speak Out.*)

The following table shows how noise levels from office machinery compare with other sources of noise

source	decibel level
leaves rustling	10 – 30
'recommended comfort level' for boardrooms	30 – 35
director's office	20 – 54
copying machine	62 – 68
electric typewriter	63 – 69
accounting office; average traffic at 100 feet; large shop; some electric fans	70 (W. German 'acceptable level')
HEARING DAMAGE BEGINS HERE	
vacuum cleaner	74
heavy traffic; office with tabulating machines; some electric typewriter carriage returns	80 (Dutch 'acceptable level')
data processing centre; single multilith printer in small room	86
most factories; addressing machine; electric staple gun; inside underground train/tube	90 (UK 'acceptable level')
food mixer at 2 feet; unmuffled motorbike	100

28

Clearly, all offices are noisy — but there are also particular danger areas.

Audio typists risk a double dose of noise. Because their cheap earphones don't keep out background noise, playback may need to be so loud that, combined with the noise of surrounding machines, the ear receives a total dose approaching 90 decibels. (There may also be a risk of irritation and infection of the ear canal.) Telephone operators' ears have been measured as receiving 87 decibels, enough to cause hearing loss.

> 'Acoustic shock can be produced while the operator is establishing a long-distance connection if there is an intense audio-discharge that exceeds the ear's capacity of resistance. Repetition may cause injuries to the acoustic nerve that will take a long time to heal. Deafness may slowly and progressively evolve: acute laryngitis (or nodular subacute laryngitis) may develop...The incidence of acoustic shock can be lessened by a regular system of inspection and maintenance of all equipment.' (International Labour Office, *Encyclopaedia of Occupational Health and Safety*, p.1377)

Data processing departments and computer rooms are very noisy. Paper bursting along the perforated line sounds like a rifle crack. The chatter of card and paper tape punches, the clatter of line printers and typewriters, high speed bursters, collators, guillotines, paper shredders, telexes, copiers — all add up to danger.

Open plan offices are not only noisy, with a lot of machinery and a lot of reflecting metal surfaces, but also pose management a security problem — you might overhear those private conversations. So rather than get rid of noise, they add to it! This might be background music, or Muzak, or it may be 'white noise'. Either way, it's known in the trade as 'acoustical perfume'! That kind of cover-up can make things worse. It upset the staff of the *New Yorker* magazine, who threatened to walk out because of the Muzak in the lifts.

Music while you work is there to increase workers' production. There is no evidence in fact that it does, but it is a cheap way of masking other noise and may be relieving job monotony. Some employers prefer 'white noise', which may be an adjustment to the ventilation system to produce a continuous whirr, or a special device which generates a hiss which can mask irritating purr tones.

Measuring the noise

Noise is measured on a decibel scale* based on powers of ten (it's logarithmic), so that ten more decibels means the sound is ten times as intense. It doesn't sound ten times as loud but it damages your hearing ten times as fast.**

Any sound source from 70 decibels upwards may cause temporary loss of hearing, which in time can lead to permanent deafness. 50 to 75 decibels is the average level in offices and this level makes speech communication difficult. The *quality* of noise is most important as a source of stress — irritation because of whines or hums, being startled because of sudden noise, the effort of trying to concentrate. The decibel level may not be very high, but that high-pitched whistle *must* be controlled — trust your own response.

There is a government Code of Practice on noise which suggests that noise at work should be limited to 90 decibels. This is not a legal limit, just a guideline. The TUC is recommending 80 decibels. The Dutch limit is 80 decibels, one-tenth as harmful as the UK level. There is a German level of 70 decibels specifically for offices, established on the basis of speech intelligibility and degree of mental concentration required at work.

If you feel you want a decibel level to negotiate around, go for that thought to be acceptable for executives' offices: 20 to 54 decibels. An acceptable level of noise is what *you* and your co-workers find comfortable to work with.

Dealing with noise

There are several ways of dealing with noise:
1   Reduce noise at source.
2   Reduce it on the way to you.
3   Reduce the time of exposure.
4   Protect your ears.

Reducing noise at source   Engineering controls to quieten machinery at source are the only acceptable answer in the long term. Management may say they can't do it, but in the vast majority of cases it can be done. Often they mean the cost would be too high. Cost to whom? Not doing it could cost you your health. Anyway, one manufacturer of typewriters reported that silencing materials on electric machines would only add 30 pence to manufacturing costs.[3] The Health and Safety Executive has a list of noise control companies

*Noise is usually measured in 'A-weighted decibels' or dB(A). This is a decibel reading with a filter switched in, which gives less emphasis to some frequencies. The filter mimics the sensitivity of the human ear over different frequencies and in this way gives a better measure of the damaging effect of noise on your hearing.

**For a clear explanation in more detail of noise, decibels, noise decibels, its damaging effects etc., see *Noise: Fighting the Most Widespread Industrial Disease*, published by BSSRS.

(although they don't keep it up to date).
In one office, workers complained of headaches and mental stress
from the noise from the key punch machines, and got the
machines modified by the manufacturers. In the meantime, they
had placed upturned wastebaskets over noisy parts of the
machines! Maybe they baffled the boss as well...

In some computer rooms noise levels are above 85 decibels *even
after* sound-proofing.[4] All this sophisticated equipment should
have been designed for quiet and comfort in the first place.
Badly maintained equipment can be noisy: good maintenance
will help reduce noise at source. Ideally, only quiet machinery
should be admitted into the workplace. Safety reps have the
right to be consulted on new equipment (see p. 164).
Offices themselves, as well as office machinery, should be
designed to be quiet. But architects are increasingly using cheap,
lightweight materials which lead to noise problems. Good floors
and structures would prevent noise in the beginning.

Reducing noise on its way to you In a badly designed office you may want some 'acoustical control'.
Thick carpeting, acoustic tile ceilings, heavy fabrics and plants
will help absorb some sound. To be effective, materials have to
be light or 'fluffy' to stop noise being reflected. Baffles cutting
off glare from fluorescent lighting should be made of sound-
absorbing material. Note that sound-proofing may prevent you
hearing the fire alarm! Alarms should be regularly checked.
Typewriters and teleprinters can be enclosed by 'hush boxes' to
reduce sound. In one workplace, felt was used on RCA print-out
equipment to lower the noise from 80 to 50 decibels. Mats
under typewriters and other equipment reduce vibration and stop
the desk being a sound box. Sometimes equipment can simply be
moved. Buzzers or lights instead of bells on the phones, and
rubber-tipped chair legs are further ways of cutting down
irritating noises. Outside traffic is one of the main noise hazards
in offices today. The Greater London Council has recognised this
and recommends that traffic noise levels in 'executive offices'
should not rise above 45 decibels. However, they find it acceptable if levels in 'general offices' rise to 55 decibels.
A survey in France found that 50 per cent of all buildings are
inadequately insulated. Builders should seal gaps round doors and
air ducts. The Building Research Establishment has also pub-

lished information on good quality double-glazing.[5]

At a General Electric plant in Ohio, in a large office area adjacent to the factory, advertising and product information employees were distracted by noise from the factory and complained about the 75 to 78 decibels noise level in their offices. They got the ceiling resuspended, the doors sound-proofed and the walls acoustically treated. Of course, this approach increases the separation of factory and white-collar workers. A joint union approach might have got the noise reduced at source.

More space and less overcrowding may further reduce noise — take a look at your boss's facilities. More than likely they're quiet and spacious.

Reducing the time of exposure

If you're working in a noisy office, an interim measure could be more breaks. This doesn't solve the problem but is a feasible short-term demand. You could also try getting noisy equipment moved to another room.

Protecting your hearing

A favourite management solution to noise in factories is ear-muffs and ear plugs. This is a classic cover-up operation which leaves the *hazard* intact. There is, believe it or not, a report on noise in offices which recommends 'ear protection' as a way of dealing with the increased use of technology.[6]

If you need to walk through a noisy factory or site, you should, however, be provided with ear protection. This also goes for protection from dust or fumes — though earmuffs and masks can never be a substitute for getting rid of the hazard *at source*. Management must be forced to clean up, not cover up!

Getting something done

Do a health survey

Ask if anyone is suffering from ringing in the ears, headaches and other symptoms of stress, giddiness, difficulty in hearing others talk, especially when there are several talking (for example, at a party). Do you have to raise your voice to talk above noise at work?

Complain

Record complaints in the accident book — useful to back up your case, and also if compensation is sought.

Get it measured

Noise does not need to be loud in terms of decibels to cause stress. By all means get it measured, but fight to get the stressful noise eradicated *whatever* the measured decibel level.

Measurement could be a management noise survey, or one carried out by a health and safety inspector, or a consultant. If you can't win this from your employer, or if you don't trust the results, check with your local trade union health and safety group if there is a helpful local college or organisation who do surveys for trade union branches. See Appendix 2 for some addresses. You may be able to borrow a noise meter from a health and safety group and do it yourself. Section 6 (2) of the Regulations for

Safety Representatives and Safety Committess refers to the reps'
right to equipment necessary for inspection purposes (see p. 164).
Try to use this section to back up your request to use such
equipment. The survey should be done during normal working
hours — not at lunchtime or at night! Make sure you get a copy
of the results and that they are in a form you can understand.
A word about hearing tests. These may be useful to prove damaged
hearing in you or your co-workers. But tests must never be
allowed to be used by management against workers (such as to
facilitate redundancies or transfers). Make sure you see the
results.

You'll miss Typewriter Noise
as you miss a Headache——

Footnotes

1 Stellman, J. *Women's Work, Women's Health: Some Myths and Realities,* New York, 1977, p.113.
2 Atherley, G.R.C. et al, 'Moderate acoustic stimuli: the inter-relation of subjective importance and certain physiological changes' in *Ergonomics*, 13, 1970, pp.536-545.
3 Hricko, A., *Working for Your Life,* San Francisco, 1976, p.D8.
4 Ministry of Technology, *Computer Installations: accommodation and fire precautions,* HMSO, London, 1968.
5 *Building Research Establishment Digest,* Nos.128, 129, 153, 163, available from BRF, Garston, Watford, Herts.
6 Winter, W., 'Noise caused by data processing equipment and noise protection' in *Zentralblatt fur Arbeitsmedizin und Arbeitsschutz,* Vol.19 No.7, July 1969, pp.201-204.

CHECK LIST

1   Regularly collect and record complaints.
2   Consider a survey to highlight symptoms of too much noise.
3   If high noise levels are suspected, get levels measured with meter.
4   If noise is outside, contact relevant safety reps or shop stewards.

Controlling noise

5   Can noise be controlled at source?
6   Is all equipment regularly maintained?
7   Has appropriate noise-damping material been provided?
8   Can noisy equipment be enclosed?
9   Are windows double-glazed?
10 Can work-time with noisy equipment be cut?

Preventing noise hazards

11 Has notice of all proposed changes or new equipment been given to safety reps?

3 Lighting

Eyestrain has been one of the traditional health hazards of office work — whether for monks copying out biblical manuscripts, Victorian clerks keeping ledger accounts, or secretaries typing up shorthand notes. Our eyes suffer from the continuous reading of documents, especially in poor light. Bad lighting in offices is a common cause of eyestrain, which in turn puts you under stress and can lead to accidents. If you try to relieve the eyestrain by moving nearer to your work it can also cause you to sit badly, bringing backache, neckache and general muscle fatigue.

Our eyes are assaulted daily at work by other hazards besides lighting. Proof-reading, filing, accounting, and jobs involving reading carbon copies, bad photocopies, handwriting or fine line drawings — all put a strain on the eyes. Similarly, reading small print such as in phone directories or working with business forms strains the eyes, and you might find the forms getting blurry as you work. Badly designed forms (very small print, with black print on stark white paper) are very nasty. Large print with buff paper is easier on the eyes.

Corridors and storerooms, toilets and stairways should all be well lit to enable you to move about safely at all times. Many injuries are caused by dim lighting. On dark mornings unlit back stairs and entrances can be very hazardous. Key switches are sometimes installed to save money and these may be controlled by porters or supervisors. As a result, people are sometimes forced to use facilities such as toilets in darkness, having the choice of stumbling about in the dark or attempting to put on lights with a paper clip, risking electric shock. This is one of the many examples of how security and economic considerations take priority over your health and safety. There should also always be a system of emergency lighting in case the normal lighting fails.

A survey by the Alfred Marks Bureau revealed that 29 per cent of office workers questioned found the lighting inadequate for their needs. Over 1 in 10 had frequent eye fatigue and 40 per cent of the secretaries and shorthand typists in the survey complained of eyestrain, due to the fact that they do 'close work' in inadequate lighting. (Alfred Marks Bureau, Fitness in the Office, 1975)

A report by the Factory Inspectorate found 'a disquieting cause of unsatisfactory lighting was due to efforts by owners to reduce the cost'.[1] Often economies are made by using single fluorescent tubes when double ones are required for the room. Some local authorities have removed every second light bulb as part of the cutbacks in public spending. Sheila Henderson, who does a lot of temp work, criticised the lighting in a solicitor's office in Birmingham:

> 'I only had a 60-watt bulb in my office in that place. A lot of my experiences counter the notion that offices are nice places to work.'

The Offices, Shops and Railway Premises Act requires that lighting in offices should be 'sufficient and suitable' (Section 8). This is a vague standard, but it can be used to your advantage. If, like the women in the Alfred Marks survey, you feel the lighting in your office is inadequate for your needs, you can argue in law that it is insufficient and unsuitable. One office worker recently complained to the Health and Safety Executive that the desk lamp he used could only be positioned so that it shone in his eyes as well as on his work: moreover, boxes were stored at the window, obliterating the natural light. The inspector agreed with the employee that the employer was in breach of the law in not providing 'suitable lighting'.[2]

While it's important to get enough light, the quality of the light is important too.

Artificial light

> By far the most disturbing aspect of the [Lloyds Bank Computer Centre] building is the relentless electric lighting. Only 15 per cent of the exterior is glazed, letting in very little natural light. 'The windows are only there for psychological reasons' said West [the architect]. 'They don't provide any working light. You see, we wanted to be very energy-conscious.' (McGhie, C., 'Keeping a low profile', Time Out, 7-13 September 1979)

Working all day in artificial light isn't good for you. In France there is a collective agreement for travel and tourist agency workers (which was incorporated into law) which provides that workers permanently employed in basements or constantly working by artificial light will be entitled to an additional eight days paid holiday, as well as to a monthly allowance proportionate to the time actually worked in the basement. In some ways this is like selling health in exchange for 'danger money'. But at least it's a recognition that there is a danger!

> *An inquiry is to be held into the apparent harmful effects on health of the fluorescent strip lighting under which increasing numbers of people are spending their working lives.*
>
> *Many people complain about strip lighting – some are even allergic to it – and it is now widely argued that ordinary white fluorescent lighting causes headaches, eyestrain and difficulty in concentration.*
>
> *More controversially, some researchers suggest that fluorescent lighting can be a significant factor in general poor health contributing to a feeling of malaise and fatigue, as well as on influence on heart disease and cancer and other serious health problems.*
>
> *The inquiry is being set up by the Lighting Industry Federation. (*The Observer, *8 June 1980)*

Many offices are lit only by fluorescent lighting. Office workers are often concerned about the effect of this. Headaches, eyestrain and fatigue among clerical workers in an Esso plant were traced to vibration, noise and glare from fluorescent tubes. Machine keyboards were difficult to read because of the glare.[3]

Glare is a common complaint, and the older you get the more sensitive you become. There are three kinds:

Disability glare

This dazzles your eyes and affects your capacity to see clearly – for example, glare from bare fluorescent tubes. Such bright lighting causes severe visual fatigue and migraine. Tubes should always be well covered.

Discomfort glare

This can inconvenience you without your realising the cause. It may come from a large area of low brightness, whose effect is similar to a low winter sun behind cloud. Discomfort glare doesn't limit your capacity for seeing properly but it wears you out. Its effects are cumulative and contribute to a sense of tiredness. It is more serious when the visual task is difficult. Fluorescent lights must be *well* covered. A good shade or diffuser has a reasonably uniform brightness, causing an equal scatter of light. A poor one clearly reveals the position of the tube. The cheap mass-produced shades for fluorescent tubes are particularly hopeless in an open-plan office.

Reflected glare

Shiny surfaces – glass topped desks, laminated work surfaces, metal cabinets – reflect distorted images of light, which can be annoying and may simply prevent you reading. A small mirror laid face up on the work surface should show which light is responsible. Reposition it or alter it, or better still find a non-reflective work surface. A large blotting pad may help.

Many people prefer desk lamps, and these are a good way of supplementing overhead lighting. They enable you to move your desk around more easily.

Strategies for reducing glare

1   *Adjust shades, screens or reflectors to reduce direct viewing of light sources.*

2   *Raise the light fittings (if suspended).*

3   *Fit diffusers around the light source (especially if fluorescent).*

4   *Use a mirror to pick out sources of reflected glare.*

5   *Reduce the number of reflecting surfaces in the workplace.*

6   *Re-site working positions to reduce glare from windows.*

7   *Redecorate to avoid heavy contrasts, especially between windows and dark walls, and ceilings and light fittings.*

8   *Fit shades or blinds to reduce glare from windows.*

9   *Alter the position of fluorescent light strips so they are viewed 'end on'.*

10 *Make sure that 'desk lamps' are properly positioned and screened.*

11 *Use matt paper if light is reflected from shiny documents.*

12 *Be careful that the light brightness is not unacceptably reduced in attempts to tackle glare. Simply cutting light levels is not enough.*

TUC Education Department: Helath and Safety at Work, No.5.

Flicker

Some people see general flickering in fluorescent lighting where others don't see it. One survey found 24 per cent saw lamp flicker and 10 per cent still saw it when they looked at their work.[4] Some people get eye irritations from this, such as watering, muscle twitch and other bodily sensations such as tense muscles, nausea, sinus trouble, headaches and chills. Some people experience a 'stroboscopic' effect, where moving machinery appears stationary. Flicker is a serious problem for many workers, and management must be forced to see the light – even if they don't see the flicker!

Flicker may also be caused by ageing of the lamps, and planned replacement is necessary. Fluorescent lights go on functioning at poor light output at far beyond their rated life — unlike ordinary light bulbs, which fade a bit but quickly conk out. The output of fluorescent tubes depreciates by some 20 per cent during their 'life'. The rated life of fluorescent lamp is 75,000 hours, for an ordinary light bulb it is 1,000 hours. Flicker may be caused by the alternating electric current, and concentrated at the ends of the tube around the electrodes.

The TUC recommends the following strategies for management to deal with the flicker effect:

1   *Screen the ends of the tube — some light fittings have screens built into them.*
2   *Use tubes with internal electrode shields.*
3   *In twin-tube fittings, wiring can be arranged so that any flickers are out of phase and self-cancelling.*
4   *Light tubes must be replaced at the end of their recommended life, or as soon as flicker becomes noticeable. They should not be left until they break down completely.*[5]

Many complaints about poor lighting in fact result from accumulated dirt and poor maintenance. Regular cleaning and replacement of worn-out lamps is a management responsibility under Section 8 (4) of the Offices, Shops and Railway Premises Act. The type of lamp used will determine how often it needs to be cleaned and changed, but 'end flicker' or a blue glow at the ends of fluorescent tubes may be a sign that they are well past their best.

Ultra-violet radiation

Fluorescent lights emit ultra-violet radiation, and there is conflicting evidence of its ill-effects. The levels emitted by fluorescent lights, according to the British Standards Institute, have 'no harmful physiological effects on a healthy person'.[6] What happens if you are less than healthy?

Slightly higher levels burn the skin and cause conjunctivitis. However, the BSI reassures us that this radiation is 'almost completely absorbed' by a one-millimetre thickness of ordinary glass or by some plastics. Bare fluorescent tubes can be dangerous to your health. But even covered tubes could be hazardous:

'One of the side-effects of certain drugs (e.g. some tranquillisers, antibiotics, diurectics) is an eruption of the skin if you work under fluorescent lights when you are taking them. What happens is that you get a photosensitising reaction from the drug and your skin on your face and hands breaks out when you are exposed to ultra-violet rays. This is the case with even small doses of the rays from fluorescent lighting or from photocopiers.'[7]

If you've used a photocopier you'll know that you can sometimes get a blast of light from it. Photocopiers work with ultra-violet light from fluorescent tubes. They are built to prevent such ultra-violet and infra-red radiation from escaping, by using glass to cut down the transmission of rays. Nonetheless there is some concern about the levels of ultra-violet radiation emitted from some copiers. It is essential, too, that you don't wait until there is an obvious fault in the machine before getting it checked.

*'After servicing photo-copying equipment while wearing contact lenses, an operator developed irritation in his eye. His doctor suggested burn on the eye.' (*Occupational Safety and Health, *December 1978)*

Miriam Crown is a schoolteacher who does some photocopying in the course of her work. She noticed a warmth in her fingers when she operated a copier. This later became a prickling effect, which lasted longer each time. She explained: 'When I lift the cover and put the paper in, it begins and lasts about an hour. Now my hands and arms feel strangely numb and painful when I do it. One time I turned my back to the machine and felt a band of heat across my back.' Miriam is seeing doctors but so far no one has been able to explain her symptoms.

The operation of photocopiers, visual display units and micro-film readers causes eyestrain, and no-one should be working on these machines as a full-time job. All work which could potentially strain the eyes must be punctuated with plenty of rest breaks. (For more information on photocopiers, see chapter 5).

Natural light

> Such vapid and flat daylight as filtered through the ground glass window and skylights, leaving a black sediment on the panes, showed the books and papers, with the figures bending over them, enveloped in a studious gloom and as much abstracted in appearance from the world without as if they were assembled at the bottom of the sea. (Charles Dickens, Dombey and Son)

Daylight views allow restful 'visual pauses' during work. Windowless offices are hazardous. According to the International Labour Office, they cause an increase in disease and weaken the body's resistance to illness. Ideally there should be plenty of daylight, and it is often said that north light is best to work in. It's certainly always preferred by artists and designers. The windows should be clean to let in as much light as possible. Your employer has a duty to keep them clean and free from obstruction (Offices, Shops and Railway Premises Act, Section 8).

Some office workers complain of glare from sunlight. Blinds and low transmission glass can help. Double glazing with an outer leaf of solar control glass and an inner leaf of clear glass will reduce glare and also control heat loss. Where large developments are built for speculative letting, architects often fail to attend to basic matters like lighting. The occupying firms later partition the building into separate units, and many areas then have inadequate or uneven lighting. It is now possible to maximise the use of both artificial and daylight simultaneously by the use of photoelectric switches. When daylight falls below a certain level, the switches bring on the electric light. In addition dimmer switches can be incorporated which gradually increase the intensity of the electric light as the daylight fades. So there is no *technical* reason why you can't have good lighting in your office.

Action

If you are fighting for better lighting in your office, go for the best you can get. Often what was put there by the architects may not be what you want. One architects' journal is quite blatant about discrimination against office workers:

> 'Some office and conference rooms may require status lighting, although discharge sources and particularly fluorescent tubes are the commonest sources for ordinary offices. Directors' suites and conference rooms often have quite different kinds of lighting, employing incandescent sources, either in ceiling mounted fittings or often, for directors' offices, in table lamps and wall brackets.'
> (*Architects' Journal*, 30 January 1974, p.236)

But why should directors have expensive lighting when office workers don't? After all, it's the clerical staff who *need* good lighting for their health. Remember, next time they say there's no money in the kitty for health and safety, it's worth finding out what luxuries the money is being spent on. The money is always there. The question is, who decides what the priorities are for spending it?

Do a survey of people's eyesight and try to find out if symptoms such as headaches are caused by bad working conditions for reading, writing and the operation of machinery. Demand a planned programme of cleaning and maintenance of all light fittings. If you think the lighting in your office is unsuitable, record complaints in the accident or incident book so that you can build up a case for improving or changing it.

Lighting is measured in units of lux, which is a measure of illumination on a particular surface. Different lighting authorities vary in the levels of lighting they recommend. The Illuminating Engineering Society (IES) have a code of lighting standards which is used as a general guideline in Britain. They recommend lighting levels of between 500 and 1000 lux for office work. 1000 lux is an inadequate level for reading small print, bad carbon copies, ink and pencilled notes, and the IES code recommends 1500 lux for 'very fine work'.[8]
But the American National Standards Institute recommends

1,600 lux for most office work. Fixed standards can be helpful, but the level you go for in your office should be *what you find comfortable to work with.* Remember that older people need more light. The lux recommendations have been assessed for people under 40 years of age. Recommended standards must be increased by 50 per cent for those over 50, and by 100 per cent for those over 60.

Some typical light levels in lux		
very bright summer day	up to 100,000 lux
overcast summer day	30,000 - 40,000 lux
'bad light stops play'	1,000 lux
shady room in daylight	100 lux
street lighting	20 lux

To find out how much light there is in your office, you can do a rough survey with a camera lightmeter (allow it to 'settle' in the light for 5 minutes), or you can get a lighting survey done by pushing management. The Health and Safety Inspector can do this too, while the local electricity board and the IES will offer advice. You might need to contact such organisations if you are not satisfied with the survey done by management.

Finally, a word about eye tests. If you think your eyes are being strained by the job, you can demand eye tests, but beware that they are not used against you. No-one should lose her or his job as a result of any kind of medical screening. Such screening is already in widespread use as a way of discriminating against the 'weak' who apply for jobs (for example, older people). Make sure you get the results of any medical tests but don't let them be a substitute for doing something about the problem. Tests can be a way of 'covering up' instead of cleaning up the workplace. A process or product that ruins your eyesight is a health hazard.

Footnotes

1   H.M. Factory Inspectorate's *Annual Report on the Application of the Offices, Shops and Railway Premises Act for 1965*, HMSO, 1966.
2   Industrial Relations Services, *Health and Safety Bulletin*, No.8, August 1976, p.2.
3   Noro, L. and Koskela, A., 'Some observations on human engineering problems in office work' in *Medical Bulletin*, Vol.21 No.2, July 1961, pp.161-168.
4   Brundett, G.W., 'Human sensitivity to flicker' in *Lighting Research and Technology*, Vol.6 No.3, 1974, pp.127-143.
5   TUC Education, *Work Hazards*, Health and Safety at Work No.5, 1979.
6   British Standards Institute, *Electrical Safety of Office Machines*, BSI No.3861, 1965, p.14.
7   Goldstein, D.H. and Orris, L., 'Diseases of white-collar workers' in *Public Health Report 79*, US Government, 1967, pp.958-962.
8   Illuminating Engineering Society, I.E.S. Code for Interior Lighting, London 1973.

CHECK LIST

Eyes and lighting

1. Are the main working areas adequately lit?
2. Are irregularly used areas such as corridors, storerooms and toilets adequately lit with easily accessible switches at all times?
3. Do those working on hard-to-read manuscripts or fine detail have adequate lighting?
4. Is the level of lighting adequate for workers over 40 years of age?
5. Are there contrasts between light and dark colours which might cause eyestrain?
6. Is glare created by unshielded lights, sunlight or from bright reflecting surfaces?
7. Are all the light fittings shielded with a good cover?
8. Are the shields regularly cleaned?
9. Do the lights flicker?
10. Is there a programme for the replacement of all bulbs at regular periods?
11. Are bulbs replaced with the correct wattage?
12. Do people complain about eyestrain or headaches from too much or too little light? Is poor lighting causing fatigue brought about by cramped posture due to peering?
13. Do you have access to a light meter?
14. Does your place of work need a survey by a qualified lighting engineer?
15. Does the level of light change so radically during the day that you need automatic adjusting equipment?
16. Do you consider lighting when rooms are redecorated, new equipment installed and work positions changed, when the nature of work changes or when new workers arrive?
17. Is there an emergency lighting system that is adequately maintained? Are lights which are governed by a time switch correctly adjusted? Are illuminated signs and notices as in liftways and exits, in full working order?
18. Are lights which are governed by a time switch correctly adjusted?
19. Are illuminated signs and notices as in liftways and exits, in full working order?

4 Sitting, standing and strains

After a hard day at the office you probably have backpain or an aching neck and shoulders. This isn't 'just you'. It means your job has been badly designed so that you are having to sit or stand in a position for a long period, possibly repeating the same movements. Aches and pains also mean that the tools of your trade — your desk and chair — are improperly designed for your needs. It isn't 'just you' because many, many others suffer from aching muscles. A study of 378 Swiss office workers found the following:

14% suffered headaches
24% suffered neck and shoulder pain
57% suffered backache
16% suffered aching bottom
19% suffered painful thighs
29% suffered in knees and feet.
(Grandjean in *Applied Ergonomics,* Vol.8/3, 1977)

Normal muscular work requires alternate contraction and relaxation. This increases the rate of blood flow, which easily removes the waste products which cause tiring. However, if a muscle is contracted for a long time without being relaxed, is held in one position, the muscle receives very little blood and quickly tires. This is what happens when you repeat movements again and again, such as filing, writing, typing or standing or sitting for long periods in one position.

Traditionally a clerk worked in a standing position and a high desk was the usual office workplace. Filing clerks still have to stand all day, and varicose veins is one result. But since the late nineteenth century office work has more or less totally become a sedentary (sitting) job, entailing a stooping posture with the head advanced and the back curved. If reading or writing are required the stomach may be compressed against the desk. This posture is bad for the action of the lungs and interferes with abdominal movement. One doctor writing in 1892 on the occupational diseases of clerks also warned: 'The sedentary position of the occupation favours inattention to the calls of nature, as well as those from the bladder as the bowels.'[1] Cystitis and constipation may be related to your job.

Badly designed chairs and prolonged sitting can also give you swollen feet or ankles. Constant sitting leads to slackened muscles, especially if you stoop while sitting, say, over a typewriter. This is bad for inner organs, especially the digestive tract and lungs. Women typists are also subject to gynaecological problems. A great number of officer workers develop back strain, caused by uncomfortable chairs and long hours of sitting with nowhere to rest your head. In the Alfred Marks survey of office workers' health, one in ten workers had *frequent* backache; 45 per cent said their chair did not support their back; 34 per cent found their chair uncomfortable. And according to the Back Pain Association, 56,000 workers in Britain are off work each *day* through backache. Who knows how many suffer *because* of their work? Many medical studies agree that more than fifty per cent of adults suffer from backache during at least one period of their lives.

Are you sitting comfortably?

In her excellent book *Women's Work, Women's Health: Some Myths and Realities,* Dr Jeanne Stellman outlines some of the problems of sedentary work in offices:

> 'A chair must allow a person to sit with a minimum amount of pressure on the thighs, which are soft and easily compressed; otherwise blood circulation can be blocked, resulting in pooling in the lower part of the body. This pooling causes the veins to dilate and can lead to, or aggravate, haemorrhoids, the very uncomfortable dilation and swelling of the veins at the opening of the anus. Blood pooling is also a complicating factor in varicose veins and other circulatory problems.' (p.103)

Ian Johnson, an ASTMS member working in a publishing firm, lost the use of his leg for two weeks when the sciatic nerve was damaged because the padding was worn away from his chair seat and the metal exposed. Lisa Christie works as an office temp in Birmingham and says that many offices still have bad seating for typists:

> 'Often they look right and are theoretically adjustable but they won't move. Yet temps have to adjust to them all the time. Also some of the backrests are hopeless. You sit forward typing in a hurry and you don't notice you are off the backrest. In the place I'm in now – a plastics firm – the typist's chair is an ordinary dining room chair! My back's killing me right now.'

The law says seats for office workers must be suitable in design, construction and dimensions for the worker and the kind of work done. A footrest must be provided unless it is possible to support the feet comfortably without one. Both the seat and the footrest must be properly supported while in use. (Offices, Shops and Railway Premises Act, Section 14) What exactly is a well designed chair? There are four key factors:

kidney-shape
backrest

porous
upholstery

movable
backrest

seat fit
for you

adjustable
height

The height

A chair should be adjustable so that when you're seated your hips and knees are at right angles and your feet are flat on the floor. If you have to move your feet to operate a foot pedal on a dictaphone, an incorrect height can seriously strain muscles in your back and legs and even lead to muscle joint disease.

The backrest

Many office chairs have adjustable heights but not adjustable backrests. These are essential. A backrest (kidney-shaped ones are best) should fit snugly in the small of the back so it supports the spine and the lower back. It is not actually the back that is primarily in need of support, it's the pelvis, so an adjustable backrest should be positioned at the back of the waist. Your chair is a bad one if you find you have to use a cushion to support yourself.

The seat

The chair seat should be slanted backward just enough to allow you to lean comfortably against the backrest, but not so slanted that you slip too deeply into the chair and have to stretch and strain to reach things. Some people prefer a seat that can also tilt forwards because they find it more comfortable. The edge of the seat should be 'scrolled' so it doesn't dig into the back of your leg and the entire seat should swivel; that way, if your work requires turning the torso your back will be supported by the backrest as you turn. Many chairs with swivel seats become unstable because of wear, so this must be taken into account when you are choosing a chair. Note that in some offices you only get a swivel chair if you've got back trouble — yet probably it was the bad seating that gave you it in the first place!

Sedentary work can actually deform your spine. Some Swedish research shows the relation between posture and risk of damage in the spine. Pressure inside the discs is considerably increased when the trunk is bent forward.[2] Typists have to constantly turn their heads to one side to read what they are typing. This can cause twisting of the spinal bones and shortening of the muscles on one side of the neck or back. An Italian survey of women operating calculating machines for many years revealed that all of them had pains and muscular spasms, and their lower back movements were restricted, especially at the end of the working day. In each case X-rays revealed spinal deformities. The introduction of swivel seats, however, eliminated their pains.[3]
A chair seat that is too long can also place undue pressure on the lower back and thighs, since it forces you to lean forward in order to work. A well fitting seat will end approximately five inches from the crease behind your knee when you are sitting against the backrest.

The material

While some upholstery is desirable, it's important that the seat should be relatively hard. The pressure in soft or 'numbum' seats is invariably distributed widely over the soft tissues, leading to discomfort and anaesthesia of the skin of the buttocks and thighs. Chair seat material should be porous to allow normal body heat to dissipate. Cotton, textured fabrics are best (the texture prevents you from sliding forward); vinyl and other plastics do not allow body heat to escape. This is particularly important if you wear synthetic materials which trap body heat and increase perspiration and may be a cause of vaginal or bladder infections in women.
All office furniture should be well maintained and cleaned regularly. Armrests are important for comfort. But they get in the way if you're typing so a good typist's chair has none.

The chair should be sturdy and firm. A shaky one may mean you have to keep back muscles permanently stiff. Office chairs occasionally fall apart when you're sitting on them.

Chairs on castors are not a good idea, for the chair doesn't give support. It has to be held in position by tightening the leg muscles, causing muscles to become fatigued and painful. Castors are also potentially unsafe; one typist sustained a cracked vertebra when a chair fitted with castors slipped from under her. Perhaps the safest chair is a five-legged swivel chair; it is sturdy and can't topple.

The supermarket chain Tesco was taken to court in 1977 because of inadequate seating provision for checkout assistants. Tesco's chairs were not adjustable, had no backrest, could not swivel and were generally uncomfortable. Tesco's were directed to provide more suitable seating for their workers.

A professor at the University of Wisconsin recently designed a special chair for office workers and said, 'Executives get the best chairs and secretaries get the worst, which is too bad because secretaries spend more time in them.' You can still find advertising brochures which offer chairs of very different quality and design according to the hierarchic order of the employees. A simple wooden model for the typist, a more comfortable chair for the manager, while the most elaborate armchair is reserved for the president. And as one medical study concluded:

> 'If every manager were made to sit for a certain number of hours today with his feet hanging, there would be an enormous increase in the number of footrests in our industrial plants tomorrow morning.'(Gilbreth and Gilbreth *Fatigue Study*)[4]

Desks and tables   Many women are sitting at desks that are too high for comfort. A chair and desk together should be considered a unit, so it is not practical to give recommended heights for the furniture. (Note, however, that the British Standards Institute recommends 28 to 29 inches for desks for clerks, to be used with chairs of 17 inches. Such standards are always based on the 'average worker'.) Ideally the table, like the chair, should be adjustable to suit your particular health and comfort needs. Required height will also depend on the kind of work performed, for example, a lower table is required for typing than for writing. And electric typewriters require slightly lower levels because the machines themselves are higher than manuals. Ideally the keyboard should be as low as possible while the cylinder (platen) should be at a level which makes it unnecessary for the typist to bend her head. (For details of the special requirements of visual display unit operators see chapter 9 .) One study in an Esso company office where workers complained of muscle and joint pains revealed that desks were too high.[5] Ideally you want an adjustable typewriting/ working desk combination where typing has to be done. It is also essential that desks allow for plenty of leg room, for legs need to be able to stretch out during work. There should be no obstructive middle drawer or moulding on the underside which could block knee room.

ALL SHORTHAND-TYPISTS
have a tendency to STOOP and should wear the
SHOULDER BRACE

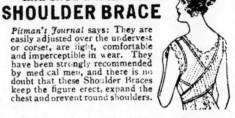

Pitman's Journal says: They are easily adjusted over the undervest or corset, are light, comfortable and imperceptible in wear. They have been strongly recommended by medical men, and there is no doubt that these Shoulder Braces keep the figure erect, expand the chest and prevent round shoulders.

Typists last century could pay for these braces to stop them stooping over their work.

It took many years of suffering by typists and key punchers, before their complaints were taken seriously and ergonomists were called on to improve office furniture design. There is now a huge and growing literature on egonomics (the design of machines and furniture). Much of it is unnecessarily mystifying, and as one contributor to an International Labour Office conference said in 1977: 'I have yet to find the textbook on design engineering which would concede so much as a chapter to the user, consumer, operator point of view.'[6]

Design of office furniture still leaves a lot to be desired. The best equipment is often prohibitively expensive. Needless to say, office furniture is BIG business and very profitable. But for all the glossy advertising and all the academic ergonomics papers, there is still no consensus on the ideal seat or desk. One study concluded, 'there is no optimum seat shape that will suit all persons'.[7] A good chair or desk is what suits you, what *you* find comfortable.

But what if you're stuck right now with a chair that doesn't fit right or sit right? Stand up and speak out. Ask if there's a better one available. Find out if others are dissatisfied too. And get your employer to obtain several types of well-designed chairs so that workers of varying builds can try them for comfort and suitability.

'At the Leeds GPO the switchboard operators didn't like their newly designed seats and desks. As one woman put it, "they didn't have any space for you to sit comfortably if you were pregnant...they must be a right load of idiots, those designers."

What did the workers do? "We sent them right back where they came from and told them to start again!"

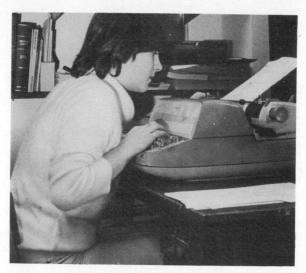

Non-adjustable seat used with a cushion, but the typist is still not high enough.

Many office jobs are badly designed. Over a third ot the women in the Alfred Marks Bureau survey said they were *hampered* by the tools of their trade. Their chair gives no support and is uncomfortable, the stationery is out of reach, the filing is made difficult, and for one in four the telephone is out of reach. Good furniture design, good lighting and ventilation will go a long way to alleviating the aches and pains and muscular fatigue of office work. But they may not solve the problem altogether. In a French study of 590 shorthand typists, many had severe back trouble even when the best design of chairs and tables were introduced.[8] The problem remains of women sitting in the same position all day, day in day out, doing the same repetitive job. If you are sitting for years doing the same thing you will suffer. Good quality equipment, a job designed for satisfaction and health, and plenty of rest breaks...when we have office jobs like that we'll see less aches and pains.

If you suffer acute muscle fatigue or backpain you should get medical attention as well as time off. Yoga exercises can bring some relief. But prevention is always better than cure.

Writer's cramp and muscle fatigue

In the past a clerk copied thousands of words and figures, often many times over, and he was plagued by the occupational disease 'writer's cramp' or scrivener's palsy. The small muscles of the fingers and hand that are used for writing or sewing or other precise motions are easily fatigued because they are small and delicate. One recommended treatment in the early part of the century was a local injection of carbolic acid! Plenty of rest would have been a less traumatic treatment. This painful cramp is not

common today, but many typists suffer from over-exertion of
the tendons of the wrist.

*Historically women were selected to be typists because of
their so-called 'digital dexterity' – their 'feminine touch'.
The reward for this talent in factories, mills and offices
throughout the world has been low wages and repetitive
work.*

For the English language, the QWERTY system keyboard imposes 60 per cent of the workload on to the left hand, with a
concentration on the middle and index fingers. Tenosynovitis, or
typist's cramp (it used to be called washerwoman's wrist), is an
inflammation of the wrist tendons which connect the muscles to
the bones in the wrist. Peritendinitus – cramping of the lower
arm – is a further occupational hazard of typing.
But it's not only typists who suffer. Visual display unit
operators (see chapter 9) and key punch operators also exert their
hand muscles on the keyboard. Extensive Japanese studies have
been done on the health of key punch and business machine
operators, and typists. This has come to be known as 'key
puncher's disease'. Complaints ranged from stiff and swollen and
aching muscles in the upper and lower arm, to finger tremor, to
pain in the spine. Tests revealed a 'significant reduction of skin
capillary width in the right middle finger of key punchers' (in
other words, the very small vessels feeding the muscles with
oxygen became smaller so less oxygen was getting to the muscles).[9]
Surveys found two kinds of disorder: 'One may be a result of
repeated static muscular fatigue. Another is a nervous disorder
almost exclusively peculiar to female clerical workers, with a loss
of sensation (hemihyaesthesia) accompanying cut in blood flow
(vasoconstricture) on the same side of the body.'[10] The suicide
of a woman key puncher attracted medical and public attention
in Japan to this illness,[11] which is now a recognised industrial
disease there.
Japanese researchers found that many typists and key-punch
operators perform monotonous jobs and are isolated from fellow
workers. They have to 'keep the same posture with the same
movement all day long and they are discontented with their
own work, always with feelings of repression'.[12] The women also
work in relatively noisy surroundings (65 to 84 decibels). Russian
studies of business machine operators yielded similar results,
adding that 'disturbances of the peripheral and central nervous
system were observed'. They recommended that these illnesses
be listed as occupational diseases.[13]

A Japanese survey of the international incidence and treatment of
key puncher's disease revealed that it was indeed widespread.
Forms of treatment varied from massage and liniments in the
Philippines, to doses of vitamin B in Peru, to cortisone injections

in West Germany! Prevention suggestions varied from reduced working hours and varied routine in the United States, to gymnastics in Finland, workers' group meetings in Sweden and adapted chairs in France.[14] A British study of tenosynovitis suggests screening, surveying groups of workers to select out those who are 'susceptible' to these cramps.[15] But like all occupational disease, this one can only be prevented where it begins: in the job itself.

Time off work and plentiful rest breaks are essential, but they don't tackle the source of the problem: repetitive work which harms the muscles of your body. Drugs and injections are no substitute. Try demanding that work be shared so that no one has to stay in the same unhealthy position all day long. And make sure that no piece of equipment enters your office before it has been vetted by those who have to use it. Remember, safety representatives have this right by law (see chapter 11).

Footnotes

1   Arledge, J.T., *The Diseases of Occupation*, London, 1892, p.105.

2   Nachemison, cited in Grandjean, E. and Hunting, W., 'Ergonomics of Posture – Review of various problems of standing and sitting posture' in *Applied Ergonomics*, Vol.8 No.3, 1977, pp.135-140.

3   Troisi, F.M., 'Lumbago with spinal disorders caused by incorrect sitting postures during sedentary work' in *Medicina del Lavoro*, Vol.60 No.1, January 1965, pp.21-27.

4   Gilbreth, F. and Gilbreth, L., 'Fatigue Study' cited in *British Standards Institute 3044:* Anatomical, physiological and anthropometric principles in the design of office chairs and tables, 1958.

5   Noro, L. and Koskela, A., 'Some observations on human engineering problems in office work' in *Medical Bulletin*, Vol.21 No.2, July 1961, pp.161-168.

6   Laner, S., *Fitting the Job to the Worker*, Paris, 1963.

7   Burandt, U. and Grandjean, E., 'The effect of office seat squabs of various shapes on sitting posture' in *Internationale Zeitschrift fur Angewandte Physiologie Einschliesslich Arbeitsphysiologie*, Vol.20 No.5, 1964, pp.441-452.

8   Mauriel, M., 'Static disorders during sedentary work in particular in shorthand typists' in *Archives Maladies Professionelles*, 27(1), January-February 1966, pp.74-78.

9   Komoike, Y. and Horiguchi, S., 'Fatigue assessment on key punch operators, typists and others' in *Ergonomics*, Vol.14 No.1, 1971, pp.101-109.

10   See footnote 9.

11   Komoike, Y., 'Effects and perspectives of the Institution on Cervicobrachial Disorders with illustrations of inspection and palpitation techniques' in *Sumitomo Bulletin*, No.13, April 1977.

12   Komoike, Y. and Horiguchi, S., see footnote 9.

13   Aramovic-Poljakov, D.K. and Kolicov, V.A., 'Occupationally induced pathology of the upper extremities in the operators of calculating and bookkeeping machines' in *Gigiena truda i professional'riye zabolevanija*, Vol.13 No.2, February 1969, pp.22-27, and Mazunina, G.N. et al, 'Clinical picture and prevention of diseases of

the hands in persons working on punched card machines in *Gig. trud.,* Vol.9 No.6, June 1965, pp.12-15.

14 Komoike, Y. et al, 'Health control on key punchers, typists and others' in *Sumitomo Bulletin of Industrial Health,* No.5, April 1969.

15 Welch, R., 'The measurement of physiological predisposition to tendosynovitis' in *Ergonomics* 16 (5), 1973, pp.665-8.

CHECK LIST

office furniture

1　Does the chair enable you to sit with your back upright?

2　Can you work without having to peer forwards (i.e. can you keep your head up)?

3　Can you work without having to constantly turn your head (eg. to see the work you are typing)?

4　Is there room enough for pregnant women to sit comfortably?

5　Is the chair adequately padded (with no exposed metal/ rough edges)?

6　Is the seat covering made of natural fibres?

7　Is the chair seat reasonably hard and firm?

8　Does the edge of the chair seat cut into the back of your legs?

9　Does the chair seat put pressure on your thighs?

10　Is the seat the right size for you (ie. ends about 5 inches from the crease of your knee when you are sitting against the backrest)?

11　Does your chair swivel?

12　Is it secure upon the floor (doesn't wobble or slip)?

13　Is the chair height adjustable?

14　Are your feet flat on the floor when you are seated upon the chair?

15　If not, is a footrest provided?

16　Does your chair have an adjustable backrest positioned at the back of your waist?

17　Can you reach things (phones, stationery) from your chair without straining?

18　Does your chair have comfortable armrests? (typists' chairs should not have any)

19　Is there plenty of leg room as you sit?

20　Is your desk at the right height for your kind of work (typing, writing)?

21　If your job involves different kinds of work, is your desk adjustable in height?

22　Is the furniture kept clean?

23　Are any repairs done quickly?

24　Do you get proper tea and lunch breaks?

25　Do you get breaks in typing work? in key punch work? in writing work?

26　Can you vary the type of work that you do during the day?

5 Dangerous substances: chemicals, gases and dusts

In offices, especially, employees run the risk of exposure to harmful products of which often they do not realise the danger. (International Labour Office, Hygiene in Shops and Offices, *1963, p. 34)*

More than a million substances are in use in workplaces in Britain, and new ones are being introduced every day.[1] 2,400 are suspected of causing cancer. Office workers use many chemicals in the form of powders, liquids, or in aerosols. Some machinery gives off harmful gases, and the air in offices is polluted with dust from insulation and ventilation systems. Yet office workers are particularly ill-informed about the health hazards involved.

Substances such as typewriter cleaning and correcting fluids, normally used daily by typists in small quantities, may contain – among others – the poison trichloroethane. If some is spilled toxic fumes can reach dangerously high levels. And the long-term effect of exposure to small quantities of many of these substances is untested and unknown.

Chemical substances find many ways into the human body. As fumes or dusts, they can be inhaled, irritating the lungs and entering the bloodstream, where they may affect other organs. In any form they can irritate the skin, causing dermatitis – which simply means 'irritation of the skin' – and possibly skin cancer after prolonged exposure. Or if you are eating or drinking, and there are fumes or dust in the air, you may be taking in chemicals through your digestive system.

If you come in contact with a chemical, your body may react to it immediately. This is known as an *acute* reaction, and it is usually easy to trace the cause. At other times you may work with a chemical substance for years and slowly become sensitised to it. Asbestos, for example, can cause cancer *twenty years* after exposure. When this happens, it is often difficult to trace the cause, since a minute quantity of the chemical concerned may cause the reaction and it could be something present at work and at home. This is known as a *chronic* reaction.

Dangerous substances damage us in several different ways:

By poisoning — The direct destruction of human tissues, such as the effect of some acids.

By sensitisation and allergy — The most common symptoms are dermatitis and asthma. Between 1972 and 1975, the Post Office had 66 reported cases of industrial dermatitis...The causes included nylon twine, contaminated mail bags and chemicals in duplicating paper.[2] One man in the German Post Office got eczema on the thumb and nose from a stamp in ink. The chemical responsible was an additive, p-aminoazobenzene.[3]

Substances known to cause dermatitis in offices include:	*carbonless copying paper* *adhesives* *carbon and copy paper* *duplicating fluid* *duplicating materials* *indelible pencils* *cleaning fluids* *plastic* *synthetic detergents*	*selenium (some photo-copiers)* *photocopier toners* *inks* *ink remover* *rubber and synthetic rubber* *type cleaners* *waxes and polishes* *audio typists' earphones*

By damage to the foetus

Some chemicals that do not harm adults can damage the unborn foetus in the womb, especially in the early stages of pregnancy. One example is lead.

By causing cancer

Numerous substances in daily use are now known to cause cancer. There is no minimum dose of such substances that can remove all danger of cancer, e.g. asbestos.

By causing fire or explosion

Many chemicals are highly flammable, particularly as gas or dust. Before discussing the chemicals themselves, a word about 'safe levels', so-called. The government has set standards for some dangerous chemicals which are known as Threshold Limit Values (TLVs) — a limit beyond which exposure to these chemicals is not supposed to go. But beware of such 'safe levels', for they are often *unsafe* levels as they are set with economic considerations as much in mind as safety. The Health and Safety Executive itself states that these levels do not protect against discomfort, aggravation of pre-existing conditions, or even getting an occupational disease! Hmmm.

TLVs are often set after inadequate testing and are set only for an 'average man'. They are set for each chemical alone — so levels don't apply when several substances are present. They vary between countries and they vary over time. So they are not scientific, objective standards. Watch out when management tells you the air is being monitored or measured and the levels of fumes or dust are below the TLV. This does not mean that you are therefore working in a safe atmosphere.

Chemical names are often bewildering but it's important to remember that they are labels — they tell you what's in a substance. You don't have to understand chemical formulae to look something up in one of the books listed in Appendix 3.

These books often explain quite simply how chemical substances affect the body.

Solvents

Many products used in offices contain solvents, which means they are able to dissolve other things. This is their use — and their danger, because they can dissolve body fats. Numerous solvents evaporate to form vapours, which are breathed in, reaching all parts of the body via the lungs and bloodstream. They may also affect your skin. They attack the liver and brain particularly. Look out for dizziness, headaches and bronchial symptoms.

The commonest solvent is also the safest: water. But the rise in the chemical industry has led to the use of many different solvents, in industry, in offices and in the home. They have various technical advantages over water, which will not dissolve all substances, and also evaporate faster. This means the job gets done faster — something office supervisors are always in favour of — but it also means they get into the air for us to breathe them in. They are more hazardous than water, and some are very nasty indeed.

Correcting fluids Those used to correct typing errors are mainly solvent-based.

Dear Madam,

Your organisation was mentioned in Woman's Own *as a source of advice regarding dangers from chemicals, especially to women of childbearing age. A colleague and I are concerned about the effect of the various types of liquid paper correction fluid which we have to use a lot at work. So far we have bought 'Liquid Paper' correction fluid because it used to say on it 'non-toxic'. This is no longer stated and it now says 'do not brush' (but dot each letter). We have to alter large parts of documents and so we do 'brush' and it gets all over our faces and round (and perhaps in) our mouths. It says 'apply sparingly' and 'not to be taken internally', 'non-hazardous when used as directed', 'contains 1.1.1 trichloroethane'.*
My friend and I are members of NALGO.
Can you advise us which is the best one to buy on health grounds. We did try one other kind, 'Tipp-Ex Mondial' (a water-dilutable fluid) but it was not possible to type over this.

Yours sincerely, Ann Law

PS: Our boss is thinking of making us buy the cheapest brand without finding out if this is harmful.

(Letter to Women and Work Hazards Group)

For example, *Tipp-Ex* fluid contains the following:

35% titanium dioxide
8 % acrylate mixture
2 % lecithin derivative
5 % special petroleum 100/1400 (solvent)
50% 1.1.1 trichloroethane (solvent)

The main concern is the chlorinated solvent, 1.1.1 trichloroethane. According to a recent report for the US Department of Health, Education and Welfare (equivalent of our DHSS) National Institute of Occupational Safety and Health, this substance has been reported to cause the following effects in humans:

'headache, dizziness, slowness, sleepiness, weakness, ringing sound in ears, prickling senation in hands and feet, liver damage, sickness, vomiting, diarrhoea, drop in blood pressure, slower heart rate, dry and cracked or inflamed skin, eye irritation.' (From 'Chloroethanes: review of toxicity', in *Current Intelligence Bulletin,* 21 August 1978)

There is also a possibility that this substance causes cancer.[4]

Until 1979 *Liquid Paper* contained chloroform and trichloroethylene (trike) which is addictive and known to cause cancer. Poor ventilation enables 'trike' to accumulate to toxic concentrations. It affects the nervous system, leading to giddiness, fatigue, headaches, nausea and vomiting at low levels of concentration (10-20 ppm).[5] In 1979, a teenager in Oregon died from sniffing *Liquid Paper.*[6] Three deaths in the past seven years were attributed to the product in Dallas Texas, where it is manufactured.[7] The manufacturers subsequently dropped trike and now *Liquid Paper* contains 98% 1.1.1 trichloroethane.

Snopake correcting fluid contains titanium resin and toluene, a solvent, which is the main cause for concern. This chemical is reported to cause eye, skin and throat irritation. Splashed on to the skin, it can cause dermatitis. Exposure to the vapour causes headache, dizziness, fatigue, muscular weakness. There is evidence that the current so-called 'safe level' of 100 parts per million* is too high and that even lower levels can cause painful menstrual periods (dysmenorrhoea). Toluene is, again, used by 'glue sniffers'.

Roneo stencil correcting fluid contains methylated spirit, acetone, ether and dibutylphthalate. These are generally irritating

---

* This figure means there is an official level of exposure which should never be more than 100 parts of the substance per million parts of air in the working environment. (See p. 54 for more details of Threshold Limit Values.)

to the eyes, throat and skin. Headaches, sleepiness, exhaustion, dizziness and loss of appetite are also recorded. Acetone is contained in some glues popular with 'glue sniffers'.

You may be wondering why manufacturers put such lethal chemicals into commonly used products. Well, they are often cheaper and quicker to make. The hazards may be multiplied if the product requires a thinner, which contains yet higher concentrations of solvent, or if you smoke while using it. For example, when smoking and using a bottle of *Liquid Paper* containing trike you used to be exposed to highly poisonous phosgene gas. The small whiff is more than 1000 times as toxic as the thinner alone. To be sure, you shouldn't smoke while using dangerous chemicals – but it helps to *know* you're using dangerous chemicals in the first place! As with many substances used in office work, you are only working with small quantities of the substance. But you may be exposed to these low levels *throughout your working life.* If you work in a typing pool where everyone is using correcting fluid you could be breathing in this and other harmful fumes all day, every day.

However, *Tipp-Ex* correction paper is harmless. If you have to use a liquid correcting agent, then use a *water-based* one. *Tipp-Ex Aqua Fluid, Snowdrop* or *Snopake* water-based correcting fluids are much safer.

Cleaning fluids for office equipment

*Chlorinated hydrocarbons and highly flammable liquids were used by office staff without them fully appreciating their dangerous properties. (*Health and Safety Inspector's report, *North East London Polytechnic, 1978)*

Chemical cleaning agents may be detergents, chlorinated hydrocarbons or other solvents. To be found in some are trichloroethylene, tetrachloroethylene, benzene, xylene, turpentine. According to the British Standards Institute (BSI) these are, however, 'not recommended' since they are dangerous, having a TLV of less than 150 parts per million. The BSI states that petrol, carbon tetrachloride and chloroform are 'not to be used in any circumstances' because they are highly dangerous, although the BSI lists them in a table of 'common solvents'! Some of the cleaners contain corrosive chemicals which can have serious effects on the eyes, skin or clothes.

Thawpitype is 100 per cent Genklene. This is trichloroethane (see above, p. 56). The label warns: 'Harmful vapour. Do not inhale. Can defat the skin.'
Roneo stencil cleaning fluid is a member of the paraffin family and a solvent.
Swallow cleaning fluid is 1.1.1 trichloroethane (see above, p. 56).
Odesco cleaner contains isopropyl alcohol which affects the

central nervous system and irritates skin and eyes. It can cause conjunctivitis. Inhalation irritates the respiratory tract and causes headaches and nausea. This cleaning fluid also contains ammonia, which burns the eyes and skin and causes bronchial disorders and headaches.

Medical textbooks recommend the wearing of respirators, aprons, boots and gloves and the use of good ventilation where these substances are used. No one with eye or chest complaints should work with ammonia at all, according to medical literature. Maybe no one at all should, in that case! If the manufacturers admit that ammonia is harmful to some people, then everyone working with it is to some extent at risk. No medical studies have been done to show the safety of low levels of exposure to ammonia. You can smell it at one-fifth of the current 'safe level' of 25 parts per million. Any sign of the odour should be taken to mean that better ventilation is required. And beware that it isn't leaking *into* the airconditioning system!

Where possible use a safe substitute. Brushes or 'Blu-tak' may be just as efficient as these deadly poisons for cleaning the typewriter — and safer. 'Kappy' sheets are also less harmful, and you just type on to the paper to clean the keys.

Self-copying paper

The National Board of Occupational Safety and Health in Finland issued a national circular in 1977 warning all firms and offices of the potential hazards of self-copying paper. They pointed out that the paper causes skin allergies in some people. A similar report from Sweden pointed out symptoms of allergy affecting the skin and mucous membranes among people handling large quantities of self-copying forms — particularly when central heating was in operation.[8]

In Spring 1976, office workers for the Inner London Education Authority were handling self-copying forms for school transfer records. There was an outbreak of eye, nose, throat and skin irritation, with catarrh, headaches and coughing first thing in the morning, among about half the staff involved. The culprit, carbonless copying paper, was a type involving microcapsule technology. The microcapsule is a polymer (plastic) containing dyestuffs and solvent, coated on the back of the upper sheet. The microcapsule burst on contact, giving you a copy but at the same time releasing a fine dust which you can't see. It gets up your nose and irritates eyes, nose and throat. The dust particles are very fine (1:10 microns) and don't get trapped in the nasal passages. Following complaints from the office workers, the education authority changed to a different kind of self-copying paper known as a mechanical transfer type, in which there is a pigment layer on the back of the upper sheet. In 1977 there were no complaints attributable to this paper.

Dusts and solvents in library work Librarians are at risk from handling large numbers of books if these are made with talc-treated paper. Talc has been linked to cancer of the lung, particularly if contaminated with asbestos (see below). Librarians sometimes use benzene or toluene to restore faded print. Both are solvents and narcotics — they damage the nervous system. Benzene can cause leukaemia (blood cancer) and on contact with the skin will cause blistering. There is serious danger from regular exposure to relatively low concentrations.

Office machinery and dangerous substances

Some processes in which office machines and data processing equipment are used involve the use of toxic substances, either as part of the process or as cleaning agents for the machine, equipment or components. Chemicals used include inks, duplicating machine fluids and developers. For the mechanical and other dangers involved see chapters 8, 9, on safety and new technology. Stencil duplicators use inks which can cause dermatitis and irritate the lungs. Spirit duplicators and microfilm developing equipment use ammonia which attacks the lungs, liver, nervous system, skin, eyes, nose and throat. Bandafluid, used commonly in schools, contains methanol. American studies have shown that machines using methanol fluid are hazardous when used 'in areas without adequate exhaust ventilation'. Tests found 400 to 800 parts of methanol per million parts of air when maximum levels should never be above 200 parts per million according to US government guidelines. The studies recommended:

1   fitting duplicators with exhaust ventilation;

2   installing air conditioning;

3   the use of the machine on a part-time basis, two or three hours per day, with a daily consumption of less than one pint of fluid (they had found that up to ten gallons per week were being used).[9]

Electrostencil machines

These machines emit carbon dust and poisonous gases. Electronic stencil cutting machines may produce the following gases during the cutting action:

Carbon monoxide Highly poisonous. Causes headaches, drowsiness, nausea, increased pulse rate, Particularly dangerous if you have a heart complaint.

Nitrogen dioxide Extremely poisonous. Irritates eyes and affects teeth, skin and hair. Can cause headaches, chest pain, asthma, mouth ulcers, bronchial disorders.

Ozone Very dangerous to lungs. (See section on photocopiers, p. 61)

Formaldehyde Highly poisonous. Irritates and burns eyes and can cause conjunctivitis, dermatitis and bronchial disorders.

Acetic acid Attacks skin, teeth, eyes and digestive and respiratory system, liver and heart.

Acrolein Extremely dangerous to eyes, lungs and skin. Can induce vomiting. No one with skin or lung complaints should work with this.

Some of these gases cause lung damage at *very low levels* of exposure if used over a long period of time. Roneo assures users that the levels of these gases are below the Threshold Limit Value (TLV). This, however, does not guarantee your safety since the basis of TLVs leaves a great deal to be desired. Moreover, TLVs are always calculated for individual chemicals. Here we have a number of gases mixing together. What is the effect of this chemical 'cocktail'?

Roneo emphasises that the gases are at a safe level when the machine is 'operating under normal conditions' and underline the need for ventilation. What happens to your health if the machine is not operating under normal conditions? And what *are* normal conditions?

The machines can be fitted with filters, filled with activated carbon and are available from Gestetner and Roneo. These must be changed very frequently, however, and still don't prevent some some gases reaching those in the room. A Gestetner's operator's manual for their model 1544 machine states, on the inside back cover, in small writing that the machine should be used in a ventilated room. Yet in recognition of the hazard, filters can be fitted and now, as a result of pressure from users, both companies have developed a 'modification'. This is a six foot length of tubing for conducting the gases to an outside window. It costs about £50.

Ventilation fans in windows near the machine are less acceptable. In all events, Roneo-Vickers recommend that the stencil cutting machine should be in as large a room as possible 'certainly not less than 1,000 cubic feet'. Further, they 'would consider a minimum of four room air changes an hour to be necessary, but as high as ten changes per hour preferable'. (For more on ventilation, see HSE Guidance Note EH22 Ventilation of Buildings: fresh air requirements 1979.

Photocopiers   If you copy only occasionally you are fairly safe. But like many other 'harmless' things, when photocopiers are used at work for hours on end, day in day out, then you may have trouble. This is because the research into making sure these new 'wonders of technology' are safe does not take into account your prolonged exposure. They rarely state the possible health hazards, just how fast, how cheap and how good their equipment is.

Process	Method	Possible health hazards	Machine type
Thermal	Uses a heat-sensitive sheet as a copying medium. No chemicals in the machine. One-off copies	coated paper ozone	Ask your management to obtain information of the processes and hazards of your copier(s). This is your legal right under Section 6 of the 1974 Health and Safety at Work Act.
Diazo	Translucent original needed. Wet process. Ammonia in the machine. Can produce very large copies.	ammonia diazo compounds coated paper ozone	
Magnetic Dry Toner	Magnetic powder ink adheres to image on sensitised paper.	toners, dust ozone, solvents vapours from dispersants, coated paper	
Electrostatic DIRECT Transfer	Uses light-induced electrostatic charge on sensitised paper. Toner in liquid suspension in the machine.	vapours from dispersants toners solvents ozone coated paper	
Electrostatic INDIRECT Transfer ('plain paper')	Light-induced electrostatic charge image on internal element is transferred to plain paper and heat fixed. Plain paper copies. Selenium, zinc or cadmium sulphide drum.	cleaning agents toners, dust, selenium, ozone carbon monoxide, nitrogen oxide	
Electrostatic	Wet process. Heat fused Vaporisation Cadmium sulphide or selenium drum. May steam in the morning.	toner, ozone, selenium, cadmium sulphide drum next to heater may split	

It has been difficult to collect information for this section because of manufacturers' reluctance to supply information. Whatever the details, the main health hazards from photocopiers are ozone, toners and carbon monoxide from dry copiers and ammonia from wet copiers. Watch out for dermatitis, bronchial complaints, dry eyes, nose and throat. Good ventilation is essential, and no one should work full-time on a copier or in the same room as one.

Selenium

Some plain paper copiers use a selenium drum (eg Xerox, Kalle) to impart the necessary electrostatic charges. While selenium is essential in minute quantities in the human diet, it is not needed as a contaminant in the air! Its oxide can cause nose and throat irritation and skin sensitisation and has a TLV of 0.2 milligrams per cubic metre of air ($0.2mg/M^3$). There is evidence that this level is too high, but the only monitoring of selenium available[10/11] revealed lower levels in the air and probably the main risk is to maintenance and production workers who handle the drums regularly.

Dermatitis due to exposure to selenium will start on the wrists and neck as distinct red, itchy blotches which then spread. Painfully throbbing nails and 'garlic breath' are clear signs of selenium poisoning. Like many other substances there are still many questions unanswered about selenium. One researcher wrote in *Nature* magazine that 'the effects of minute volatile emissions [of selenium] from copiers cannot be predicted with confidence'.[11]

Ozone

Note: For more information, see page 169

Photocopiers normally emit very small quantities of ozone. Ozone is a gas produced by high voltage electrical equipment. The image most people have of ozone is of a substance that makes air 'fresh' and makes sea air good for you. Both are false. Ozone is a sweet-smelling, highly toxic gas. The 'official' maximum level (TLV) to which the 'average worker' should be exposed is one part in ten million parts of air. The US Department of Health warns: 'This concentration (0.1ppm) is objectionable to all normal persons, and irritates the nose and throats of most persons.'[12] *If you can smell it, the level is too high.*

> *There is no exposure to ozone without some risk to health. On this basis, all unnecessary exposure of humans to any concentration, however small, should be avoided. The danger of undesirable health effects far outweighs any benefits presumed to be derived from the industrial or institutional use of ozone for control of odors or bacteria in air. Even in low concentrations; inhaled ozone may cause dryness of the mouth, throat irritation, coughing, headaches, and pressure or pain in the chest, followed by difficulty in benefits presumed to be derived from the industrial or concentration of ozone and the period of*

exposure, ozone can produce many other injuries. It impairs the sense of smell, disguises other odors with a continuous odor of ozone, alters taste sensation, and reduces the ability to think. Ozone also depresses the nervous system, thus slowing the heart and respiration and producing drowsiness and sleep. Exposure to relatively small concentrations for an hour can cause the lungs to fill with fluid and start bleeding...' (US Public Health Service pamphlet, quoted in Nader below)

The long-range effects of ozone exposure show that ozone can significantly alter the structure of cells and tissues, most importantly in the lungs. (Ralph Nader, Bitter Wages, *p. 34)*

Several companies have carried out tests on the ozone concentrations. IBM carried out measurements in a small room with the only ventilation an open door. After several thousand copies they found a level not exceeding 0.05 ppm, which is irritating to some people.

In 1980 American scientists tested 10 photocopiers for ozone emissions.[13] The worst machine (Xerox 3400) gave off 50 times as much ozone per copy as the best (3M VHS – Rank Xerox 7000) and a maximum rate of use produced levels 50 per cent above TLV. The researchers emphasise that:

> ...copies are often installed in small, poorly ventilated areas which are not useful for other purposes...With inadequate ventilation, even relatively low ozone discharges can produce an exposure hazard.

They found that servicing caused a dramatic reduction in ozone levels (5 to 30 times lower), but that three weeks later, they were back to normal. This indicates poor design of the machines.

In the United States Anita Reber, a secretary at the Sperry Univac Corporation, complained of nose and sinus irritation as well as serious breathing problems. She also began to lose her co-ordination, and could not understand what was causing all these troubles. After several months she traced her ailment to the Remington 530 photocopier about three feet from her desk. She was told by a Sperry official: 'You'll have a hard time proving it.'* So she complained to the National Institute of Occupational Safety and Health, who found that other employees were similarly affected when the copiers were near their desks. They recommended that the machines should be confined to areas away from desks; that mechanical exhaust ventilation should be provided; that machines should be checked *before* they break

* Sperry are also the manufacturers of Remington copiers!

down; that people should be monitored for ill-effects; and that more ozone measurements should be made.[14]

Although the recommendations were soon carried out, Anita Reber was first demoted, then sacked for her responsible action. This again argues for strong union organisation, because there had been considerable stress put on this woman's life in carrying through her case against the company, which did not help her recovery. She suffered serious lung and sinus aggravation, and only after several months did her sense of smell improve. Philaposh, the local trade union health and safety group picketed the health and safety inspector's offices and pressured them to take Sperry to court.

Nitrogen oxide

Nitrogen oxide gases may be produced where there is a sparking created in the process in the electrostatic photocopiers, although the levels are likely to be very low. The symptoms are similar to those of carbon monoxide (see below) so if you get any air measurements done make sure these gases are included in the survey.

Carbon monoxide

Carbon monoxide is a well known poisonous gas which will be produced wherever carbon (eg. toner) is heated in an inadequate air supply. So it is present when a 'plain paper' photocopier is used ('direct transfer' copiers use presses rather than heat to fix the toner). Rank Xerox have taken measurements of carbon monoxide in their relatively well ventilated room and found levels of 20 to 25 parts per million around their 9200 machine, and less than 5 parts per million around the 3100 and 3103 machines. A level of 25 ppm is just half the TLV. This indicates that where there is anything less than properly installed ventilation, you are going to get hazardous levels. So if you find you've got a splitting headache, drowsiness or faintness, or an increased pulse rate, it may not only be the boss, but the carbon monoxide that is causing it. (Even so, it's his responsibility to fix it.)

Toners

Toners of one sort or another are used by most photocopiers. Dry powders are used in the dry-toner and plain paper copiers to develop an image on the paper. In the liquid processes the toner is mixed with a solvent and so is less likely to become an air-borne contaminant. Toners usually consist of a mixture of plastic resin and carbon black. The resin can consist of a number of polymers (plastics). For example:

Minolta Electrostatic uses aliphatic hydrocarbons (petroleum distillate).

Toshiba Fax BD-601 uses two toner resins, a styrene/acrylic copolymer or an epoxy resin.

Remington 530 uses a copolymer of vinyl/toluene/styrene

Other polymers used include polyvinyl acetate, polystyrene and polymethacrylate of butyl.

Scientists in the USA are concerned about chemicals in carbon black toners eg. nitropyrene which was found to cause cancer in animal tests. On the basis of these studies scientists at the University of Texas are 'worried about people who have worked all the time in confined copying areas'.[15]

Unfortunately the Threshold Limit Values for these new chemicals either don't exist or are completely inadequate. They are presumed to be just 'nuisance' dusts, although some of the chemicals used to make them are considered to be cancer agents and may be present in minute quantities in the final product. For example, epichlorohydrin, used to make epoxy resins, is treated in the United States as a cancer-causing substance. It seems that the particle size of these dusts is between 3.5 and 15 microns, which means that they can be inhaled (see p. 67 for the health effects of dusts).

The other constituent of toners — carbon black — has a Threshold Limit Value of $3.5mg/M^3$ (3.5 milligrams of dust per cubic metre of air) and can accumulate in the lungs. All in all, until more research is done — or made public — these substances should be considered as a possible danger to your lungs. Certainly the big companies have their doubt about the safeness: while each insists the toners are non-poisonous, Toshiba says 'avoid inhalation of dust', Rank Xerox recommends 'avoid dust inhalation' and IBM tells you to 'avoid excessive dust inhalation'. So in future you'd better stop breathing...Most of the companies' research has gone into checking the toners for skin irritation and possible skin sensitisation (allergy). They all reckon that, following tests on animals, there is no sensitisation. However, when we checked up with the manufacturers of some of these toners, they weren't helpful. For example:

> Dear Sir,
> We regret that we cannot reveal the compositions of our products except to the HSE or to medical practitioners under conditions of strict professional confidence.
>
> Yours faithfully,
>
> Group Chief Scientist
> Coates Brothers & Company Ltd.

Ann Bateman works as a reprographics assistant in an oil company office. She described her work:

> 'It's my job to clean the machines and change the toners. Even where there's a cartridge of toner you still get some spillage on your hands and clothes. And you breathe it in. Same with the cleaning fluids — the stuff stinks. I haven't a clue what it's doing to my lungs.'

Workers at Columbia University, New York, complained of nausea when working in the vicinity of a Minolta Electrostatic photo-copier. The National Institute for Occupational Safety and Health (NIOSH), found that aliphatic hydrocarbons and ozone were contaminating the air and were probably responsible. These hydrocarbons can also cause central nervous system depression and loss of appetite. NIOSH recommended that because of poor ventilation, 'the copying machine be used for no more than a small fraction of the work day (less than two hours a day)'. They recommended that the ventilation be improved.[10]

Dispersants

In liquid toner machines the dry powders are dispersed in 'hydro-carbon mixtures' or dispersants — a vague term that can mean anything. For example, in Toshiba machines the liquid is a mixture of isodecanes, which can cause headaches, nausea, depression, respiratory irritation, and should be kept well below the Threshold Limit Value of 400 parts per million. Other solvent mixtures include paraffins, ethyl alcohol, diethyl ether, acetone and octane, all of which will be mildly irritating to mucous membranes. Get management to have the vapours of these chemicals measured if you have any doubts.

Developers

Developers are used to impart the necessary electrostatic charge to which the toner sticks. They consist of glass, sand or iron powder with a lacquer coating. The particles are relatively large (200 to 400 microns) so are not likely to be inhaled.

Diazo process photocopiers

With these copiers there is the combined risk of ammonia and diazo compounds. The health hazards of ammonia are dealt with on page 59. Two chemicals present in the diazo developer, hydroquinone and resorcinol, have been reported to cause liver abnormalities.[16] However, little published research is available. At Brent House in Wembley, NALGO members complained of ammonia fumes from a Dyeline copier. The staff rep said: 'It was a running sore for many months, with a noticeable increase in colds, nose and throat irritation.' Consistent pressure forced the management to put in ventilation.

If you're worried about health hazards from a copier in your office, follow the 'Strategy for dealing with a health hazard on p. 169. The checklist on p. 75 and the guidelines for action against dangerous substances on p. 72 will also help. A short health survey asking people if they're suffering from symptoms such as dry throat or dry eyes could be useful (see Appendix 1) For information on photocopiers and ultra-violet light see p. 39.

Remember: No one should work full time on a copier. No one should work in the same room as a copier in frequent use. Good ventilation is essential.

Cleaning agents used with office machinery

A range of other chemicals is used in cleaning office equipment, for example, isopropyl alcohol (see p. 58).

Dust in the machine There may be a build-up of paper dust in some kinds of office machinery, including photocopiers. Near electrical components it is liable to cause sparking, and is therefore a fire hazard. Paper dust is classified as a 'nuisance dust' and there is no strict maximum amount to which you can be exposed. But if it is combined with other dusts, such as toner dust, it could aggravate coughs and so on.

Dangerous substances in the office building

Asbestos Many offices, including many government departments, have asbestos as a building material. It has been traditionally used as insulation in partitions, pipe lagging and cable ducts. It crops up in the home too, for example on your ironing board. At work you will find it in some unexpected places: inside some 3M photocopying machines there is a curtain of woven asbestos. Fire blankets are mostly asbestos and many doors are still fireproofed with it. In one London Department of Health and Social Security office the new ceiling fell in on the workers. Happily no one was hurt, but the ceiling was discovered to be insulated with asbestos. Asbestos is a known killer. A US government report released in 1978 estimated that more than two million American workers will probably die of cancer because of asbestos exposure at their work.[17] Here in Britain it has been estimated that more than half a million workers could die due to asbestos-related diseases in the next 30 years.[18]

There is *no* safe level of exposure to this killer dust — though the latest government standard (TLV) says workers may be exposed to 2 milligrams of asbestos in every cubic metre of air ($2mg/M^3$). It doesn't sound much, but this means you are permitted to breathe in two million fibres of this lethal stuff in every cubic metre of air you breathe in a day!

The smallest particles and fibres, which we cannot see and which, in the case of asbestos, cannot even be seen under an ordinary microscope, are the most dangerous.

How damaging the dusts are depends on the size of the particle or fibre, the type of dust, the amount received (which is determined by the concentration of fibres multiplied by the period of exposure). In other words, you are more at risk if you breathe in a dust over months and years. But dust-related cancers do *not* depend on how much you breathe in: one tiny fibre can cause the disease (eg. glass fibre or asbestos, both of which have been found in the airconditioning systems of offices).

Acute (immediate) reactions to dusts include irritation to eyes, nose and throat, coughs, dermatitis, allergic reactions. *Chronic* (long-term) effects are bronchitis, asthma, lung diseases such as asbestosis (scarring of the lung), heart disease, heart failure, and cancers such as mesothelioma, an extremely painful cancer of the chest or abdomen which is always fatal: over 85 per cent of cases of mesothelioma are due to asbestos. This and other cancers may take twenty years to show up. The accumulation of 'nuisance' dusts can also make people more prone to infections such as colds and 'flu.

A study by Mount Sinai School of Medicine in the United States found dangerously high levels of asbestos fibres in office buildings all over New York. Dr William J. Nicholson, who ran the study said:

> 'We are seeing inside the office buildings concentrations that are as high as we saw in areas near asbestos plants or where spraying was being done, where there has been illness or death. This significantly increases the risk of cancer to people who work in those buildings on a day in and day out basis.' (*Newsday,* 22 November 1975)

Thousands of offices have asbestos in them. It crumbles in time and the fibres come loose and can circulate through the office, sometimes via the ventilation system.

Other fibrous materials

Glass fibre, Rockwool and other brand-named insulation materials present some of the same problems as asbestos. They too are constructed from tiny fibres which can be breathed in and have been found to cause lung cancer. Glass fibre can cause severe skin irritation or dermatitis.

> '150 NALGO members at local authority offices in Essex refused to move into a new building because it was insulated with Rockwool fibre.
> The safety rep refused to believe management's and manu-facturers' reassurances that the material was safe. The

Health and Safety Executive was worse than useless. They told him their documentation on the hazards of Rockwool was 'classified information' and covered by the Official Secrets Act!

The rep got evidence from the TUC Centenary Institute showing that Rockwool is potentially more dangerous than glass fibre: 36 per cent of the fibres are below 3 microns in diameter and can be inhaled into the lungs, compared to 26 per cent of glass fibres. Like asbestos, it is these minute fibres which carry the greatest lung cancer risk.

Angry NALGO members picketed the new £500,000 office block, and Council managers gave in under the pressure. They agreed to the workers' demands for regular monitoring of the air, release of test results and acceptance of the level of permissible exposure to the same as the Threshold Limit Value for asbestos (1 milligram of dust per cubic metre of air). This is a victory, since Rockwool is officially classified as a "nuisance dust" with a TLV of 10 milligrams per cubic metre.' (From *Hazards Bulletin* 14, December 1978)

The Health and Safety Executive now recommends 5 milligrams per cubic metre of air: note that at this level you breathe in around 30 million fibres a day! At the Department of Health and Social Security office in Brighton, CPSA representatives got a survey done to find out levels of glass fibre particles in the air when they found there was fibre-glass insulation behind the tiles. They pressured management to carry out regular monitoring of the air.

'Nuisance dusts' Some dusts, like paper or houshold dust, are classified by the Health and Safety Executive as 'nuisance dusts'. This means they are known to irritate the nose and throat but not enough research has been done on the long-term health hazards. Until very recently glass fibre was classified thus. It was assumed that the particles could not be breathed in and were not so tiny or the sort of shape that would penetrate the lungs. But now the Man-Made Fibres Committee of the Health and Safety Executive is recommending that it be reclassified and the level of exposure reduced.

Dust in filing rooms can give you a sore throat. If not cleaned properly, books and files can become dust traps, harbouring spores which can cause allergic reactions in some people. Office workers at St Thomas's Hospital in London complained about the levels of dust in the filing room. They pressed management, who called in consultants to do a survey of the dust in the atmosphere. The room was thoroughly cleaned and reorganised to minimise dust, and redecorated.

Other dangerous substances

For more on smoking and why women do it, see the excellent Pluto Press publication The Lady Killers *by Bobbie Jacobson (London 1981)*

Improperly cleaned and maintained airconditioners can also harbour hazardous spores (see chapter 6 on ventilation). Pollution from cigarette smoke is harmful to health and can affect even those who don't smoke. A Toronto office worker, Murdeena Johnson, was awarded 'workman's compensation' after being subjected to high concentrations of tobacco smoke. The Ontario Workmen's Compensation Board said that the level of smoke was a precipitating factor in giving her bronchial asthma.[19] Many office workers smoke while they work as a way of coping with the job — as a reaction to stress. But others do not, and there is an increasing resistance to smokers always getting their way. Perhaps there is a need for separate smoking areas in offices as there are now in cinemas and in aircraft.

Office workers are exposed to a host of other toxic substances indirectly, such as telephone disinfectants and toilet cleansers, furniture polishes and paints, air fresheners and fly killers. Many of these are in aerosol containers which are pressurised, causing the lungs to be at risk, and they are also potential bombs. If you have a cut or sore and any of these substances leak into the cut, it can be very nasty. Look at the list of cautionary instructions on the aerosol cans — that's enough to establish these are dangerous substances! Women in particular are at risk here because many of these products are also used for cleaning purposes at home, and women could be getting a double dose.

There is a severe hazard arising from the mixing of cleaners and bleaches or disinfectants. This can generate chlorine gas — a hazard in both home and office. Cleaning substances should not be made of such potentially dangerous stuff. The burden should be on the manufacturer to make a safe product, not on the consumer to 'be careful'.

Janet Carpenter works in the office of a large shipping firm: 'In our office they were laying new carpets. The fumes from the glue used to lay the carpet were overwhelming, especially near the hot pipes. This lasted three weeks, and I got so ill I had to stay at home.' In one government office the place was infested with rats, but the pesticide put down for three weeks to kill the rats nearly finished off the staff!

In the 1920s and '30s office workers suffered from an industrial disease known as chemical necrosis of the fingers. This was due to pricking with aniline pencils and particles of aniline remaining for some time within the tissue. A number of office workers lost fingers as a result.

Storage of chemicals Chemicals are often stored in large quantities in offices and in factories. As they get used they eventually end up in the atmosphere and in your body. Chemicals stored for office use may

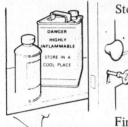

include benzene, petrol, methylated spirits, paraffin and ammonia. Stored chemicals can also leak, catch fire or explode.

'A near-disaster happened in a London office, when two thousand office workers were evacuated from office blocks in Berkeley Square in August 1978. Ammonia fumes spread through a ten-storey block and 21 people were taken to hospital and the area sealed off.' (*The Times*, 19 August 1978)

Find out what chemicals are stored, and why. There are some useful regulations limiting the storage of some chemicals. One safety rep used these as the basis of a warning letter to the management at the Greater London Council:

'It has been brought to my attention that propane gas cylinders are being stored in Room 214 at County Hall. In my opinion this practice contravenes the Highly Flammable Liquids and Liquefied Petroleum Gases Regulations 1972:

　　　　Regulation　6(1)
　　　　　　"　　　7(1) (d)
　　　　　　"　　　7(2)
　　　　　　"　　　7(4)
　　　　　　"　　　7(5)
I hope you will remedy this situation immediately.

NALGO Safety Representative.' (Copy to Senior Officer, Health and Safety)

Where possible, other substances should be used which do not present health hazards. In the meantime, they should be kept in a proper storage room and be clearly labelled, and workers alerted to their existence and the ensuing risk. The health and safety inspector and the fire brigade should inspect them. Precautions should be taken in the dilution or transference of such stores: the closed suction method is safer than open pouring into containers.

Pollution from outside

As well as chemicals and dusts used inside offices, office workers are also exposed to harmful substances in the air from outside, from factories, traffic and heating systems.

'Office staff in central London are exposed to more sulphur dioxide gas than in any other part of Britain. And sulphur dioxide levels in the City of London are among the highest of all Europe's capitals.

These observations — surprising, since the clearing of smoke from London's air is said to be a great environmental success — were made today by a spokesman for the Greater London Council's air pollution department, Dr David Ball. He said sulphur dioxide was heavily concentrated in the City because of the large number of office heating plants which burn sulphur-rich oil. In winter it could reach an average of 150 micrograms per cubic metre — about twice the level recommended by the GLC.

Sulphur dioxide is a colourless acidic gas which can cause aggravation of some respiratory problems like bronchitis. But there is considerable medical dispute about how serious it might be.' (London *Evening Standard*, 3 October 1978)

If you work in any large town you will be exposed to some sulphur dioxide, carbon monoxide gas and diesel fumes from traffic pollution. Double glazing and a high quality efficient air-conditioning system are essential. P.J. Taylor, the Chief Medical Officer for the Post Office, said that trichloroethylene (see p.56) has been found 'seeping into manholes' from factories where it is used in massive quantities as a degreaser. He pointed out that the 'trike' would pollute the air of offices situated next to one of the factories. Workers in the office of a Nestlé factory in London suffered from asthma when exposed to a minute amount of TDI (toluene di-isocyanate) pollution which came from the factory next door. TDI is an extremely dangerous yet widely used indus-trial chemical in the manufacture of paints, inks, adhesives, enamelled wire and polyurethane rubbers and foams.

If you suspect pollution from adjoining plants, get your employer to have the air in your office sampled.

Action on dangerous substances: if in doubt, check it out

Office health hazards are likely to become more serious as more machines are introduced. More research, with publicly available and accessible results, is needed. Meanwhile, new substances are introduced into the workplace at a dizzying pace of one a day on average.

Try to get an agreement with management that they won't introduce any new substances without prior agreement from you.

Find out whether there are any alternatives which are safer.

Get hold of a chemicals manual: See Appendix 3 for some titles.

Make sure (under Section 7 of the Offices, Shops and Railway Premises Act) that where any chemical is getting into the atmosphere there is 'suitable provision for circu-lation of adequate supplies of fresh or purified air'.

Monitor the amount of the chemical, using a Draager Tube (simple to use — see Appendix 2 for addresses of where these can be obtained).

Check the information that suppliers are supposed to provide (under Section 6 of the Health and Safety at Work Act) regarding health effects, testing, chemical constituents, etc. see standard letter requesting information.

Dear Sir/Madam,

I am writing to ask if you can supply me with information about the possible hazards to health of one (some) of your products: (give full name(s) of substance(s) here).
I understand that, as required by Section 6(4) of the Health and Safety at Work Act 1974, you maintain information about tests relating to the toxicity of substances which you supply.
I am (shop steward/safety representative/union secretary etc.) at (name of company) and I (my members) use (name of substance) at work.
(If you have already seen a 'hazard data sheet' or similar information from the company on this substance, add the following paragraph):
I have already seen some information published by you on (name of substance). This is (Give name of leaflet or publication. If you can, also give the date, any reference number on the publication and the name of the author.) Can you please supply me with any additional information that you have.

Can you tell me:

> *What are the chemical ingredients of (name of substance), the chemical formula of each, and the rough proportion in which they are mixed. (You only need to ask this question if your substance is identified by a 'trade name' such as 'Bostik' or 'Genklene'. Leave this question out if you already know the proper chemical name of the substance or the ingredients.)*

> *What harmful effects is (this substance/each of the ingredients in this substance) known to cause or suspected to cause in humans? What harmful effects have been found in animals on which the substance(s) has (have) been tested? Please include reports of both short-term and prolonged exposure.*

> *At what concentration or dose, and what period of exposure, were any ill-effects observed? (Please supply references to textbook or journal articles in which full details of these reports can be found.)*

> *What precautions should be used when working with or near (name of substance?)*

> *What symptoms indicate that over-exposure to (name of substance) has occurred, and what first-aid measures should be used in such cases?*

I shall be most grateful for your help with these points and I look forward to hearing from you.

Yours sincerely,
(Your name)

You should question everyone about the health effects of any substances they are exposed to, not forgetting cleaners and porters, who are also at risk from substances being used in your department. A short questionnaire is very useful, listing questions like 'Do you get a sore or dry throat at work?' (see Appendix for sample questionnaire.) Watch out for respiratory complaints, dermatitis, menstrual problems, fertility problems in both men and women, headaches, drowsiness, depression.

Your employer may try to put the burden of safety on to you by simply emphasising that you must 'take care' when handling nasty chemicals. This isn't good enough. It also ignores the fact that you are probably breathing in the stuff forty hours a week, year after year, and no amount of 'taking care' will prevent lung damage from this kind of slow build-up. It is your employer's legal responsibility to provide safe and healthy working conditions.

Footnotes

1   *TUC Health and Safety at Work 7,* A Course for Union Representatives, TUC Education, 1979.

2   Taylor, P.J., 'The Post Office Occupational Health Service' in *Journal of the Society of Occupational Medicine,* 26 (2), April 1976, pp.65-68.

3   Brown, W.P., 'Contact Dermatitis from a Stamp Ink in the German Post Office' in *Contact Dermatitis,* 1 (3), June 1975, pp.189-90.

4   In Animals some liver cancers have been observed. (World Health Organisation Monograph on Carcinogens, Vol.20, 1979)

5   *Special Occupational Hazards Review of Trichloroethylene,* NIOSH publication No.78-130, Maryland, January 1978.

6   *Mother Jones,* New York, May 1979.

7   Phone interview with Dallas County Medical Examiner, Dallas, Texas, 27 November 1979.

8   *Vern og Velferd,* No.3, 1976, p.45.

9   McAllister, R.G., 'Exposure to Methanol from Spirit Duplicating Machines', *American Industrial Hygiene Association Quarterly,* Vol.15, March 1954, pp.26-28; and Goss, A.E. and Vance, G.H., 'Methanol Vapors from Duplicating Machines may be a Health Hazard' in *Industrial Hygiene Newsletter* (US), Vol.8 No.9, September 1948, p.15.

10   National Institute for Occupational Safety and Health, *Health Hazard Evaluation Determination, 73-195-152,* November 1974, US Dept. of Health, Education and Welfare.

11   Harkin et al, 'Evaluation of Selenium Levels in Air by Xerography' in *Nature,* Vol.263, 21 October 1976, p.708.

12   National Institute for Occupational Safety and Health, 'Industrial Exposure to Ozone', 1973, and *Safer Times,* No.7, Philadelphia Programme on Safety and Health, April 1977, p.1.

13   Selway, M. et al, 'Ozone production from photocopying machines' in *American Industrial Hygiene Association Journal,* Vol.41, June 1980, pp.455-9.

14   National Institute for Occupational Safety and Health, *Health Hazard Evaluation Determination, 76-70-367,* March 1977.

15   *The Guardian,* 14 April 1980; see also *Wall Street Journal,* 14 May, 1980.

16   Gaydos, J.C. and Mornson, A.S., 'Study of Abnormal Laboratory findings in Workers Exposed to Diazo Developing Chemicals', in *Journal of Occupational Medicine,* Vol.17 No.8, August 1975, pp.502-505.

17   US National Institute of Environmental Health Sciences, Report on Asbestos, 1978, quoted in BSSRS, *Asbestos − Killer Dust,* 1979, p.7.

18   See footnote 17.

19   Toronto Globe and Mail, 3 February 1979.

CHECK LIST

dangerous substances

Do staff complain of:

1. Irregular painful menstrual periods?
2. Irritation of eyes, nose or throat?
3. Headaches, dizziness, sleepiness?
4. Skin rash or irritation?
5. Difficulties in sleeping?
6. Do these symptoms appear with any particular materials?
7. Do these symptoms appear in any particular departments?
8. Is there any pattern of disease/complaint (eg. cancer/back trouble) among retired workers?
9. Is there any pattern of disease/problems amongst staff (eg. inability/difficulty in having babies)?
10. Do you know what chemicals you are using in the office?
11. Are any of them known to be: toxic/corrosive/inflammable/explosive?
12. Are they labelled to show contents, danger, precautions and first aid?
13. Are there warning signs in danger areas?
14. Will management identify all chemicals?
15. Can safer materials be used?
16. Can the dangerous work process be moved to another area?
17. Is there local exhaust ventilation to extract dust and fumes?
18. Is there good general ventilation to dispose of air contaminants?
19. Does the employer get the air tested regularly?
20. Do you take toxic materials eg. asbestos dust, home on your body or clothing?
21. Are permanent monitoring devices installed to detect very dangerous substances?
22. Are they set to warn of the smallest concentrations?
23. Are medical tests carried out regularly?
24. If so, are results made available to staff?
25. Is emergency breathing apparatus readily available?
26. Could bulk storage of chemicals, fumes or dust be a community hazard?
27. Are waste chemicals disposed of safely?

6 Temperature and ventilation

'M.D. Marsh & Co. supply accountancy and secretarial services in Sheffield. Their offices are in the attic of a hundred-year-old building converted from a pigeon loft in 1973. The local authority inspector served an Improvement Notice on Mr Marsh because of insufficient ventilation. In the secretary's room the fan heater on the wall was inadequate and there was no window. Mr Marsh appealed and said he was willing as a compromise to remove a sliding door to create draughts. The appeal was dismissed. Note that the industrial tribunal thought the inspector was being "somewhat overzealous".

The most common complaint voiced by office workers is poor ventilation, and one in three office workers in the Alfred Marks survey said they found office heating inadequate. It's often too hot or too cold and draughty; the temperature is uneven in the building and the air is dry; dusts and fumes give people sore throats and bunged-up noses.

Many large employers are expanding their copying and duplicating departments piecemeal until they become full-scale printshops, housed in totally unsuitable basement rooms whose ventilation was never designed to deal with the resulting air pollution. The severity and extent of ventilation problems has been greatly underestimated. If you're working in a poorly ventilated environment forty hours a week, year after year, these conditions are irritating and stressful and dangerous to your health.

Temperature

Modern office blocks are particularly prone to overheating. The Factory Inspectorate's reports are informative:

Many inspectors encountered the increasing problem of maintaining suitable temperatures in modern buildings with large areas of glass. Examples of room temperatures of over 40º C have been recorded in new office blocks, and there have been cases of employees suffering from heat exhaustion. [author's emphasis.]

Excessive heat builds up on sunny days, yet paradoxically the heat lost through the glazing during the night or on dull days can cause difficulties in maintaining a comfortable

*temperature. Thus the temperature in part of a building
exposed to the sun can be intolerable whilst the temperature on the shaded side can be below the required level.*

*Solar gain in modern buildings is a structural problem and
is closely related to the type of building, its ventilation and
heating systems, its design and aspect. Architects often
underestimate or ignore its effect. Little can be done after
the design stage because it is so expensive.*

*Tinted glass, reflective plastic film, blinds and airconditioning can be utilised to reduce its effect. More research into
structural solar shields and structural insulation of modern
buildings is needed before there is a really satisfying
solution.* [2]

Christine Adams, who works in a large oil company's office in
London: 'Our heating would drive you crazy. I work in a high
rise office block where it gets colder as you go up. One side of
the building is always hotter than the other.'

Modern construction techniques are geared to building office
blocks where fewer workers can be concentrated and work reorganised for efficiency. But tall buildings provoke wind currents
outside, and thus it is actually dangerous to open a window
because this can cause severe draughts. So permanent airconditioning, or 'canned air', becomes a technical necessity. You have to
struggle with a controlled 'microclimate'.

If the air temperature is too high, your body temperature rises,
your heart action increases, and your powers of concentration are
reduced. You might get dizzy spells. Exhaustion and drowsiness
may follow, which increase the chance of accidents. If the
temperature is too low, the body loses heat so that you shiver
and you get stiffness in muscles and joints. Your powers of concentration decrease and you notice even minor draughts. If the
humidity is too high, your sweat can't evaporate, which reduces
your body's resistance to high temperatures. If it's too low, you
get dryness of the mouth, throat and nose. The upper respiratory
tract, with its passages and sinuses, is lined with mucous mem-
brane which is supposed to be moist. It acts rather like a moat
which deters offensive organisms from crossing. If it gets dried up
even the most geriatric microbes can limp across and settle there.

Any of these symptoms may be attributed to the lack of efficient
airconditioning in your office — yet so often they are dismissed
by doctors and personnel managers as 'your imagination' or 'too
much smoking'.

Isobel Stewart described the customs and excise office where she
works:

'The heating and ventilation systems in our place are very inefficient and members complain of not enough oxygen. The stuffy atmosphere causes us to feel drowsy all the time.'

Some office workers have developed a 'winter itch' in the summer by being constantly in an airconditioned environment. The lowered indoor humidity, increased air movement and lack of sweating contribute to dehydration of the skin and damage to its protective barrier. These factors, coupled with the 'excessive use' of hot water and soap, can cause itching and dermatitis.[1]

By law a 'reasonable temperature' must be maintained in all workrooms other than those used only for short periods. Where the work does not involve 'severe physical effort', the Offices, Shops and Railway Premises Act, Section 6(1) states that after the first hour the temperature shall be at least 60.8°F (16°C). Less than this is deemed unreasonable in law. It's a pathetically low standard — really only a starting point. In 1967 the Factory Inspectorate officially admitted that the legal minimum is too low for workers who sit at their job.[3]

Directives on heating from a Midland firm in 1852.

Overshoes and topcoats may not be worn in the office but neck scarves and headwear may be worn in inclement weather. A stove is provided for the benefit of the clerical staff Coal and wood must be kept in the locker. It is recommended that each member of the clerical staff bring four pounds of coal each day during cold weather.

The Civil Service unions have succeeded in negotiating a slightly higher minimum of 65° F (18.5° C) and they are pressing for more. Where the heating system fails to produce 65° F and employers don't succeed in quickly restoring the agreed temperature, the unions recommend branches to take appropriate industrial action. Note that by law a thermometer must be provided in a conspicuous place on each floor (Offices, Shops and Railway Premises Act, Section 6). In the winter of 1977 the temperature at the London local government office, Brent House, fell below the legal minimum and 400 staff walked out. They came back the following day when management turned up the heating controls and maintained temperatures *above* the legal minimum thereafter.

Existing suggested levels are low, especially if you are not moving around in your work. A Swiss study found that 68° to 73° F (20° to 23° C) was the most agreeable temperature for the office workers in their survey.[4] You might want to negotiate this range. The British *Institute of Heating and Ventilation Engineers* (see Appendix 2) recommend a minimum of 68°F for offices. Whatever method of heating your employer supplies must be safe. The Offices, Shops and Railway Premises Act, Section 6(1) also states that no heating system must be used which 'results in the escape into the air...of any fumes of such a character and of such an extent as to be injurious or offensive to persons working [on the premises]'.

Overheating is a serious problem in some offices, yet there is no maximum temperature limit given in the Offices, Shops and Railway Premises Act. However, the Act does say the temperature shall be 'reasonable', which is negotiable between you and your employer. DHSS workers in Brighton protested about high temperatures in their office during the hot summer of 1976. The CPSA branch went through the usual negotiating channels but nothing was done, so over fifty of them walked out. Only then were fans installed. In winter they again had to walk out in protest at the cold before getting supplementary heating. But they won!

The increasing use of office machines producing heat requires more thought to be given to the design and construction of rooms in which these machines are installed. According to the Factory Inspectorate:

> 'One report investigated the complaint of lack of ventilation in a computer room and found temperatures in the range of 29° to 32° C (upper 80s F) not uncommon. Recommended temperature for efficient operation of computers is 21° C (70° F), and the airconditioning plant which was the only means of ventilation *was* designed to

maintain this temperature in the computer room. Several faults were found and remedied in the airconditioning plant.

Investigations also showed that similar high temperatures were being recorded in a large room in which data processing machines were being used. The ventilation, which was by means of windows and extractor fans, was found to be inadequate.[5]

And in 1978 secretaries at Aston University walked out of their office when the temperature rose to the 80s due to overheating of the visual display units and other office machinery in the room where they worked (see p. 140).

Ventilation

Where there are photocopiers, duplicators, electrostencil machines in use, good ventilation is absolutely essential for your health. The same goes for chemical fluids of any sort (see chapter 5). Heating systems can also cause problems. Carbon monoxide may be present in the flue gases of some heating installations. The staff of the accounts department of a firm housed in a single large room on the third floor of a multi-occupancy building complained of severe headaches, particularly in cold weather. It was thought at first it was caused by poor general ventilation. However, tests showed high levels of carbon monoxide coming from a residential flat below the office. The flat's gas-fired central heating boiler was to blame. Diesel fumes from some boilers have been known to cause sickness among office workers. An office cleaner on early morning duty was killed from poisoning caused by fumes from a small sink water heater which needed external air vents. Make sure the heating system for your building is well maintained and regularly serviced, and that rooms are well ventilated.

There are two kinds of ventilation: general — which is airconditioning — and exhaust — which removes dust or fumes from a dangerous process.

General ventilation Airconditioning, or general ventilation, should be a *total air cleaning system*. Its purpose is to distribute fresh air throughout the building at a comfortable temperature and humidity. But it's not very effective in controlling hazardous substances since it relies on fresh air merely to dilute such substances. To remove them you need exhaust ventilation (see below, p. 82).

General ventilation is not a fan on the wall. Fans are useless, at best only sucking some cigarette smoke and germs across the room and out the window. Ventilation from another room is not good enough either. The *Department of Employment Gazette* reported that in London, 'internal offices in warehouses and within larger offices, reception areas and telephonists' cubicles rarely had adequate provision for the circulation of air'. The only provision was often indirectly from another room.[6]

Clean, fresh air is a vital requirement for healthy working conditions.

> 'It has been known for a long time that if the thermal conditions are poor, that is if the ventilation is inadequate or the temperature is too high or too low, employees become discontented and accidents and sickness occur. Such conditions may also affect the supply of suitable labour because these days higher standards of comfort are demanded by employees than in the past.' (Dr G. Socrates, *Management Services*, March 1978, p.44)

Office workers in London's Kensington and Chelsea Council offices moved into the new town hall in 1978. Ever since they have complained of very dry air where it's difficult to breathe. There have been complaints of many sore throats and an increase in the number of colds and 'flu. NALGO departmental reps communicated the complaints to management and health and safety inspectors and doctors have confirmed that the lack of humidity is a health risk. Workers with contact lenses suffered from eye irritation due to the dry air. NALGO members voted to have a walk-out every week at 4 pm as long as was necessary to get something done. The Council has now agreed to install a humidifying system. As part of their cutback in public expenditure the Council had taken out humidification in the air-conditioning plan to save £40,000. To install the system now will cost a lot more.

> *There are two ways to work out general ventilation air flow rates. Either relate ventilation to the number of people in the room, expressed as cubic feet of air per minute per person. Or relate it to the size of the room, expressed as cubic feet of air per minute per square foot of floor area. The Health and Safety Executive's Guidance Note EH22* Ventilation of Buildings: Fresh Air Requirements, *1979, gives recommended air movement rates for different offices. The level recommended for offices where people smoke is 30 ft^3 per minute per person or at least .02 ft^3 per minute per square foot of floor area. Humidity should be controlled between 30% and 70%. It's useful to know this minimum recommendation exists if you get a ventilation survey done and someone starts quoting figures at you.*

Depending on the kind of building you work in, you may feel air-conditioning is necessary — but you'll have to fight for the best system available. Many systems cause more problems than they cure.

Exhaust
ventilation

When there is any dust or fumes, such as from photocopiers or duplicators, exhaust ventilation is *essential*. The fumes or dust must be extracted as near the source as possible, before they reach you. Exhaust ventilation consists of a hood positioned close to the health hazard, a funnel, air cleaning device and fan. In a good system, nasty fumes are destroyed and *not* spewed out into a corridor or street. *The ventilation system should be regularly maintained and cleaned and the air regularly monitored to check that it's working.*

You have a legal right to good ventilation in your office. The Offices, Shops and Railway Premises Act, Section 7(1) states:

> 'Effective and suitable provision shall be made for securing and maintaining, by the circulation of adequate supplies of fresh or artificially purified air, the ventilation of every room comprised in or constituting premises to which this Act applies.'

For a piece of health and safety legislation, these are strong words, and the duty on your employer is clear. It is *not* weakened by the words 'as far as is reasonably practicable'. The law states that provision of ventilation shall be made, and so it shall (with a bit of pushing from you).

In the Civil Service, the National Whitley Council has agreed the following standard:

> 'Mechanical ventilation is to be provided where fresh air supplied by natural means is insufficient (for example, in rooms which have no access to external air) or undesirable (for example, rooms in which openings to external air would permit the entry of unacceptable dirt or noise).[7]

Problems of
ventilation

Ventilation itself can be hazardous. Poor ventilation can make the air dry or create draughts; it can redistribute the pollution round the building instead of cleaning it; it can spit stale air straight into the community or the corridor; it can be noisy. All these problems can be rectified — don't put up with them. If you're plagued with draughts you may need *both* systems. Draughts are a common complaint in offices, causing aching muscles and stress as well as colds. An efficient general ventilation system replaces the air removed by the exhaust system and evenly distributes it throughout the office so that cross-draughts are avoided.

There is a kind of fatigue which you only experience from air-conditioning. However, there doesn't seem to be any evidence that this is in fact due to a lack of oxygen. It seems more likely that the fatigue is caused by being constantly in a 'microclimate' which, unlike a natural environment, is unvarying. According to one German medical report, some people develop a 'pathological aversion' to the atmosphere in airconditioned places. They fear the effects of it, and 'anxiety, degenerating into depression, can occur'. The report recommends that people working in such environments have regular contact with natural fresh air in rest rooms, for example.[8] Breaks allowing you to leave the building may also be necessary.

Some serious problems can be created by airconditioning and ventilation systems. According to a study carried out by Mount Sinai School of Medicine, crumbling asbestos from the insulation circulated through the air system in some office buildings has reached dangerous levels. A thousand New York office buildings used asbestos in their systems of fireproofing. The hazard is greatest in buildings erected between 1958 and 1970 when asbestos was most widely used for fireproofing and insulation. Some of the asbestos fibres are now coming loose. Exposure to asbestos — even a few fibres — can cause cancer (see p. 67).

Some airconditioning systems use ozone to sweeten the air and counter smells. Ozone, even in minute quantities, irritates the mucous membranes, gives you a sore throat, and even low levels can cause pains in the chest and harm the lungs (see chapter 5, section on photocopiers for more details). Ozone doesn't neutralise smells, 'but by its effect on the mucous membranes of the nasal passages it does in fact mask them'.[9] Effectively, the air is poisoned but smells nicer...Beware of ioniser airconditioners hailed in the press as the wonder cure for all office ills. Some emit ozone and some are cheap and nasty, being found to give out significantly hazardous levels of this gas.

Humidifiers   Some airconditioning systems also humidify the air, and this has caused a new occupational disease: 'secretary's asthma' or 'humidifier fever' (see *Observer* article below). The symptoms include intermittent chills and fever, coughing, vomiting, aching joints, tightness in the chest — usually for a few hours on return to work after a break. The disease has been mistaken for a feverish cold or virus infection and dismissed by some managers as malingering or 'just a bug'. Attacks are extremely debilitating and distressing but long-term effects are unknown as studies have not been done. But it is particularly hazardous to those suffering lung and heart ailments. The disease is similar to 'farmer's lung' which farm workers get if they work with mouldy hay, and there may be some connection with 'legionnaires' disease. Humidifiers, drip trays and entire duct work must be regularly maintained and thoroughly cleaned. In one workplace, to eliminate the contamination, the water supply system was removed and cooling was accomplished by electric refrigeration of the air stream. The whole system was thoroughly steam cleaned. Disinfectant should not be used as it only slows up the growth and spread of the spores, and the smell invades the whole place.

If you feel feverish at the end of the first day back at work after the New Year break, it may not be the shock of returning to the grindstone or even a touch of 'flu. It could be the airconditioning.

Doctors at the Health and Safety Executive's Employment Medical Advisory Service (EMAS) believe that many outbreaks of illness written off as minor attacks or influenza are probably caused by amoebae breeding in the water reservoirs of airconditioners. They suspect similar organisms are causing some cases of fibrosis of the lung, an irreversible disease similar to asbestosis.

The first illness, 'humidifier fever' (but not the fibrosis), was identified at a rayon factory in Gwent, South Wales, where about half the office staff went down with aches and pains, shivering, and high temperatures on Monday nights. By Tuesday mornings the mystery illness had disappeared again.

The management called in the Cardiff branch of EMAS who, after visiting the workers, had no doubt, says Dr Alan Jones, one of the experts, that 'these people were acutely ill'.

The Medical Research Council's Pneumoconiosis Unit in Penarth, which was asked to discover what was responsible, believes the cause lay in the factory's airconditioning system. They found that the reservoir of water used to humidify the air was an ideal place for the amoebae (which can be naturally present in water) to breed. In Dr Jones's words, it had become 'a living organic stew' of the amoebae and other organisms.

The system was cleaned periodically and the sludge containing the amoebae put on the floor of the reservoir area. It then dried into a fine dust, which was distributed not through the airconditioning system but by the normal movement of air.

This sort of dust, the medical detectives think, can cause both the fever and fibrosis of the lung. No cases of fibrosis, which is probably caused by some different organism in airconditioning sludges, were found at this factory, despite careful medical checks, but they are strongly suspected to have occurred elsewhere.

The Welsh staff got the fever only on Mondays because they built up immunity during the week. This disappeared while they were away from the office at weekends, and by Monday they were vulnerable again. Two people had only to walk through a room in the office block to become ill. To get rid of the fever the company had to evacuate the offices and strip them bare, at a cost of £750,000.

Outbreaks of the fever are being recognised 'on an increasingly wide scale', says Dr Jones, who made a report to the

*Nineteenth International Congress on Occupational Health
held in Dubrovnik in the autumn.
Several cases have been found in paper mills in Britain, and
others have been reported from the United States. Dr
Jones thinks the cellulose in paper and rayon may be a
factor in the growth of the amoebae in these outbreaks. But
he believes that airconditioning systems which recycle
water through a reservoir are not safe, whether cellulose is
present or not.
He said at Dubrovnik: 'I personally have little doubt that
systems should not be designed with recirculating water.
This is fraught with danger.' (From the* Observer,
31 December 1978)

Action

Demand a survey where the air is measured and sampled and
temperatures recorded while people are working. If you are
suspicious of a survey, check with the Health and Safety
Inspector, or a local polytechnic department may help. Demand
the best in airconditioning and see that it's regularly checked and
maintained.

If a survey is done, they may use a machine which measures
thermal comfort, assessing things like the face temperature of the
skin. This is called the 'comfy-test'. That's fine, but make sure
they also ask people how they feel. It's a good idea also to do a
union health survey. You can draw up a short questionnaire asking people to record their symptoms, for example, 'Have you
noticed an increase in colds?' (see Appendix 1 for draft health
survey) Record too their complaints about draughts, overheating
and so on. Some people find total airconditioning depressing,
causing extreme fatigue. Demand good restroom facilities with
windows which open and plenty of fresh air. It's a good idea to
get a system with thermostats that you can control. However,
watch these! One firm in Boston was very keen on 'worker
involvement' and made a big play about involving employees and
giving them some control. They installed individually controlled
thermostats, which was great. Just one problem: you could
adjust your own thermostat OK — but it wasn't hooked up to
anything!

You may have to start campaigning for a new building altogether.
Safety reps have the right to be consulted on plans for new
ventilation systems for their present workplace and for new
buildings (see p. 164). Many faults occur at the design stage.

If you want a system where the windows can be opened, you
may get the 'security' argument. Often, says a Factory Inspectorate report, 'windows are nailed permanently shut, or even bricked

up'.[10] The law says ventilation shall be provided and such criminal activity on the part of employers should not be tolerated. You'll be up against some old problems, like money. 'It'll cost too much and put us out of business', or 'With the cutbacks in public expenditure we don't have funds for ventilation systems.' In other words, your health is not a priority. You'll have to negotiate on this one, just like you do on wages — don't take 'no' for an answer.

A lot of research on airconditioning and ventilation is done because it promotes 'worker efficiency' and 'higher productivity' (see Colt advertising). A fortunate by-product sometimes is that it promotes health. But in preparing your case for better air-conditioning systems you can always point out that you'll all be more alert and more contented workers in a more comfortable environment. Anyway, computers stop working if the air-conditioning is of a poor standard. Some office workers might too.

Another slogan accompanying this advert reads 'If working conditions are healthy, business is healthy too.'

WHEN IT'S 82°F IN A HOT STUFFY FACTORY, IT'S NOT JUST THE WORKERS THAT SUFFER.

Footnotes

1   Goldstein, D.H. and Orris, L., 'Diseases of white-collar workers' in *Public Health Report,* 79, US Government, 1967, pp.958-962.

2   H.M. Factory Inspectorate, *Report for Offices, Shops and Railway Premises Act for 1963-1973,* HMSO, 1974.

3   H.M. Factory Inspectorate, *Annual Report for Offices, Shops and Railway Premises Act for 1966,* HMSO, 1967.

4   Grandjean, E., 'The effect of various heating systems on office microclimate' in *Schweizerische Blatter fur Heizung und Luftung,* Vol.33 No.1, Zurich, January 1966.

5   H.M. Factory Inspectorate, *Annual Report for Offices, Shops and Railway Premises Act for 1970,* HMSO, 1971.

6   *Department of Employment Gazette,* HMSO, October 1971.

7   Civil Service CSD General Notice GEN 78/55, *Civil Service Handbook,* p.506-7.

8   Peters, T., 'Volklimatisierte Raume' in *Zentralblatt fur Arbeitsmedizin, Arbeitsschutz und Prophylaxe,* Vol.26 No.11, 1976, pp.243-6.

9   May, J., 'Warmth and Ventilation in Offices', in *British Journal of Industrial Safety,* Vol.6 No.70, 1964, pp.225-230.

10   H.M. Factory Inspectorate, *Annual Report for Offices, Shops and Railway Premises Act for 1971,* HMSO, 1972.

CHECK LIST

temperature and ventilation

Temperature and ventilation are often controlled together but they are split up in the following checklist to help identify specific points.

Temperature

How warm you feel is affected not only by the air temperature but also by the humidity of the air, how draughty the room is and by what sort of work you are doing. The following figures are therefore variable.

1   Get management to do a survey of the whole office during a normal working day to produce a report which gives clear details of the temperature in all parts of the building. Combine this with a questionnaire to your members which will bring out personal responses to balance the 'facts' of the survey.

2   Make sure that there is a thermometer on every floor placed where it can be easily seen.

3   Recommended temperature levels: 67-73° Fahrenheit 19.5-22.8° Centigrade.

4   Minimum temperature by law 60.8° Fahrenheit, 16° Centigrade.

5   Maximum temperature: 80° Fahrenheit, 27° Centigrade.

CHECK LIST

Ventilation

1   Find out how the ventilation system is supposed to work. More often than not there will be basic mistakes in the way that it is being run. Equally, it may not be big enough to do the job properly.

2   Get a survey done of the ventilation rates in the various different office areas. Humidity should be controlled between 30% and 70%.

3   Getting enough air in total is usually the major problem, however, the following is a checklist of other points worth looking at:
(a) Where does the air come from? It should not be drawn either from street level where exhaust levels will be high or from the roof where there may be fall out of dust from factories near by.
(b) Does the heating system give off fumes which then get circulated around the building?
(c) Is the water in the airconditioning tanks pure?
(d) If ozone is used are the levels being used safe?
(e) Was asbestos used in the construction of the system?

4   Maintenance systems need to be set up for all the ventilating plant on site. This should be undertaken by specialist ventilation experts.

5   In the long run the only really sensitive way to assess the heating and ventilating plant is to see whether people like working in the office!

7 The basics: welfare facilities and hygiene

You spend much of your life at work. You give your labour and your time in return for money to live on. Decent working conditions should not be an added extra. They are a basic right – hardly much to ask for in the 1980s. By law, employers must ensure the welfare of their workers, as well as their health and safety.

'It shall be the duty of every employer to ensure, so far as reasonably practicable, the health, safety and welfare at work of all his employees.' (Sec. 2(1) HASAWA)

Offices vary in the welfare amenities provided for the people who work in them. Some are grim, dirty places to work, with only minimum amenities. Others are spacious and bright. But many offices, both old and new, leave much to be desired.

Fiona McNally, author of *Women for Hire: A Study of the Female Office Worker,* worked as a temp at the 'XYZ Credit company'. She described her workplace:

> 'The firm occupied eight floors of a large, modern office block…The locus of higher management was adorned by wall-to-wall carpets and elegant furnishings, that of lower management by fairly stylish fittings and bright paintwork, whereas the filing department, where I was to be employed, was a barren wasteland of rickety chairs and tables, with not so much as a calendar to grace the fading, dirty walls. This enormous room was dominated by tall, rusty filing cabinets which effectively prevented the sunshine from entering.' (London, 1979, p.161)

The Offices, Shops and Railway Premises Act (OSRPA) sets down some specific minimum requirements, and you will probably have to fight to get more. But beware! One book written for management gives the following guidelines:

> 'In providing amenities, any suggestion of paternalism or generosity should be avoided. "We like you to have the best conditions to get from you the best work" is not only a realistic approach, but one that breeds confidence. (H. Cemach, *Work Study in the Office*)

Space

Each person must have a minimum of 40 square feet of floor space in an office, exclusive of furniture and fittings. Your employer has an absolute legal duty to provide this (Offices, Shops and Railway Premises Act, Section 5(2)). Where the ceiling is lower than 10 feet, at least 400 cubic feet per person must be allowed. Forty square feet isn't much. Standards as usual vary all over the place for what is deemed a basic minimum. In Ireland the minimum is 50 square feet, and the International Labour Office recommends 75 to 90 square feet per worker. A British government inquiry into conditions in the Civil Service recommends 60 square feet for a clerical worker and 40 for a typist.

An overcrowded office is a health hazard. It means more risk of injury, more stress, less light and increased risk of infection. Lack of space means desks and filing cabinets become an obstruction, causing bumps and bruises. Adequate working space round office machinery is essential to enable adjustment, repairs and cleaning to be carried out safely.

In spite of the legal requirements, offices are still overcrowded. In one Ministry of Defence building in South London, 160 office staff are currently working in three converted corridors. The Factory Inspectorate had occasion to prosecute a firm employing hundreds of clerks, and did; 37 persons were working where the permitted number was 23, and 17 other offices occupied by the firm were found to be also overcrowded.[1] Overcrowding can occur in both old and new offices. Employing 'temps' at peak work periods, can cause serious overcrowding problems because sufficient space has just not been created.

Office workers in NUPE in Birmingham called in the Health and Safety Inspector because of overcrowding and she issued an Improvement Notice, threatening the employers with a £1,000 fine if something wasn't done in three weeks (see p. 159).

Typists are often crowded in the 'pool', but you'll never see an overcrowded manager's office. Often, the higher the concentration of women in a particular area of the office, the lower the standard of decor and the less space for each individual. The 'mixed' areas are next. And the smartest are usually the men-only bastion (boardroom, executive lounge). Women tend to receive the same proportion of office space as they do of pay: 20 to 50 per cent less than men. Space is officially allocated according to status and not health and safety. Have you ever been asked how much space you need to work in? Or whether you prefer open plan or partitioned offices?

Open plan

Open plan offices can cause problems: individual requirements for air and warmth vary, and there's noise from telephones and machines. The management philosophy behind the open plan office is that it ensures uniform work with no slacking, since it's harder to talk or read in the open than in the privacy of a separate room. Open plan makes for easier supervision. Open plan offices are sometimes partitioned as an afterthought. An inspector states:

> 'It is when offices are inspected after partitioning that interior offices with screens extending to ceiling height are sometimes found to be without ventilation, with borrowed natural lighting and often overcrowded.'[2]

Developers of high rise office blocks cannot estimate the number of people likely to be employed in the premises, so they often fail to provide amenities such as washing facilities on a sufficient scale. Such problems could be cut down if office buildings were *designed* for flexibility, taking into account the needs of those who have to work in them. Offices should be open plan only if you want them to be. They could be reorganised, with open plan areas together with a 'thinking room' and a 'reading room' which people could share and use when necessary.

Washing and toilet facilities

At the Bexleyheath office of the Pearl Assurance Company office workers refused to merge with another office unless more toilets were installed. Four women and three men worked in the office, sharing one toilet with 15 agents who also regularly used the office. The ASTMS Branch Secretary pressed the public health inspector to issue an Improvement Notice, which he did, although Pearl appealed. After a great deal of union pressure Pearl agreed to build new sanitary facilities. Pearl repeatedly said they couldn't afford to spend

*the necessary £20,000 (although meanwhile they were
spending £80,000 on an advertising campaign).
The Branch Secretary said staff will soon have decent
toilet and eating facilities – but only after 18 months 'of
bitter struggle'. He personally believes that other Pearl
offices are probably contravening the Offices and Shops
Act on requirement of toilet facilities'.*

There must be at least one toilet for every 25 people, according
to the law (Offices, Shops and Railway Premises Act, Section 9).
If there are more than ten women workers, there must be suitable
and effective means for disposal of sanitary towels. Like all the
legal standards, this is a basic minimum and a pathetic one at
that. There should be towel or tampon vending machines,
although there is no legal requirement. Toilets must be conveni-
ently accessible and they must be clean, private and well
ventilated by law. Detailed requirements for toilet facilities are
outlined in the Sanitary Convenience Regulations 1964.

There must be a supply of clean, running, hot and cold water.
Soap, clean towels or equivalent must be provided and kept clean.
There must be one basin for 15 workers (Offices, Shops and
Railway Premises Act, Section 10). Separate toilets and washing
facilities for men and women must be provided if more than five
people are employed. Many office workers' sanitary facilities are
still a disgrace, with broken washbasins and mirrors, inadequate
standards of cleanliness and lighting. Most employers only provide
the minimum, or less.

Cloakrooms

Provision of suitable and adequate cloakroom space for clothing
not worn during working hours is the employer's statutory duty,
following Section 12 of the Offices, Shops and Railway Premises
Act. Nails on the wall don't make a cloakroom. Ideally you'll
want space for changing footwear. Space for drying of outdoor
clothing should also be provided.

Have a look at your boss's facilities – this will be a good guideline for the kind of standard to aim for.

Eating and drinking facilities

Wholesome drinking water must be in plentiful supply. The
regulations for this (Offices, Shops and Railway Premises Act,
Section 11) are often met by fitting taps over wash basins in the
washrooms. 'This', said London's Chief Public Health Inspector,
'is potentially dangerous and aesthetically unacceptable.'[3]

There should be suitable provision of eating facilities. A canteen
with good food at reasonable prices should ideally be provided
by your employer. BP's office staff in Central London get a three-

course lunch for five pence, and Pearl Assurance workers in their head office have free lunches. Bad catering can mess up your digestive system, and can cause stress symptoms. Good facilities are particularly necessary for shift workers. In many business areas of large cities, thousands of office workers pile into snack-bars or queue up for take-away sandwiches at high prices to take back and eat at their desks. This is testimony to how few of the shining new office blocks dominating our cities have amenities for the people who work in them.

There should also be canteen facilities for tea and coffee breaks. Carrying hot drinks to your desk or making them on the premises yourself can be dangerous. What happens if someone is burned? Some employers just supply tea and coffee by machine, but these frequently break down. The drinks are far from wholesome, and some office workers are now refusing to use them since the drinks have been found to cause chronic constipation.

Microwave ovens

Microwave ovens are now in use in many pubs, canteens, restaurants and private homes. The manufacturers claim that the microwave radiation which heats the food is contained within the glass and metal case of the oven. All ovens are fitted with automatic locks which are supposed to switch off the radiation as soon as the door is opened or even if the door is not firmly shut due to build up of grease, dirt, etc.
The British Standard Institute specifies that the radiation level emitted should be not more than $5mW/cm^2$ (5 milliwatts per square centimetre) at a distance of 5 cm from the door of the oven.
Many normally functioning ovens without faults have been found to leak microwave radiation, whilst in use, at *levels above the $5mW/cm^2$ standard*. Indeed, after one survey, the American Consumers Union refused to recommend as safe *any* model of microwave oven.

Environmental Health Officers Association put forward four safety rules:

1   Ovens must not be sited where workers sit for long periods
2   Ovens must be regularly serviced and maintained.
3   Servicing must include a check on the level of microwave leakage.
4   Do not use any microwave cooker if the leakage level exceeds the recommended maximum.

One survey in Cambridge showed that almost three quarters of commercial microwave oven users were unaware of the hazards.[4]

Hazards of microwaves

Cataracts (clouding of the lens of the eye)
In one canteen two women worked sitting either side of the microwave oven. The one on the left of the oven developed a

cataract in her right eye and the one on the right developed a cataract in her left eye. The management denied that the oven was responsible.

Behavioural effects
Fatigue, drowsiness, nausea, dizziness and irritability.

Fertility effects
Abnormality of the foetus in some pregnant women exposed to microwave radiation. Increased number of mongol offspring if father is exposed to microwave radiation.

As with many health hazards in the workplace it is the *long-term effects* of even low levels of exposure that are the most insidious.

Cleanliness

All premises, furniture and fittings must be kept in a clean state by law (Offices, Shops and Railway Premises Act, Section 4). Dirt and refuse must not be allowed to accumulate, and floors and steps must be washed, or if appropriate swept, at least once a week. Sue McKenzie, safety representative, on her first inspection found hundreds of unhealthy, unsafe or dirty areas of the tax office where she worked. Among these she listed:

1   The filing room is generally cramped and overcrowded and it is dusty and dirty. The lack of space in a room which is critical in the event of fire and evacuation is particularly undesirable.

2   Boxes and waste sacks obstruct the main walkway through the general office, which also leads to the fire escape.

3   The counter room is generally dirty and dusty, behind radiators and pipes being the dirtiest.

4   In the ladies toilet there is a very low standard of cleanliness. The door gets jammed open on the uneven floor. One strip light is not functioning. The wash basin supports are broken.

The list goes on and on.

Some office workers complain of skin rashes resulting from dirt and dust at their work. There are stories of vermin, of rats and mice and various creepy-crawlies residing in offices. The spread of infection, including dermatitis and colds and flu, is often compounded by unhygienic toilets, washrooms, cooking and eating facilities.
In many cases management employs contract cleaners who usually work at night or very early in the morning and have to clean huge blocks. As a result they're often unable to do the job properly. Often they don't clean storerooms, cupboards or eating facilities, it not being in the contract. It is preferable that permanent cleaners are employed to do a good job. Try to contact

the cleaners and if possible link up with them on health and safety (see chapter 11 on organising).

There is some evidence that the incidence of sickness diminishes notably if telephones and intercommunication equipment are systematically disinfected.[5]

Decoration   In addition to cleanliness, comfort and colour are also important. Bright and pleasant surroundings affect your morale and your mental health. Yet often it's only the area which is open to the public — the reception area — which is well furnished and pleasantly decorated. This was underlined in the *Department of Employment Gazette* in 1971:

> 'While there was a reasonable standard [of cleanliness] in many offices and shops, in those parts of the premises not open to the public the standards often continued to be poor. In many premises the standard of decoration was again reported to be poor, which caused cleaning difficulties and gave the building a dirty appearance. According to one authority, redecoration "has a profound psychological effect on the staff and public alike, and the mere act of redecoration results in improved cleanliness".'[6]

The drab office that can't be changed by any amount of effort (for example, plants and pictures) is depressing. But possibly more of a strain in some ways is the glossy, decorated office which must not bear any sign of the personalities of those who work there.

In May 1926, W. Keay, General Secretary of the National Federation of Professional Workers, wrote in a leaflet:

> 'It may come as a surprise to many that in several of the public services the conditions are nearly as deplorable as in offices under private control. People, when speaking of, for example, the Civil Service, think of the front rooms in Whitehall and are more or less unacquainted with the miserable, damp, unhealthy accommodation frequently accorded to, say, customs officers at the Ports, or the sickly, dark kennels in which many of those engaged in Inland Revenue duties and in the work of Labour Exchanges throughout the provinces have to spend their working hours. *Cuts in expenditure* on such services have been secured in several instances by the maintenance of premises never intended for permanent habitation.' (*A Much Needed Measure: The Offices Regulations Bill*)

This leaflet was one of the thousands written in the fifty years of trade union campaigning to obtain protective legislation for offices.

There is little doubt that with the passing of the Offices, Shops and Railway Premises Act in 1963 the standard has improved. But many office workers still work in damp basements, in windowless rooms, in converted warehouses and corridors. In the public sector, many clerical staff work in appalling conditions which are a result of the cuts in public expenditure — a feature of life now as in 1926.

In October 1980 an edict went out from the Property Services Agency (part of the Department of the Environment), forbidding redecoration of government buildings. *The only exception to this cutback in public expenditure will be where redecorations are necessary for health and safety reasons.*

Restrooms and First Aid facilities

A first aid box or cupboard containing only first aid requisites must be provided for the use of all employees and must be readily accessible. Where there are more than 150 employees, an additional box or cupboard must be provided for every 150. The regulations made under the Offices, Shops and Railway Premises Act list minimum contents of a first aid box (Section 24). Deirdre Hunt, who is a file clerk in a plastics firm, said the manager keeps the key to the first aid box, which is locked away in his room! In one large bank, the box held nothing but a rusty screw!

Where there are more than 150 employees, someone must be trained in first aid and must always be available during working hours. They should have a refresher course every three years. If your office is within the boundaries of a factory or electrical station, a trained first aider is necessary for every 50 workers. But one first aider is simply not enough where you have two hundred or so people working somewhere. As many people as possible should be trained — in your employer's time and at their expense. The Inner London Education Authority pays trained office first aiders £50 a year extra. Many companies also pay people to take on this responsibility. There should be a first aid room or restroom with a sofa or comfortable chairs where you can go if injured or feeling unwell. Restrooms are especially important for pregnant workers and women with menstrual cramps. There is no legislation which gives you this right, however.

Some of these rooms, where they are provided, are worse than useless. One first aid room in a customs and excise office in the south-east has kitchen stores in it which require open windows; the result is a cold, draughty restroom. Many have nothing in the medical cupboard and no toilet. Another, in a large government building, is a total shambles, full of stored furniture, and next to the kitchen so that the sick get sicker from the smell.

Action

Why not find out what you can do about the basic health hazards and welfare problems in your office? Raise the issue at your union branch and see what action people want to take. You will have to negotiate to improve standards and get what you want. As one ASTMS safety rep put it: 'All aspects of your life in the office should be a subject of negotiation — from the colour of the decor to the number of people to a room.'

You can try calling in the Health and Safety Inspector or Environmental Health Officer. They are usually quite efficient on things such as basic toilet facilities and drinking water. With some pushing they will see you get the basic minimum. But don't just settle for that.

Childcare

Many office workers are parents. Childcare during working hours can be a desperate problem and affects a worker's welfare. In this society childcare is seen as the responsibility of the mother, and working mothers often have to carry this heavy burden alone. Very few employers provide workplace nurseries. In 1975 there were only 90 in Britain, mainly in hospitals and academic institutions. With the cutbacks in public services, state nurseries are being slashed.

97

The Civil Service Creche Campaign (CSCC) is a national campaign
being waged by several unions for creches for Civil Service
workers' children. Daycare facilities for the children of both male
and female workers have been won by a number of unions, for
for example the Inland Revenue Staff Federation (IRSF) at
Llanisten in Wales, where the nursery was financed by the Civil
Service, administered by a joint union/management committee
and run by the local authority. (The nursery was closed — another
'luxury' to be chopped from public expenditure.) In Edinburgh

the IRSF's members are negotiating for premises for a nursery. One childcare worker will be employed full-time and members plan to help out at the creche using flexitime provisions. Camden NALGO's nursery is administered by a committee of parents, union and management. Thought should also be given to the provision of facilities for school age children after school and during holidays. The service must be seen as a right and not a privilege. This point is emphasised in an excellent handbook produced by NALGO, *Workplace Nurseries: A Negotiating Kit.*

What you can do

1   *Do a survey of need throughout your workplace.*
2   *Contact all your workplace unions, either through staff side or by setting up action groups.*
3   *Hold open meetings to discuss needs and tactics.*
4   *Build a contact list – and include even those who do not have or want children. Involve everyone.*
5   *Contact your union and demand support. Write to their journals.*
6   *Contact your local Trades Council and find out about local authority provision.*
7   *Propose motions in your branch supporting the* Civil Service Creche Campaign; *urge affiliations, if appropriate.*

Type of nursery demanded by the CSCC

1   *Full-time – at or near the workplace.*
2   *Union/parent controlled.*
3   *Professionally staffed at proper rates of pay.*
4   *Civil Service Department subsidised to enable parents in all grades to afford the nursery.*
5   *Run on non-sexist lines (i.e. no stereotyped roles for either sex).*
6   *Open to children of all staff.*

Footnotes

1   HMFI, Report on the application of the Offices, Shops and Railway Premises Act for 1967.
2   *Municipal and Public Services Journal,* 28 January 1966, p.272.
3   p.267.
4   Keerie, J.G., 'Results of a survey of microwave ovens in Cambridge-shire in 1977' in *Environmental Health,* March 1979, pp.54, 55.
5   International Labour Office, Encyclopaedia of Occupational Safety and Health, Geneva, 1972, p.979.

CHECK LIST

basic facilities	1	Does each worker have at least 40 square feet of space exclusive of furniture and fittings?
	2	Is there adequate space in all areas to allow easy movement and safe machine-adjustment?

Washing and toilet facilities	1	Are all toilets clean, private and well ventilated?
	2	Is there at least one toilet for every 25 people?
	3	Is there at least one basin with hot and cold running water along with soap and clean towels provided for every 15 workers?
	4	Are separate facilities for men and women provided where more than five people are employed?
	5	If more than ten women are employed, has management provided suitable means for disposing of sanitary towels?
	6	Are sanitary towel and tampon vending machines provided?

Cloakrooms		Is a cloakroom provided, adequate to store and dry out clothing not worn during working hours?

Eating and drinking facilities	1	Is there a wholesome, plentiful supply of drinking water?
	2	Are there suitable eating and tea break facilities?

Cleanliness	1	Are all floors and steps washed or swept at least once a week?
	2	Are all accumulations of dirt and refuse immediately removed?
	3	Are all premises, furniture and fittings kept clean?
	4	Are all telephones systematically disinfected?
	5	Is the general office environment bright and pleasant?

Restroom and first aid	1	Is a first aid box kept readily accessible?
	2	Where more than 150 employees work is there an additional box for each additional 150 workers?
	3	Where more than 150 people work, is there a trained first aider, retrained every three years?
	4	Is there a warm, comfortable and well equipped restroom for injured or unwell workers?

Childcare facilities	1	Is there a suitable site which could be used for a nursery?
	2	Is the negotiation of adequate childcare facilities high on your union's list of objectives?

3 Physical Hazards

8 Injury and fire

Five thousand injuries every year cause office workers to be absent for more than three days. Contrary to the message on most safety posters, injuries at work are rarely caused by individual carelessness or by 'accident prone' workers. The real causes are poorly designed jobs, pressure of work and bad maintenance of equipment and fittings, so most 'accidents' can be *prevented*.

Many factors contribute to the cause of an accident: temperature, humidity, noise, tiredness, monotony, time of day, stress, production pressures, poor equipment, lack of staff, inadequate funds spent on safety precautions. The cascade of safety magazines (eg. put out by ROSPA and British Safety Council) flooding the market, are mainly for managers and safety officers and a vehicle for advertising protective clothing. Safety is big business. The main thrust of most safety propaganda is that accidents are caused by careless workers. These firms (who are so concerned

Sexist adverts like this one degrade and insult women

about your safety) say little about how to file a claim for compensation. There is hardly a word either about stress or toxic hazards in the workplace. Putting the burden of safety on to the individual saves a company money.

The five thousand serious injuries sustained by office workers in Britain each year are only the *reported* accidents. The level is probably nearer twenty thousand. A study by the National Institute of Industrial Psychology in 1971 showed that in companies with medical centres between 55 and 70 per cent of observed accidents were reported; where no medical centre existed, the accidents that got reported were as low as 5 per cent![1]

Trips and falls

Almost half the injuries in offices are due to trips and falls. And three-quarters of the falls in an American survey of office safety were due to defective surfaces, holes or loose floor coverings. Check the following in your office, following Section 16 of the Offices, Shops and Railway Premises Act:

* Are floors, steps, stairs, passages and gang-ways soundly constructed and well maintained? Are they kept free from obstruction and slippery surfaces? Some manufacturers claim their floor coverings are non-slip when they're not. Special anti-slip material should be used at lift and building entrances.

* Do all staircases have a substantial hand rail on any open side? Iron steps to a boiler house in a new office block were railed on one side only, and a worker was seriously hurt in falling off the unrailed side. An inspector, recently visiting a London cinema found unlocked doors which directly lead to cavities with drops of 4 feet 6 inches!

* Are files and stationery stacked out of reach? Do you have to risk breaking a leg to reach equipment you need? There are step stools that lock into place, with spring mounted retractable castors, and a rubber mat on the stepping surface.

* Are telephone leads and other cables and wires near walls battened down, over seven feet up out of the way, or laid under foot? Ramps can reduce risk of tripping. If there is a spaghetti junction of wires, there are not enough power points. Jenny Malcolm received a permanent back injury from tripping over a telephone wire in her office. Twenty years later it is still causing her enough pain to prevent her working.

* Are all accesses, staircases and stores well lit?

* Are company car parks and pavements around the office building kept clear and safe?

Lifting

The second most common cause of injury is strain from over-exertion. Office machines, supplies, file drawers, furniture, often require moving. If lifting is required, don't risk your back — get someone to help you. Remember, there is often no cure for back strain. If things need to be regularly lifted, then pressure for more staff. In the Civil Service and in some companies, porters are specifically employed to transport supplies.

By law, you have a right to refuse to lift or carry something. Section 23(1) of the Offices, Shops and Railway Premises Act states that 'no person shall in the course of his work...be required to lift, carry or move a load so heavy as to be likely to cause injury to him'. The firm Western SMT were prosecuted under this section, in Edinburgh. A woman who injured her back while lifting an 85 lb cash box with another woman won £3,242 damages in court. The court decided that 85 lbs was too great a load to be lifted by two people.

You are also protected by Section 7 of the Health and Safety at Work Act:

> 'It shall be the duty of every employee while at work to take reasonable care for the health and safety of himself and of other persons who may be affected by his acts or omissions at work.'

You could argue that you'd be breaking the law by carrying something heavy which could injure you. This is a favourite section of the Health and Safety at Work Act usually used by employers to discipline workers and quoted at the top of their safety policy. Now you can quote it back. There is no relevant legal maximum weight that office workers may carry, so it's best to use the above bits of law to refuse to carry weights *you* believe are too heavy. However, in the Civil Service only weights 'within each person's capacity up to a maximum of 35 lbs should be lifted, otherwise help should be called for'.[3] There is often no reason why a load should be heavy; for example, the cash box mentioned above could have contained less. You can negotiate with your suppliers to pack goods in smaller quantities.

Shelving and stacking areas should be rearranged to reduce lifting height and carrying distances. Trolleys could be on hand for easy moving of equipment, and felt pads under typewriters mean they can be pushed short distances.

Employers and safety officers like to blame workers for not lifting 'properly'. Well, you can probably ignore all the propaganda about 'proper lifting techniques'. According to the *American Industrial Hygiene Association Journal,* 'In spite of enthusiastic promotion of lifting training — "straight back, bent knees" — the percentage of back injuries in the working population has not materially decreased over the last forty years.'[4] And the International Labour Office says that there is no published evidence that lifting instruction reduces backpain. The danger of employers emphasising lifting techniques is that they are covered if there's an accident, and you are not. The burden should be on *management* to make the workplace safe and healthy.

Machinery and mechanical hazards

There's hardly an office in the country without machinery. Automation, and therefore, danger, is increasing (see chapter 5 for chemical hazards of machinery and chapter 9 for the health hazards of 'new technology').

> An office worker leaned over an addressing machine and her hair became entangled in a roller spindle. She got a bruised temple and jaw.

> An experienced operator suffered amputation of a finger when he opened the side panel in a drawing office printing machine after he'd started it up. He was replacing an ammonia bottle.

> A man got his finger bones crushed by a stapler and was off work for six weeks.

> A woman was cleaning the cylinder of the office 'multilith' printing machine, which was not switched off at power. The rotating cylinder caught her bracelet and pulled her thumb under the cover guard, breaking it.

Guarding

Section 17(1) of the Offices, Shops and Railway Premises Act requires fencing off of hazardous office machinery. There are photo-electric guards (using a curtain of light beams), where a hand moving across the light makes the machinery shut down, and transparent guards, eg. on a multilith offset duplicator, which let you see the work safely. Ideally, all machines should be designed so that they won't operate without guards, but too often safety features are advertised as 'optional extras', and if left off allow faster output while the supervisors turn a blind eye. Some jobs have been speeded up so much that under pressure people remove the guards to work faster. Like productivity deals, pressure to work fast is an insidious cause of injury and death in all kinds of work.

Where there is a roller, a fixed guard should be placed in front of it, and it is advisable for the upper roller to be spring-loaded so that it rises if the fingers are put into the gap. Machines with a larger gap between the rollers may seem safe, but if a ringed finger gets caught it will be injured.

Office machinery and its safety hazards

photocopiers/addressing machines/ electrostencil cutters/duplicators/ paper shredders/inking rollers/ rota printing machinery/postal franking machines	*can trap and damage fingers, trap and entangle hair*
multilith offset duplicators	*some have gaps in the periphery into which the mechanism for holding the plates is fitted; if you try to remove misfed paper while the machine is running, can damage fingers and even break a wrist*
guillotines	*can slice flesh*
hand presses/stitchers/paper drills	*can damage fingers*
staplers	*can crush bones, lacerate fingers*
Electronically moving shelving	*can trap and squash a whole person*
lifts	*can trap limbs; especially hazardous for elderly and disabled workers*
jogger machines	*vibration can cause 'dead finger'*

Where the machine is power driven it also presents a fire hazard and a risk of shocks (see below, p. 106).

> *A woman working in the students' union office at a London polytechnic used a jogger machine for five years. The machine vibrated a great deal, so did the operator and the floor. There were no instructions and no proper base for the machine. The woman's fingers and toes developed a numbness which interfered with her daily use of her hands and feet. The doctor diagnosed the condition as 'white finger' (Raynaud's Syndrome) caused by the jogger machine.*

Faulty siting and/or congestion of machinery will increase the hazards by impeding the operator's movement and make inspection and maintenance difficult. Machines should not be placed near the edges of desks or tables. They should have slip-proof pads or anchoring.

Section 17(3) of the Offices, Shops and Railway Premises Act forbids those under the age of 18 to clean moving parts. But should *anyone* perform such a task if there is risk of injury? According to Section 19, no one must operate a paper cutter or guillotine unless they are trained or supervised.

All office machinery should be regularly serviced to ensure safe operation. Any new machinery or equipment should be red-tagged for danger until all operators know how to operate it safely. Safety representatives should vet new machinery before it's put in operation. If a sales rep is on the scene, get him or her to test for mechanical and electrical hazards. If they or your boss insist the equipment is safe, you could request that they prove it by putting their fingers in between the rollers or whatever...

Electrical hazards

These include shock, fire and certain risks to the eyes and lungs from ozone and radiation (see p. 62). Faulty electrical equipment can electrocute you. Get management to watch out for the following:

loose connections
unearthed equipment
damaged cables
defective insulation
overloaded circuits
broken switches
worn or damaged appliances
trailing leads
(from HMSO, *Is My Office Safe?*)

Many machines give no indication whatsoever that they are switched on, such as light or noise. They could be left on all weekend. This 'stresses' the electrical equipment and makes it more hazardous. All equipment should have a clearly marked mains switch. Where several different types of machines are brought together, such as an addressing machine and guillotine attached to a stapler, each from a different manufacturer, there will be a shock hazard because each machine will have a small amount of leakage current, which adds up.

The fuse is probably the most abused bit of any electrical circuit. Fused plugs specifically designed for a specified type of mains wiring known as the 'ring main' are commonly known as 13 amp plugs. But if a machine only consumes 3 amps of power, then the fuse in the plug should also be 3 amp. Otherwise, if the electrics fail there may be a fire before the fuse blows.

Although normally safe, ordinary mains voltage of 240 volts such as that supplying office lighting and most simple machines can give rise to dangerous currents. There are 38 reported electrical accidents in offices in an average year and these are often caused by not switching off machines. Also electric fires can get knocked over and are dangerous if used for drying wet clothes; safe drying facilities should be provided.

Some electrical equipment contains liquids (for example, some photocopiers) which may be spilled on to the electrical components. The resultant corrosion can lead to electrical failure. If the liquid conducts electricity, there is a danger of shock to the user via the wet machine and possibly wet hands. Some machines use flammable liquids (for example, spirit duplicators). If these are spilled where there's an unshrouded electrical switch they can ignite, or the vapour can cause small explosions in the body of the machine. In some electrical machinery you can put your hand into the electric works (for example, some ventilation fans). If you touch a mains voltage, say with a paper clip, it could kill you. And some machinery gets overheated — it's a bad design if it gets too hot to touch or if you can touch the heating elements. Some are a fire risk (see below, p. 111).

The covers of dangerous areas should not be removable with the machine on, or else the machine should switch off automatically if they are removed. Some new photocopiers have this system. Badly designed equipment should be put right, replaced; or it should remain unused by the office staff — although this might shock the boss! All machines should have automatic power cut-outs. This means they should have control and interlock circuits which shut them down at the first sign of trouble or interference. Only qualified electricians should check and maintain electrical machinery.

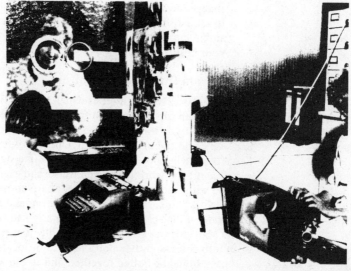

Note the dangerous trailing lead

Static is generated by a number of things: nylon carpets and upholstery, vinyl floors, formica desk tops, plastic chairs, synthetic
clothing. Metal furniture aggravates the problem and you can get
nasty shocks from touching filing cabinets and switchboards.
Electrostatic photocopiers also generate static electricity. Static
can be painful on contact and can cause heaviness and pains in the
legs. It can be stressful and is especially dangerous if you have a
heart condition. There is some evidence that static has an effect
on the nervous system of laboratory animals.[5] It may create a
fire and explosion risk if it occurs in areas where solvents are
stored.

Possible solutions Furniture can have earthed conductive mats and plates
over non-conductive surfaces. This avoids the build-up of
static charge.

Increased humidity reduces the risk of static. Humidifiers
can be installed (but see p. 83 for health hazards of these).
Indoor plants properly watered will add moisture to the air
and improve the atmosphere.

Carpets may be inserted with earthing wires, or can have
metal or carbon coated fibres incorporated. Carpets may
be treated with anti-static agents to increase their conduc-
tivity, but this is really only a temporary measure. You
could demand the installation of carpets with special
guarantees against static shock. These are always found in
computer rooms, where floor coverings must be anti-
static to protect the *computer's* health...

Cotton clothes may be worn. There is no good reason why
you should *have* to change your clothes (it's better to
change the office carpet!), but you should have the *right*.
In some offices it's compulsory for women to wear skirts
and nylon tights — a basic infringement of your rights and
your health needs.

Injury from fittings and furniture

Crowded offices lead to injuries. Open bottom file drawers can
trip you, open top drawers can fracture your nose or bang against
your head. If you lean back on a chair on castors it can overturn
and you could fracture your skull. One safety rep in the Civil
Service broke her nose on the corner of a free-standing screen. She
was absent from work for several weeks and ever since has been
plagued with frequent sinus trouble. Sharp corners, drawers that
stick, swing doors, knobs, are all dangerous and can be modified
to be safer. Filing cabinets are particularly bad. A CPSA member
in the Midlands was crushed by one. File drawers should not
open into aisles, and they don't have to be located behind doors!
Cabinets should be bolted together, and to the wall, so they

cannot fall over. A piece of hardwood or strip metal about half an inch thick can be inserted under the front end of a cabinet to improve stability. There should be a fail-safe catch at the back of each drawer to prevent it coming right out and dropping on your foot. The filing of papers in a tightly packed drawer causes finger cuts. More filing space would prevent this.

After the event

If someone does get hurt in your department, make sure they get medical attention (see also section on first aiders, p. 96) and that the incident is recorded in the accident book, with all the details about how, where and when it happened. Do not say or sign anything. This may be used against you later (this goes for safety reps or victims). The only person you must give a signed statement to is a health and safety inspector. Make sure you're involved when the employer is filling in accident report forms. Always enter near misses as well as injuries. The accident book should be readily accessible to everyone. It is useful to analyse it and to use the information and statistics to argue for prevention of further injuries. Is everyone, including the people who clean your office, aware of the whereabouts of the accident book?

Safety representatives should always get to the scene of an accident quickly to record what happened. This could be crucial later if the injured person claims compensation. D.A. Castle, a solicitor, warns management that union safety representatives are liable to be quick on the scene:

> 'The line manager, if properly trained, should get all the witnesses to an accident together immediately and take statements from them. He should then fill in the accident report form. This is the ideal situation: in reality things happen differently. It is more likely that safety representatives, being workmates, will be on the scene quickly and begin asking questions first. Employers who answer these questions may well make admissions in the emotion of the moment which they would otherwise never have made. A safety representative looking for evidence of what occurred would have an admission to report to the solicitors representing the prospective claimant. The employer's insurance company would start with an immediate handicap...*the problems really begin* when safety representatives ask to see accident reports and seek to interview employees who witness the accident.' [author's emphasis] *New Law Journal*, 28 September 1978)

It's bad enough having an accident, without being up against this kind of thinking!

This approach to safety results from the conflict of interest between safety and profit. How many windows are locked shut and fire escapes blocked for security purposes and to protect the property rather than the employees? How many employers are willing to spend money on an efficient ventilation system or a safe photocopier when you demonstrate that these represent a hazard to health?

A Factory Inspectorate report on the working of the Offices, Shops and Railway Premises Act 1963 analysed 35 fatal accidents in premises covered by the Act to see how far each accident could have been prevented, and by whom. They concluded:

number of fatal accidents	accidents could have been prevented by
8	management
6	deceased
1	fellow workers
3	management and deceased together
3	deceased and fellow workers together
14	unforeseen circumstances
35	

They say: 'Most of the failures of the management were related to the supply of proper maintenance of equipment, or its inspection and control.'[6] A large proportion of workplace accidents can be put down to *bad management*.

Trade union organisation is the best way of approaching safety. The election of safety representatives who inspect regularly and pressure management to fulfil their legal duties will do more for health and safety at work than all the commercialised safety propaganda in the land. Get a good safety agreement (see chapter 11) on organising for safety). Safety reps have the right to vet new machinery. Training is important, since new workers have more accidents than experienced workers. However, the point of training is not to learn how to avoid the danger; the point is to *eliminate* the dangers. There should also be training in fire prevention and in first aid, and safety reps must be involved in all training programmes.

Fire

Fire is one of the biggest causes of death and severe injury at work. Much of the material and equipment used in offices is combustible and much of it a very dangerous fire hazard. Here are some examples:

> cleaning materials and solvents
> paper and paper dust
> electrical and mechanical equipment, especially if badly maintained and unguarded
> gas applicances
> furnishings
> insulation materials
> wax on floors, especially with underfloor heating
> timber frame structures
> refuse

Machines using paper in large quantities collect a great deal of paper fluff, which gets into inaccessible cavities and acts as blotting paper for flammable liquids. All that's then needed is a spark. A ventilation fan caught fire in one of London's big libraries, and an electrostencil cutter burst into flames in one Edinburgh school office.

Photocopiers may contain infra-red heaters. If the exhaust fans break down heat soon builds up. Once the heater is on fire, toners and dispersants may be set alight.

Old timber frame offices can be a serious fire hazard, but many are safer than the modern ones. In Brazil a glass office block fire killed 174 people in 1974. Wall-to-wall carpeting, plastic furniture and combustible partitions are all dangerous. Open plan offices permit an instantaneous flash of fire across the ceiling if the soundproofing is of combustible material. Some plastics and other synthetics, if set alight, give off fumes which can kill instantly.

Carpet backing und underlays, if set on fire, emit huge quantities of smoke. The Manchester Woolworth's fire killed ten people mainly as a result of fumes from burning polyurethene foam. It started in the furniture department.

Death in a fire is mostly caused by asphyxiation due to inhaling smoke and gases. Paraffin, acetone and ammonia are highly dangerous, and may be stored in your office. The vapours from most flammable liquids are heavier than air and can be carried by ventilation to other areas where a source of ignition may be present. And it's not only chemicals. As Janet Ross, a clerical worker in a small office, said: 'We are all very afraid of fire, since hundreds of files are not in metal cabinets but in open bookshelves along the room.'

Fire certificates

If more than 20 people are employed (or more than ten work anywhere other than on ground level), your employer must be issued with a fire certificate. This lays down legal requirements for fire precautions in your workplace: means of escape, particulars of highly flammable materials, and so on.

Safety representatives can inspect and take copies of the fire certificate as part of their rights to information (see chapter 11). You can use the certificate to make up a checklist for inspection to help you monitor whether it is being correctly applied by management. Note that they must report any changes (for example, of exits, or in the use of inflammables) to the fire authority, who issues the certificate. Fire precautions in Crown premises are dealt with by HM Inspectorate of Fire Services. Small workplaces are covered by the rire Precautions Act 1971 and special regulations made in 1976.[7] The legal requirements here say nothing about means of escape, alarms or drills, so you will have to negotiate these.

Fire precautions and disabled staff

Special consideration must be given to the needs of disabled staff in fire situations. Some of the aspects for consideration are:

1 Identification of everyone who may need special help to get out.
2 Allocation of responsibility to specific able-bodied staff to help disabled staff in emergency situations.
3 Consideration of the best escape routes for disabled staff.
4 Developing procedures to enable lifts to be used where possible (eg. to identify unaffected lifts, to prevent power loss to lifts being used to evacuate the disabled).
5 Procedures for disabled staff to summon assistance in emergencies.

While these aspects need to be considered, the problems they raise are not great, and management should not refuse to employ disabled staff because of problems in emergencies. They should be pressed to tackle other barriers to the employment of disabled people, eg. access and toilet facilities. (From TUC Education Department: Health and Safety at Work, No. 5)

Appliances which become hot should be modified, and meanwhile sited away from combustible materials. The flammability factor of carpeting, plastic components and sound proofing should be investigated before they're installed, but furnishings can have flame-proof treatment. Flammable liquids should never be used in a confined space. There are special requirements for storing flammable materials. These will be laid down in the fire certificate and in the Highly Flammable Liquids and Liquefied Petroleum Gases Regulations 1972. These lay down the types of containers and storerooms required for various quantities of highly flammable liquid.

Safer substitutes should be used where possible. Check the safety certificates of all fire appliances and machinery. Containers for disposal of scrap and waste and their locations should be safe and designed to prevent fire. Fire doors and automatic sprinklers should be installed where necessary.

Prevention of fire and fire extinguishers

Fire extinguishers should be regularly checked. Christine Hamilton, safety representative in a local authority office, found (1979) on inspection that one of the fire extinguishers was sited between two cabinets. Half the people working in the room didn't know it was there, and its last inspection date was June 1973! There are several different kinds of fire extinguishers and hose reels are more efficient than water extinguishers. Water, foam, dry chemical or carbon dioxide extinguishers are designed for different kinds of fires. The Workers' Educational Association *Safety Representatives' Guide to Fire Precautions* by Dave Bennet contains details of the various types of extinguishing equipment and their uses.

Dear Hazards Bulletin,

A young girl who sometimes does temp work for our office burst in and threw lighter fuel over a newspaper, set light to it and rapidly puffed it out with a fire extinguisher (which she was carrying around in a briefcase).

She had answered an ad in the Evening Standard for salespersons. When she went along initially to the office that produced the fire extinguishers, she had to sign a form saying she realised the fire extinguisher was not recommended by the Fire Offices' Committee (ie. the insurance companies). She also asked if the contents were safe and the man demonstrated that they were by drinking the stuff.

Anyway, back at the Central London Poly, we were all very impressed (though not with the price – £28) and were thinking of placing orders right, left and centre. I looked at the fire extinguisher label and noticed it said 'Contains TCF & SGM'. Pat Kinnersley's book has about half a page on the toxicity of TCF and related substances. Amy, our temp, has now handed in her fire extinguisher. She was advised to ring the HSE Occupational Safety and Hygiene Laboratories at Cricklewood for more gen on TCF & SGM. She was put through to a Dr somebody who said words to the effect that if the company said it was a safe product she should take their word for it and if everybody acted like her then how would any work get done! She was very upset by this response.

Best wishes,
Netta Swallow
Central London Poly, 309 Regent Street, London W1

The fire safety department of the local fire brigade will help you if you need advice on the phone. They're usually happy to give lectures and demonstrations. Training in the use of fire-fighting equipment is usually given at the fire station and the employer charged for the service. Note that no one should attack a fire if it puts them at risk.

The fire service, like the Health and Safety Inspector, has the right to enter premises and inspect the fire precautions. They will investigate complaints, anonymous or otherwise. If you are a safety representative you could send the fire safety officers a list of safety reps from your place of work and ask them to have the reps contacted about inspection of the offices. It's also worth contacting the firemen through the local Fire Brigades Union if you need more information.

Escape

Workers in Cheshire County Council's Warrington offices are working in a potential fire trap, although it was built in 1974. A new fire escape was to be built to meet legal specifications. The fire officer has told the NALGO reps that the building is unsafe. But the proposed alterations were scrapped as part of the cutbacks in public expenditure! One NALGO safety rep had this to say:

> 'This means there are 40 people on each of four floors with literally no escape from their workplace. If the central staircase — the only present escape — is blocked, 160 people could die. I think this is outrageous. Local government is supposed to be a good employer, working in the interests of local people. Yet here they are letting us, their own employees, work in a time bomb! They *knew* it was unsafe! It didn't even fit the regulations when they moved into the building. The reality of the cutbacks is that every day people's lives are put at risk...It's not a natural risk it's deliberate cutbacks. We're not going to let this issue go.'

If there's a fire, what you'll want above all is an easy way to get out. Yet many fire escapes are locked or blocked with stores or refuse. In one insurance office in Colchester, the fire escape was blocked because it was next to a loading bay. Make sure you can't be trapped in your office in event of fire.

Escape routes must be clearly indicated, and particular attention should be given to escape routes for basements and windowless premises. Provision should be made for disabled staff. In computer rooms there should be easy escape, since in the event of fire the fail-safe systems which protect the computers often flood the place with carbon dioxide.

There should be full-scale fire drills at least every six months. In one DHSS office in the London area there were no fire drills until a safety rep was elected. Management simply said it was unnecessary! APEX carried out a survey of their members' offices and found 68 per cent lacked proper fire drills. Workers should have regular fire practice so they are familiar with escape routes. If you have an irresponsible management like the one above it might be worth just setting off the fire alarm one day as a test. Ursula Hughes worked for the Schools Council in London, and there had been no fire practice for two years:

> 'The branch pressed for fire drills, but we got nowhere. So then we said we'd organise our own fire practice. The threat was enough, and management organised regular ones after that and unblocked the fire doors.'

There are now automatic systems which can detect heat, smoke or flames and raise the alarm. Alarms must be audible or visible everywhere. Some soundproofing prevents inefficient alarm bells being heard. For example, can the bell be heard in the typing pool and in the toilets? The bell should be tested or examined every three months at least. Make sure alarms are well maintained − often the hammer is missing.

If you are dissatisfied with anything concerning fire precautions, it should be a matter of negotiation or dispute. Fire precautions are only adequate if *you* think they are.

Footnotes

1 Workers Educational Association, London District, teaching material, 1978.
2 *National Safety News,* USA, October 1975.
3 TUC checklist for Civil Service trade union representatives, ref. LAO Code, paragraph 14.
4 Brown, J.R., 'Factors contributing to the development of low back-pain in industrial workers' in *American Industrial Hygiene Association Journal,* January 1975, pp.26-31.
5 TUSIU, *A Workers' Guide to Office Hazards,* North East Trade Union Studies Information Unit, Newcastle, 1979, p.6.
6 *HM Factory Inspectorate Annual Report for 1971,* HMSO, 1972.
7 Fire Precautions Act 1971 (Non-certificated Factory, Office, Shop and Railway Premises Regulations 1976).

CHECK LIST

general office safety

Trips and falls

1   Has management checked that the premises come up to safety standards?

2   Are the floors of all offices and passageways, corridors, storerooms, or stairways
     (a) kept free from any obstruction?
     (b) properly maintained?
     (c) made of non-slip material?

3   Are staircases provided with a substantial handrail or hand hold?

4   Are all corridors and stairways well lit?

5   Is there any alternative to storage at height?

6   Are the surfaces of all car parks and pathways around the building kept free of pot-holes, ice, etc.

Lifting

1   Have any members been injured due to heavy lifting?

2   Is there any agreement with management about maximum weights?

3   Are there any mechanical aids to help with the moving of heavy items?

4   Is there any way in which jobs can be redesigned?

5   Does any training given to new workers include advice on the use of lifting equipment?

6   Can goods be packed in smaller units?

Equipment hazards

1   Has management checked that all machinery is up to safety standards?

2   Are workers (or their representatives) consulted on the safety aspects of new equipment?

3   Are all the dangerous parts of any machines effectively guarded to prevent people coming into contact with them?

4   Where possible, is the guard constantly kept in position?

5   If the guard has to be removed, is it interlocked with the controls so the machine cannot be worked unless it is in the 'safe' position?

6   Is the 'off' or 'stop' control clearly marked and close to the operator's work station?

7   Are desk top machines placed so they cannot fall off?

.8   Does management provide adequate training so that all workers know how to operate machines which they may be instructed to use?

Electricity	1	Has management developed a system for immediately fixing faulty equipment?
	2	Do all machines give a clear indication that they are on?
	3	Are all electrical machines fitted with the correct fuses?
	4	Does all electrical machinery clearly state the name of the service engineers?
	5	Have precautions been made to prevent any build up of 'leakage current' between machines connected together?
Hazards from fittings and furniture	1	Are all offices large enough to prevent any hazards arising from overcrowding?
	2	Are all filing cabinets, cupboards and so on attached to the wall/floor to prevent them falling over?
	3	Are they fitted with locking devices to prevent more than one drawer from being opened at a time?
	4	Are they sufficient for the storage needs of the office?
	5	Are they kept clear of doors, corridors, and frequently used passageways?
	6	Can sharp corners of furniture, etc. be situated so as to avoid a hazard to people passing them?
Fire	1	Is the means of escape properly maintained?
	2	Is the means of escape free from obstruction?
	3	Are all exit doors, and all doors leading to them, kept unlocked during working hours?
	4	Are all exit doors, and windows used as fire exits, clearly marked?
	5	Is there an effective fire alarm?
	6	Is it tested every three months?
	7	Is fire fighting equipment provided?
	8	It it suitable for the types of fires likely?
	9	Is it properly maintained?
	10	Is it kept ready for use?
	11	Is there a fire certificate?
	12	Is it kept on the premises to which it refers?
	13	Is it readily available for safety reps to check?
	14	Are provisions regarding the storage of inflammable materials adhered to?
	15	Is appropriate training in fire precautions given to employees?
	16	Are there regular fire drills?
	17	Have there been any changes in the workplace which could affect fire safety, including any increase in staffing levels?

4 New Technology

9 Microelectronics: what computers are doing to office work and office workers

Microprocessors, visual display units, microelectronics, new technology, silicon chips, word processors — all have suddenly become household words. One Monday morning you go to work and find a machine that looks like a television sitting in your office. Nobody asked you. Nobody explained why it was being introduced. Will it mean fewer jobs? Is it safe to operate? Why is everyone talking about the 'new technology'?

A visual display unit (VDU) is the common name given to a TV-like screen, often with a keyboard, used to 'read' information into and out of a computer. The use of these in offices, banks, airlines, the GPO and Civil Service is growing very fast. Silicon chips permit a miniaturisation of computers (very cheap), and these microprocessors are enabling employers to increase automation in libraries, offices, storehouses, hospitals, restaurants, shops, agriculture, aviation and all industries. Meanwhile thousands of postal and other workers lose their jobs.

Soon you'll be able to call up on your television screen information on travel, sport, news or hundreds of other subjects, through Ceefax or Prestel. Microelectronics have already brought an explosion of new consumer goods and cheaper products: calculators and cash registers, TV games, digital watches.

There's no doubt that this new technology will make enormous changes to the way we live and work. On the one hand, technology has increased standards of living and created some new jobs. On the other, its introduction has resulted in massive redundancies, loss of skills, and more monotonous and alienating jobs. New technologies also bring new health hazards. If employers get their way, microelectronics in offices mean a massive cut in clerical staff, another danger to health and more inhuman ways of working. Microelectronics bring great advantages to employers. They cut costs, are never sick, never on holiday, need never stop or go

118

to the toilet, never ask for a pay increase or better working conditions.

Job loss is the greatest health hazard of new technology. More than a third of Britain's working population is employed in offices, and office costs have risen to about half of the total business costs. Thus, the pressure is great to reduce these costs, and it can be achieved by the introduction of new technology. Every form of office work is under threat.

In this chapter we will look closer at microelectronics — what is it? How is it being introduced into office work? What is happening to jobs? What are the health hazards to operators? We'll discuss some union responses to the new technology and look at what you can do about it. Finally, we'll look at the wider social implications: the computer is now affecting all aspects of our lives, and the impact on ways of working and on patterns of employment could mean massive social and political upheavals.

What is new technology?

Machines capable of storing large quantities of information on a few square millimetres of a silicon chip* can now be manufactured at a fraction of the cost of the circuits of traditional computers. The cost of one microprocessor varies from 50 pence to a million pounds. The size of these microprocessors means that they speed up any computer operation and they are portable and easy to operate. The most widespread application of new technology, and the area where the largest number of jobs — mainly women's jobs — is immediately at risk, is within the office. Here the rising cost of labour — even women's labour — is the incentive to automate.

* The basic logic circuits of the processor can now be etched into the surface of small silicon-based wafers. A piece of wafer with thousands of integrated circuits is known as a 'chip'.

The most common microelectronic device is the visual display unit attached to a computer terminal keyboard. You may have seen this type of machine in an airline booking office or bank, with words and figures flashing on the screen in response to the push of a button. The image produced is usually yellow-green or blue-white with a dark background; black on white is common too.

Computers and calculators

Office work has been constantly changing since the days of ledgers and quill pens. The introduction of typewriters at the turn of the century was part of the first stages of mechanisation. This didn't change office routines greatly. Typewriters, calculators and other small hand-operated machines were mostly worked by women and developed during a time of expansion in clerical work. The second phase was characterised by punch-card machines, some electrical. These were more complex counting machines and were boring to operate, and used by low-paid women. The next stage was in the 1950s, the era of 'galloping technology', characterised by the 'automatic digital computer', large expensive electronic machines which were sometimes called data processors. These systems required the employment of key punch operators, whose conditions of work were horrific. They were machine operators working in stressful, noisy offices at a terrific rate. Many complained of mental and physical fatigue, and the turnover rate was very high.

'New technology' therefore isn't all that new. It is part of a continuing trend of mechanisation and automation, which together with 'scientific management' methods has attempted systematically to reduce the number of workers doing a job (one woman, one task), to change the nature of work and to reduce the level of skill needed. The cost of secretarial labour has risen in the last few decades, as has the demand for that labour. The pressure to automate offices to save on labour costs has now produced the 'word processing revolution'. The capital investment in new office technology is now accelerating rapidly and is having dramatic and visible effects on the workforce. Office workers are going through many of the same experiences that factory workers suffered over the last 150 years.

Word processors

The word processor is like an electronic typewriter with a video screen instead of the usual cylinder and paper. Its computer may be in another part of the building or elsewhere in the world. Others contain a small computer with a memory for previous correspondence and the ability to prepare, edit, store and retrieve text: this is the 'stand-alone' type. Once prepared, text may be transmitted for printing by pushing a button.

The word processor automatically centres, indents and justifies margins as instructed. The skill required to produce a neat, well laid-out document is eliminated. It will produce any number of error-free copies of an original text once this is in the memory. The operator can automatically interrupt standard material to insert text specific to each letter, such as a name and address and account number. Complex editing, including re-ordering of paragraphs, inserts and revision of layout is possible. This eliminates the need for retyping an entire text as documents are edited before the final draft. Until now, the number of errors and the need to go back, white them out and retype has been the limiting factor on a typist's speed. Now errors can be retyped at the touch of a key, and less skilled typists can work at the same speed as more accurate ones (this advantage of word processors is much vaunted by advertisers).

Examples of use of word processors in offices

Insurance	*Updating information on policies and interest rates or retrieving this information.*
Banking	*Obtaining current bank balances from the computer or processing cheques.*
Printing	*Checking and correcting the text which has been entered into the computer by operators before it is used to generate photographically produced type for the actual page.*
General office work	*Taking customers' orders over the phone and entering them into the computer.*
Secretarial	*Producing intermediate drafts and final copies of documents. Allowing the assembly of letters and other documents from phrases and paragraphs stored in the computer memory. Automatically setting, centring and tabulating. Once a piece of information is typed in it need never be retyped.*
Civil Service and local government	*Checking records and cataloguing. Filing will become a thing of the past. All records can be stored in a central bank and called instantly on to any video screen plugged into the computer.*

Unemployment

A study carried out by the research department of the Association of Scientific, Technical and Managerial Staffs (ASTMS), which represents many banking and insurance staff, estimated that the effect in Britain of increasing office automation in this economic climate will be to raise unemployment to the five million mark by the early 1990s. Barrie Sherman of ASTMS research said: 'It's happening already. Just this year the Friends Provident Insurance Society, to give one example, introduced televisual policy displays in all offices, which could produce a 40 per cent cut in jobs, to do three weeks' work in three minutes' (1979).

Some people estimate that the new technology will raise the level of unemployment to that at the peak of the 1930s slump: this would mean 10 to 15 per cent of the workforce. Professor George Ray of the National Institute of Economic and Social Research suggests that employment in the service industries 'could fall by 1¼ million' in the next 12 years (*Financial Times*, 24 July 1978).

> *Suicides are increasing in number and one reason could be growing unemployment. According to the Samaritans suicide attempts have gone up by 30 per cent in parts of the north-east of England where unemployment is already high.*

New technology destroys jobs. But doesn't it also create them? In March 1979, an optimistic American consultant forecast that one million new jobs would be created by microelectronics by 1987. These, however, would be spread over Britain, France, West Germany and America, with the latter taking 60 per cent! It seems unlikely that those who lose their jobs to micro-electronics, can be transferred to other industries. A Confederation of British Industry (CBI) paper states: 'World trade cannot be relied upon to expand sufficiently to provide the jobs needed.' (*Financial Times*, 30 October 1978)

> *In Britain in August 1980 there were 14 people registered as unemployed for every job vacancy.*

Your boss may try to reassure you that the VDUs coming into your office won't mean job loss. Look into it carefully.

Women and new technology

The importance of clerical work to women in this society cannot be overstated. In Britain no less than two in every five working women are in clerical or secretarial jobs (that's three million). In November 1978 typists in the National Association of Local Government Officers (NALGO) at Bradford Council voted 128 to 16 against the introduction of word processing. Management tried to introduce a time and motion study (see p. 11) and the typists came out on strike for two and a half weeks. They went back after management agreed to call off the study while a working party looked into the whole question of new technology.

A recent estimate by Siemens suggests that by 1990 40 per cent of present office work could be carried out by computerised equipment. In West Germany this will mean a staggering loss of two million out of five million secretarial and typing jobs. In Britain there are already many instances of office jobs being slashed. At the British Standards Institute, for example, one-third of the typists lost their jobs on the introduction of word processors. Word processors are relatively cheap. It's reckoned that some can pay for themselves through savings on typists' wages in less than nine months. Thousands are now in use, with numbers increasing every day. Already unemployment among women is rising faster than for men. The result could be a devastating destruction of the one slightly better paid fields of employment for women.

Women's earnings are essential to family budgets. 30 per cent of working women with children are the sole family income earner. With rising unemployment among both men and women, will we see an increased reaction against women who do paid work? It is being argued by some government members such as Patrick Jenkin, that women should be the first to go. Lord Spens told the House of Lords in June 1979 that married women should leave paid work to men and stay at home. He said women with children 'should not compete in the market for paid jobs'. And will the limited effects of the Equal Pay and Sex Discrimination Acts be dissipated as women workers in offices, banks and shops find their traditional job opportunities blocked and their promotional prospects lessened still further?

Already many jobs have been lost, but in small groups, many by 'natural wastage' or redeployment rather than massive redundancy. This kind of job loss doesn't make the headlines, but the effect on job opportunity is the same whether people are sacked or just not replaced. Job opportunities for women are under severe attack and their potential for wage-bargaining decreased.

Microprocessors will also affect women in the other side of their working lives — at home — with link-up facilities like View-Data using the domestic phone and TV to receive information. Increasingly it will be possible to work from home. This has advantages, but there is the danger of an increase in the number of workers, particularly women, suffering the isolation and low pay of existing home-workers. Such workers are more easily exploited and more difficult to organise into trade unions.

Health hazards: tomorrow's technology, today's headache

But what if you're one of the 'lucky few.? Say you get a job as a word processor operator. What about the health effects? Are VDUs safe? Will this 'labour-saving device' save *you* labour and make *your* job easier?

> 'Employees working with computer display screens are showing a range of alarming physical symptoms, ranging from just discomfort to pain and extreme visual fatigue.' (Dr O. Ostberg, *National Board of Occupational Safety and Health, Sweden*)[1]

In this section we shall look at some of the 'alarming physical symptoms' together with ways of improving your working environment to cut down risk. This does not imply that the answer to health problems with visual display units is simply better machines — how they are introduced and operated, including staffing levels and hours of work, are equally important.

The Swedish National Board of Occupational Safety and Health did a survey of operators engaged in 'full-time sedentary visual work'.

75% felt discomfort in their eyes
55% felt discomfort in their back and shoulders
35% felt discomfort in their head and neck
25% felt discomfort in their arms and wrists
15% feld discomfort in their legs

Eyestrain and visual problems

Many VDU operators complain of sore and tired eyes, sometimes including prickling, dryness or burning sensations, twitching of the eye muscles, and conjunctivitis. Sitting staring at a VDU for hours tires the muscles of the eye. You may get a throbbing behind the eyeballs, or tense, heavy lids, often tender to pressure. You may feel nauseated. Headaches and feelings of strain occur especially if you work in front of a display screen for long and uninterrupted periods. In one study, continuous intense terminal work during an eight-hour day led to various types of visual strain for 75 per cent of the operators.[2] Strain which affects the ability to see can be dangerous for anyone coming off a VDU shift and then driving home.

You may have trouble watching television after work. One VDU operator in Birmingham puts a tea towel over her TV in the evening because she literally can't face it — even when it's switched off!

Much eyestrain is actually muscular fatigue caused, like other aches and pains, by the muscles having to work for long periods doing the same thing. Eyes have a very small range of focus changes, so the operator needs the opportunity to gaze periodically at some distant point, thus resting the eye muscles. This is normally achieved by turning the gaze away from bright light, focusing on the distance, or closing the eyes. If you are required to work at the pace of the machine this becomes impossible.

Glare from a wrongly adjusted screen, excessive heat emitted by the machines, the dryness of a poorly airconditioned atmosphere and the flicker effect of the VDU add to the resulting problems, which include difficulty in focusing, double vision, disturbed colour vision, or a coloured fringe round things. Research suggests, however, that in the case of both eye fatigue and colour distortion, particularly red-green blindness, sight rapidly returns to normal *with rest.* Tests on long-term effects have been inconclusive. A study of users on air reservation terminals for Air France concluded after a year's monitoring that although there was an increase in short-sightedness of ten per cent of the group tested, sight deterioration was anyway a feature of age. However, nearly all of the 216 VDU operators suffered eye fatigue at the end of the day.[3] Safety representatives on a number of trade union courses have reported that significant numbers of VDU operators' eyesight deteriorated after a while and they have to start wearing glasses.

Danger! Eyes at risk

I became a VDU operator in 1976 and stuck it out for nearly three years. My job was to process information by typing on a computer terminal. The job demands that you sit still all day, staring at a screen which is about 25 inches from your face.

It's potentially damaging to your health for several reasons. First, you are prevented from exercising most of your body, you can only leave your seat to go to the toilet. Where I worked we had no fresh air and the central heating was stifling. I suffered from continual colds and coughs.

Our chairs were supposed to be adjustable, but most of them were broken and the firm didn't waste money mending them. Most women had backache or neck cramps.

The lighting was the fluorescent strip variety, which shone on the screen so that you couldn't see the print without turning up the brightness, and this really hurts your eyes after the first couple of hours. What we needed was soft, individual lighting which we controlled. The print on the screen was lime green (this is the cheapest to buy) and it makes you feel sick. Other colours are available, cream and soft pink are more comfortable to look at.

Having done this work for a few months, I realised that my eyesight was affected. When I left work I could hardly see across the road, although this used to wear off after a couple of hours. We all suffered with frequent headaches and carried aspirins around with us. When I left that job, I got my eyes tested and was prescribed glasses to compensate for my blurry short-sightedness. But I realise how lucky I was – my eyes have improved and I don't wear glasses now. But one girl I worked with went blind in one eye very suddenly. She went to the hospital and they asked about her work. They thought it probably contributed to her

condition. She left the job, and fortunately her sight re-
turned. She didn't come back!

We had three short breaks in an eight-hour day. I've heard
it's recommended to have a five-minute minimum break
every hour, just to rest your eyes. It has been said that
VDUs only exaggerate existing eye troubles – but the vast
majority of people have potential problems with their
vision anyway.

The only thing that VDU operators can do to improve
such dangerous working conditions is to organise through
trade unions, with specific health and safety demands.
Regular visits from an eye specialist would help, and a
shorter working week is vital, not only to share the few
new jobs which are replacing the old ones, but also to
prevent unnecessary risks to operators' eyesight.
(Heather Bryden, letter to Womens Voice, *December 1979)*

If you are using a VDU together with other material, for example
checking figures or invoices against it, or writing down information taken from it, then your eye has to refocus from screen
to paper and back again repeatedly. This can cause fatique in the
muscle used to focus the lens of the eye. In other words, eyestrain.
A union representative in the French Post Office received a
number of complaints from women in the telephone information
centre. They suffered from excessive eye fatigue and had difficulty in focusing. Through union pressure they succeeded in
getting more rest breaks and better conditions.
If you are taking drugs, your eyes may be more at risk, and the
combination of VDU work and drugs could adversely affect your
vision.

Microfiche viewers Microfiche readers units are a form of visual display unit now
widely used in libraries and some office. Pages of information are
photographed and reduced for storage on a small sheet of film.
Light is passed through the film and a magnifying lense is used to
recall the tiny images. Sometimes computer output is directly
transferred to microfilm.
The health hazards of microfiche viewers are mainly visual,
causing eyestrain, headache and nausea after prolonged use.

Most of the guidelines for VDUs in the previous section apply
also to these reader units. But here there is the additional problem
of 'scrolling'. Finding the right page on a film means that unwanted images flash across the screen in a rapid blur leading to a
feeling of nausea. No manufacturer to date makes provision for
blocking out this blur. Blurring occurs also as a result of a poor
focusing system, bad maintenance and poor siting of the machine.
Eyestrain also arises from peering at images with low contrast
between light and dark areas. Letters reproduced in negative, i.e.
light against dark, are thought to be easier to read, because the
letters appear larger. However, there is generally conflicting

evidence on screen colours (see p.129). So you may have to reject some types until you find one that suits you.

Almost all currently available viewers demand that you operate them from close-up. This forces your eyes to focus on a close-up image, and could cause a form of eyestrain known as asthenopia. This can occur because our eyes have evolved over time to focus easily on distant objects 'at infinity'. The eyeball muscles are then relaxed. When you focus on a close object (eg. the tip of your nose) the eyeballs have to turn inwards, creating *tension* in the inner muscles. It is this tension that causes headache, fatigue, discomfort and ultimately double vision. A large screen viewed from a *distance* is always easier on the eye muscles than a small screen viewed up close.

ASTMS makes the following recommendations for microfiche viewers:

Recommendations

1   Larger screens should be preferred to smaller, and documents should be reproduced at least to their original size. Optimal is A4 reduced to 24X then magnified 24X at the screen. Higher magnification than 24X should be avoided, as this introduces graininess into the image and enhances the speed of the moving image.

2   Brightness of screen should be variable to adjust to surrounding lighting conditions; it should contain no 'hot spots'. Ratio between screen brightness and ambient illumination should be around 3 to 1.

3   Contrast of image should be high; machines that cannot guarantee uniform, sharp focusing ability should be absolutely rejected.

4   The screen should be protected from reflections, either by a hood, or by a matt finish that does not destroy image quality. Hoods should not cast a shadow across the screen.

5   Viewers should be solid enough to absorb vibrations from passing people, for example, without shaking the image; controls should be flexible and not jar the image.

6   Masking should be introduced to cover the image while the right document is being found, to avoid nausea.

7   The screen should always be sloping at least gently away from the vertical and be viewed from above; looking *up* at a screen becomes very tiring.

Continuous work at even the best designed microfiche viewers will result in related illness unless frequent breaks are taken. One Russian study recommends a 30 minute break after 45 to 60 minutes of reading microfilm.[4]

This section is largely based on an ASTMS article. For more information on microfiche see ASTMS *Health and Safety Monitor* No.3.[5]

VDUs and lighting Ambient, or room lighting should be below 300 lux according to VDU manufacturers, and some recommend levels of 100 to 300 lux for background illumination for older types of VDU (see chapter 3   for more on lighting levels). In normal offices lighting is between 500 and 1,000 lux. So these recommendations are for *dimly lit* offices. Is this what we want in the office of the future — working practically in the dark? Local lighting to supplement general lighting is often recommended, especially where the operator is also writing or reading written material. However, specially designed lamps may be necessary, since ordinary desk lamps are unsatisfactory here. The eye has to keep adjusting from light to dark when moving from screen to paper.

VDUs are being introduced at an alarming rate, often in offices with totally unsuitable fluorescent lighting. Baffles and diffusers must be fitted to overhead lighting to help prevent glare and reflection.

Glare and reflection A significant cause of eyestrain is glare on the screen produced by light from windows, from shiny work surfaces, key boards and lighting that is too bright or incorrectly positioned in relation to the machines. This *reflected* light makes it difficult to see the characters on the screen. This may also be a cause of neck and backpains as the operator contorts her body posture to minimise the glare.

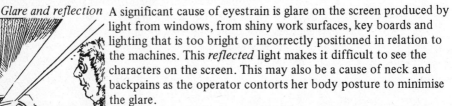

The General and Municipal Workers Union (GMWU) recommends the following:

> 'Tests should be made to ascertain glare and reflection on the display screen and to remove this glare or reflection by either moving the work station or installing screens in sufficient quantity as to remove these stressors. In some cases experience has shown that reflection can be largely eliminated by removing the transparent screen of coloured glass in front of the display tube.'

Anti-glare filters and adjustable screen angles can reduce glare. But marketed VDUs for offices are rarely equipped with any form of anti-reflection filters of the type always used in aircraft cockpits. Some manufacturers have filters as an option, but because they're not standard they are often not purchased. An anti-glare coating on the screen may be better than an anti-glare filter, which can allow dust to collect. Note that anti-glare modifications may make the screen more difficult to read.

As pointed out above, lighting is crucial. Only indirect and deflected light should be permitted so as to minimise the problem of glare on the screen. The National Union of Journalists states:

> 'Reflective surfaces — desk tops, screen surrounds, even the typing keys — should be dark-coloured [or neutral—author], and if necessary shields should be provided around the

screens. The Visual Display Terminals should be positioned to avoid the operator having to face unshielded windows and/or other strong lights or screen. As the level of ambient lighting suitable for continuous Visual Display Terminal work is lower than ideal for other types of work, VDT areas are best kept separate from the areas where other work is to be carried out.'

Even where the isolation of the operator is simple to arrange, you may want to question whether this is the best way to deal with a health hazard. This looks like a classic case of modifying the person rather than the process. Ideally we want processes that are inherently safe and healthy to operate. The isolation of VDU operators in dimly-lit rooms could easily add to the stress and boredom of the job, thus creating more hazards.

Flicker

Flicker can be distressing and it causes severe eyestrain. There is a small possibility that flicker on the screen can precipitate epileptic fits and migraine attacks in some people.

The characters on the screen are not illuminated continuously but are flashed on a large number of times every second. This is known as the 'character refresh rate'. This rate should be no less than 60 times a second (60 Hertz).* All VDUs flicker, but the problem is made worse if there is fluorescent lighting or flicker from multiple VDUs in use. To reduce flicker the operating frequency should be increased to 100 Hertz. (Note that in many units the rate is between 25 and 60 Hertz.) Manufacturers say that few customers specify this fairly simple modification, so most units flicker at 50 Hertz, which is mains frequency. To keep the price down, virtually no VDUs for offices have a flicker frequency above 60 Hertz, and they all cause complaints from their operators.

Screen and character size and colour

VDU screens and characters vary in colour. Swedish studies recommend yellow text against an amber background for office VDUs,[6] while the TUC says that yellow-green symbols on a dark green background is most acceptable. Try demanding a variety of trial units to find out what people in your office find most comfortable — if any. Negotiate the right to send back what you don't want. Too low a level of screen brightness makes the characters difficult to read; too high a level results in disturbing glare. Luminosity contrasts should be adjustable. Beware of management attempts to limit brightness control to cut costs and extend the life of the machine.

The characters on the screen are made up of tiny glowing dots. The more dots there are, the clearer the character will be. The number of dots in a character will be shown by the 'dot matrix'.

---

* Hertz is a unit of frequency, expressing the number of cycles per second.

The TUC recommends a minimum dot matrix of 5 x 7 (35 dots) or preferably 7 x 9 (63 dots). The dot matrix print displayed on many terminal screens is exhausting. You constantly have to try to bring the characters into focus, forcing the eyes to work harder. If the individual dots are visible to the operator, this makes the light appear to 'dance' within the letters, causing annoyance and stress.

Characters should be 'squared' and in upper and lower case for long texts, and lower case for intermittent work. There are recommended minimum standards for character sizes, together with recommended sitting distance from the screen, published by the TUC Printing Industries Committee (see addresses below, Appendix 2).

You should monitor carefully how much information is being placed on the screen. Pressure to put the maximum information on the screen should be resisted, since the use of the screen edges significantly reduces the quality of presentation.

Tubes should be inspected regularly, since worn tubes will blur the edge of the screen display

Eye defects

Up to one-third of the working population have uncorrected or insufficiently corrected visual defects. The likelihood of visual fatigue associated with close work or work requiring constant visual attention increases with age, and is increased if an operator wears reading glasses. Vision changes with age and experience. As the lens in the eye hardens over time, the curvature changes and an inability to read text close to the eye develops long-sightedness or presbyopia. Most glasses prescribed for correcting your vision assume that material will be read at approximately 33 cm. VDUs are usually situated at a distance of 50 to 100 cm, so the glasses are often unsuitable. Similarly, standard bifocal lenses are not suitable for display work. In addition, these may provoke neck and arm pain through straining to focus on reading the screen. Spectacles and contact lenses need to be specially designed for display operation, and if required should be paid for by the employer. But special glasses can never be the answer to visual problems *created* by this technology. It must be more carefully designed and the work organised in such a way that it suits all our health needs — if we are going to have it at all.

Computer terminal operators at the French Post and Telephone Office have compiled a dossier on health and terminals. They are accusing the employer of making statements to the effect of 'Give us your health — in return you will get a modern word processing machine, a bonus and a pair of spectacles'. Their colleagues operating a microfiche system for directory enquiries are demanding rest-time allowances.

Screening workers

As outlined above, there are many kinds of eye defects and our
eyesight does not remain constant. It is impossible to say how
many people have absolutely perfect eyesight and how many
have some kind of defect at some time in their lives. Yet some
trade union guidelines and most medical studies recommend
regular eye tests and screening tests to prevent those with eye
problems being employed as VDU operators. Many also recommend that no one over the age of 45 work with VDUs. This is
essentially recommending a *selection process.* The danger of
selection processes is that they divide workers into the healthy
and employable, and the susceptible, disabled and unemployable.
The latter group (over 45 or short-sighted in this case) are quite
simply discriminated against. And it's not just in work with VDUs
that this screening-out process goes on: pregnant workers, people
said to be accident-prone or stress-prone, those with a weak back,
and so on.

Yet we *all* have weaknesses, we all have our area of susceptibility.
Who is really in a position to make the division between the
superworker and the 'susceptible, weak worker'? Who controls
the eye test results? What happens to those whose eyes were
perfect on beginning work with a VDU and tests show up subse-
quent damage? Do they get compensation? Are they tossed on
the rubbish heap to join the other susceptible workers, to make
room for a young, healthy worker — who then goes on to get eye
trouble from the work...? This aspect of the new technology
underlines its sheer brutality. If your branch decides on eye checks
it is important to include safeguards in the agreement. The GMWU
in their checklist for using VDUs recommends:

131

'...eye checks should test vision on a regular basis and should be done at the place of work during the normal work day so as to reflect the effects of the normal work-load on the eyes. Eye tests must not be used to screen out those workers with less than perfect vision. Machines like VDUs should be designed and manufactured to suit all workers, whatever their differences in age and physical condition.

The purpose of eye tests is 1) to check on the health effects of VDUs over a period of time, and 2) to *prevent* possible deterioration in those workers who already have serious eye defects and who are likely to be adversely affected by the VDU work.

The results of the tests should be explained to the workers and given to them (or their GPs) and safety reps if required. The tests should be performed by qualified personnel, agreed by unions and management.'

Medical tests often come across as progressive management practice. Your employers are seen to be doing something for your health and safety. But remember, screening saves the employer money by keeping down disability expenses.

ASTMS recommends that people with eyesight problems should *refuse* the work — a very different position from being told you can't do the job.

Body fatigue

There is a rising tide of complaints from VDU operators of aches and pains during and after work. AUEW/TASS states:

'The standard layout in current use, "screen above key-board", imposes an immobility which can lead to back-ache, aching muscles in head and shoulders, and headaches. Well designed supportive seats, desks of the correct height and regular breaks are essential to avoid posture problems.'

It is all too easy for management to blame 'poor posture' for your aches and pains. Poor posture is usually caused by bad seating and inadequate lighting — that is, by badly designed jobs. (For more information, see chapter 4)

Working with VDUs (Letter to Womens Voice, August 1979)

I read with great interest your article about visual display units. I work on a VDU in Bradford, doing the clerical work for a mail order catalogue firm. Until recently there were four pregnant women in our department. It must be worse for them than the rest of us because the chairs we use sort of push you over on the machine.

The VDUs not only record how many times you touch the keyboard (correctly) in an hour, but also when you signed on and off. If you're one minute over the time you have to make it up out of your tea breaks. We are allowed 50

minutes for lunch, three 12-minute breaks for respite, and
two 20-minute breaks for tea. The respites must be spent
in a grotty wee room, where there is a vending machine
which hardly ever works, and bad ventilation.

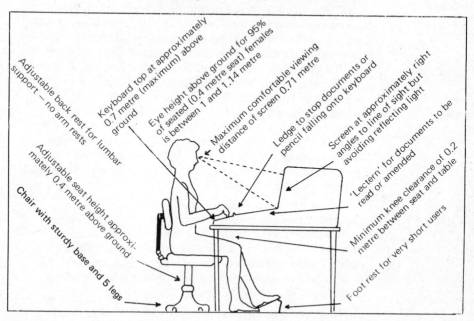

From Visual
Display Units and
their application
(D. Grover, ed.)

Screen and keyboard console should be separate so that operators
can arrange them to suit themselves. Equipment can then be
individually positioned for either left or right-handed operators.
Height, screen angle and seating should be adjustable. Some
Swedish equipment (eg. Facit) incorporates gas infilled legs on
their furniture so that the operator can adjust the screen and keyboard with little effort. Ideally, the keyboard should swivel from
left to right. Typing or 'keyboarding' should be possible with the
forearms horizontal, the feet comfortably on the floor or a footrest, and back supported. The keyboard should be as low as
possible on the desk, but the console must not be too steeply
inclined as this tires the wrists. The keys should be 'dished' to
help the operator to locate them. Hand rests should be provided
which should be approximately 60 mm deep and continuous with
the keyboard. ASTMS recommends also that a paperholder of
some kind or some system to reduce neck movement in reading
should be installed. The work station should ideally provide two
different height working levels for activities involving paper and
console work, and should be sufficiently large to give you enough
room to spread out material and to develop a comfortable work
posture. Provision should be made at the work station for all
ancillary equipment.

Communication with other operators should be possible, and vast, impersonal layouts should be avoided. Walkways, floor areas and work surfaces should be kept clear of obstructive wiring. Storage space should be provided for your belongings.

Flexibility in work is crucial. Adjustable equipment so that posture can be varied is essential, as are regular breaks to prevent tensed muscles. Note that breaks, together with varied jobs throughout the day, are even more important in combating fatigue than 'ergonomically well-designed' equipment. Any job which forces you to work in one position for long hours will give rise to body fatigue, but there is evidence that while the new technology is perhaps more efficient for employers, it is more fatiguing for the operator. The International Labour Office has said:'The fact remains...that machine operation is still more tiring for many operatives than straightforward manual methods of copying or calculating and can in some cases be a serious drain on their physical resources.'

Working a VDU

To find out what it's really like to work with a visual display unit, and the sort of conditions which prevail in Leeds, the Trade Union and Community Resource Centre (TUCRIC) interviewed a worker in the order processing department of a large local manufacturing and distribution firm – a typical application of the new technology.

Q. How long have you been working with VDUs?
A. About three and a half years, but only continuously for the last six or seven months.
Q. What do you mean by 'continuous'?
A. We work a 7½-hour day, with half an hour for lunch. We have a ten-minute break in the morning and another ten minutes in the afternoon, but the afternoon one isn't official. We've been on flexitime for about two years, but now it looks as if they're trying to get rid of it. All the word processing machines are switched on and off at the same time, and they want us to make a record of all the work we do, so they can monitor how many orders each person is dealing with. We're against this. It isn't our fault if an order takes a long time. You can get one order that's a page and a half long that could take fifty minutes to deal with if it hasn't been properly checked by the scrutineers. Sometimes you have to query just about every item on an order.
Q. How would you feel about losing the flexitime system?
A. Well, a lot of us really depend on it. You can leave early to do your shopping or whatever one day and then make up the hours the next day. It would be difficult for a lot of the women here if it goes – especially those with kids.

Q. Do you think the hours you're spending on the VDUs are too long?

A. Definitely. We've found out through the union that in some other places in Leeds nobody's allowed to use the machines for more than four hours a day — and that was introduced by the *management.*

Q. What are the effects on your health?

A. When you get home you feel tired and tense and irritable. All the girls here complain about headaches and waking up in the morning with puffy eyes. Sometimes when you're working you get very dizzy and have to have a break. A friend of mine went to have her eyes tested because the headaches were getting so bad. The optician said she had long vision so it's very bad for her to be working so near the screen (it's about 18 inches away). He said she'd have to wear glasses if she went on working under these conditions. He'd been getting people in practically every day from working with these things.

Keyed up:
VDUs and stress

'It has been shown that workers who work for machines have a far higher incidence of neurotic pathology than workers who work for (other) men.' (Dr E. Krapf, *Chief Mental Health Secretary, World Health Organisation, 1957)*

Eyestrain and body fatigue cannot be separated from mental fatigue or stress; for example, in some systems, if you make a mistake on the keyboard, messages of warning flash across the screen until the error is rectified. These incessant flashes are exhausting to the eyes and the mind.

A telling description of the everyday effects of working with VDUs comes from a worker for a large supermarket warehouse in Leeds. He doesn't work with VDUs but remarked: 'The VDU operators are always round the coffee machine during their breaks. They seem to need nine or ten cups a day; the rest of us will only have two or three at the most — and it's not exactly what you'd call a nice cup of coffee.'

The risk of stress from work is greater for those already under strain, such as working mothers, or those taking tranquillisers.

The list of stress symptoms is long and the causes complex (see chapter 1). On stess and work with VDUs, NUBE (the National Union of Bank Employees) had this to say:

'VDU work is inherently stressful: the operators' work pace is subordinated to that of the machine. It is necessarily fraught with problems where VDU work involves manuscript reading, which has an entirely different set of environmental requirements. It also tends to be highly monotonous. These problems persist even where the "technical" and environment conditions are adequate, and they are far more difficult to tackle.'

Linda McVeigh, a secretary of seven years' standing, found work on a word processor intolerably boring. She worked on an Olivetti system in an estate agent's where the job made little demand of her intelligence:

'The only time it wasn't boring was when it went wrong and there was something to do! On the other hand, that could be irritating. It would flash up all the symbols in completely meaningless succession, zooming along at a rate of knots. Then it would go dead. The engineer would come and it would work perfectly; he'd leave and it would conk out. He'd say it was my fault; I'd say it was the machine's. Without it the agency ground to a halt, as we'd thrown away all the name and address cards once the processor was programmed. Worse still, it once wiped out the memory discs. I'd be constantly frustrated by its illogicality.'[8]

The job of VDU operator may require a high degree of concentration, and under the conditions of the job as it now stands in most places, this is stressful. So is the lack of rest or relief pauses. VDU operators might *seem* to have an opportunity to gain relief during the frequent delays that show up at send-and-receive operations. But these delays are in reality stressful since you don't know exactly when and for how long the pauses will show up, so you can't really take a break. Instead you are spending your time *waiting* for the computer response. When computer technology was in its infancy, computer operators were highly trained and highly skilled. They were familiar with the elements of computer design, memory storage, coding language and similar skills. Now computer terminal display units have been made simpler to operate; the work has been deliberately broken down into a series of simplified tasks, and is more easily controlled and managed. It has been *deskilled*. Stress is greater. Word processor operators are often employed purely to key in text, with virtually no prospect of further learning or advancement.

Noise

While VDUs are certainly quieter than their forerunners, teletype, they still whirr, roar or hum due to cooling fans or transformers. Such low noises can be stressful to operators. The main potential noise problem is high-frequency noise from the VDU, which can cause discomfort and stress. Manufacturers should ensure that noise levels are minimal. The fan removing excess heat should not produce irritating humming, nor draughts. The printing machines can also create noise, particularly with several word processors in one room. It is possible to transfer printing facilities to a separate room.

Breaks and hours	Machines are expensive and there is pressure on employers to get the maximum possible use out of them before they deteriorate. This means an increase in pressure to do shiftwork. (For more information on shiftwork and health, see p. 16) The 'twilight shift' has already existed for some time in many offices, eg. mail order firms in Bradford. This trend is likely to spread with the use of the special telephone lines which can transmit typed copy from one word processor to another and which are cheaper to operate in the evenings. There are moves in some firms to eliminate the dubious advantages of flexitime and to increase shiftwork and/or to employ more part-time women workers on VDUs. At Barclaycard in Northampton, VDUs are used extensively. The 'auxiliary staff' bash details from the forms into the computer. The women work two hours at a time, then get a ten-minute break.
	Working shifts, working at the pace of a machine, goes against your body's natural rhythms and causes untold mental fatigue. The body's primary reaction to stressful work is a powerful urge to stop doing those actions which promote further fatigue, i.e. *to stop work.* This goes for most muscle fatigue and general stress. Many VDU operators complain regularly about general fatigue. The degree of fatigue is directly related to the amount of data processed, the more data processed, the greater the fatigue.
Here are some union recommendations and agreements	This can only be reduced by frequent breaks as well as a *reduction in workload.* *All workers should have adequate regular work breaks from the VDU.*
ASTMS	Maximum two hours, with half an hour break. Maximum work in any day should be no more than four hours. Shorter work periods with a greater number of breaks are advisable, eg. 50 minutes work followed by a 15-minute break. All breaks should be taken away from the work station.
NALGO (GLC branch)	Total time spent working on a VDU should not exceed 100 minutes per day. Fifty minutes should be the maximum period of continuous work, followed by a break of at least 15 minutes.
CPSA	At the GPO, CPSA members have agreed a code of practice whereby normal time spent with VDUs is 100 minutes a day maximum (180 minutes during abnormal work peaks). No operator is required to work more than 50 minutes continuously without a break of at least 15 minutes.
TUC Printing Industries Committee	*Minimum* of 30 minutes break from the screen in each period of two hours continuous work, and there should be an agreed maximum of work on the screen during any one shift. Whenever possible the work pattern should be programmed so that periods of work at the VDU alternate with periods which give the eyes an opportunity to become restored.

APEX	Twenty minutes rest in every hour for operators involved in continuous VDU work throughout the day. Wherever possible the work pattern should be arranged so that periods of work at the VDU are alternated with periods which give the eyes an opportunity to become restored.
AUEW/ TASS	Maximum of four hours work at a VDU during a working day. Regular breaks from screen working are essential — at least twenty minutes break in each period of two hours continuous working.
GMWU	All workers should have regular fixed work breaks away from the display unit, preferably every hour. If it is inconvenient for the worker to leave his(!) work station on a regular basis, there should be provision for the display screen to be turned off or made dark at regular intervals.
BIFU (Banking, Insurance and Finance Union – formerly NUBE)	There should be an agreed maximum period of operation of VDUs during any one shift: this maximum will depend on the concentration needed in any one task. However, the following should be observed: (a) the operators must work *no longer* than two hours continuously at a VDU; (b) the relief period between spells of work on a VDU must be no less than thirty minutes.

Some medical studies have also made recommendations. A French study recommends 90 minutes maximum time without a break, and a six-hour day.[9] A report for Air France carried out by the French Institute of Health recommends that no staff be employed full-time on VDUs.[10] A German study noted that while a system of short breaks is preferable as regards output levels, this is 'a source of great fatigue which can only be overcome by longer breaks and periods off work'.[11]

There is a danger in adopting a rigid attitude to rest periods, because their length and type must vary according to things like the overall workload and your own health needs. Go for a flexible agreement with minimum safeguards with your employers on the subject of rest pauses. Ideally what we want is a shorter working day and a shorter week for all. More holidays and periods of paid educational leave or long service leave, together with good maternity and paternity conditions, are all things you should consider in any agreements you draw up with management. In fact, the trend in British workplaces seems to be *away* from these recommendations — as long as employers get their way:

> 'Employers are tending to ask an increasing number of their staff to spend more of their day looking at displays.' (Roy Gladman in *Visual Display Units and their Application*, edited by Derrick Grover)

APEX surveyed its members and found many working on VDUs for 7½ hours a day. And operators at ICI's Millbank headquarters work all the time on word processors. But one VDU manufacturing boss suggests that this is in fact an *abuse* of the equipment. In a letter to *Computer Weekly,* 9 December 1978, Bill Ross, European Manager of Informer Inc. said:

> 'VDUs are basically transitory devices and should be regarded as ancillary devices to help a store keeper, bank teller, etc. do their normal work at their usual desk… Used in this way, no complaints have been received of fatigue, dizziness or claustrophobia.'

No one should be working full-time on a VDU. Breaks must be plentiful and long, and tasks varied. *You* should choose when to use the machine and when to take a break. The equipment should be designed so that you have control.

> 'Mental hazards caused by inhumanely designed computer systems should be considered a punishable offence, just as endangering bodily safety.' (A suggestion from a working party of the *International Federation of Information Processing*)

VDUs, radiation and heat

VDUs emit X-rays, infra-red rays, ultra-violet rays or microwave radiation. When functioning correctly VDUs are supposed to emit very little ionising (X-ray) radiation. Tests show exposure levels below the limits set in both the UK and USA at which it is necessary to wear film badges to record exposure.
Older models of VDU may pose problems from ionising radiation and must be checked periodically.
As with most dangerous substances, what may be considered a 'safe level' by one authority one day may be considered dangerous another day by someone else; there are many examples of this among industrial chemicals. The NUJ recommends new, more sensitive radiation detectors for operators to wear. TASS recommends:

> 'To minimise risk from radiation, VDUs should be frequently serviced by qualified engineers. The front of the cathode ray tube should be covered by a glass panel and the set enclosed in a metal case to give maximum protection in case of explosion.'

Cataracts

In 1976, two copy editors working for *New York Times* developed cataracts, a disease which clouds the eye and leads to blindness if not surgically corrected. They work at VDUs all day long. Both were in their thirties and blamed the radiation from the VDUs. Ordinarily cataract victims average sixty years of age; it is highly unusual in people in their thirties. Neither of the editors had any significant medical history that would lead to the development of cataracts.[12] However, the US National Institute of Occupational Safety and Health held an inquiry and found that radiation levels were not high enough in their view to cause cataracts.

In March 1980 Dr Milton Zaret, who had acted as a consultant to the Newspaper Guild of New York during the dispute, informed the Guild's shop stewards that he disagreed with the inquiry's findings. He now believed that there was a greater danger for VDU operators than in 1977 when he first investigated the problem.[13]

Amounts emitted are thought to be small, and GPO tests, for example, have shown no detectable level, yet there has been no study on the *long-term* implications of the operators being exposed to such low-level radiation. Nor do we know of any studies on the possible fertility hazards of this work.

This equipment is new. What happens when it's been around for thirty years? Will we be exposed to leaking radiation from old and faulty machinery? The risk of low-level radiation may be an unknown, but it is enough to argue against the installation of VDUs in small rooms.

A single VDU can produce 400 watts of heat, the power of a small electric fire. A survey for Air France found that reservation centres often had several units placed close together producing 'hot spots' due to problems of overheating and poor airconditioning. Existing ventilation provisions were obviously inadequate.

Office worker s at Birmingham's Aston University downed tools and walked out when the VDUs and other office machinery heated to such an extent that work became impossible. Ann Lee, the NALGO safety rep, explains:

> Early in 1979 new word processors/VDUs were introduced. The typists were just given brief training, and an instructor then stayed at the university for a week to monitor the machines in operation.
>
> During that week the build-up of heat was noticed, even by the instructor, and was complained of by the operators, until one day one of the machines wouldn't work. It was discovered that this machine wouldn't function at an internal temperature of over 80° F. The manager informed the university's estates department and they referred it to the Maintenance and Minor Works (M&MW) Committee. This committee only meets once a year and happened to be meeting in just over a month's time.
>
> The heat continued, and the women complained of discomfort, headaches, tiredness, etc. With still nearly three weeks to go before the M&MW Committee was due to meet, and the temperature at 92° F, we stopped work. The non-members all joined the union and NALGO became involved. Emergency measures were agreed with

NALGO, including installing fans and temporarily moving two of the operators to a nearby room.
The M&MW Committee met and agreed to find a permanent solution (possibly an airconditioning system).'

In March 1980 Dr Tjonn, the medical director of the Department of Occupational Health in the Norwegian Directorate of Labour Inspection reported some possible cases of occupational dermatitis among ten VDU operators. Symptoms included a reddening of the face and an itching rash between half an hour and a full working period on the VDU. They disappear some hours after the operators stop work on the machine. At the time of writing this book, there is no satisfactory explanation as to the cause. Radiation has been discounted by the investigators. A number of reports of apparently similar symptoms have come to light in Britain.[14]

Safety and VDUs

VDUs present the usual electrical hazards (as described in chapter 8) and in addition they have internal high voltages. Paper clips, hair pins, hot drinks and inflammable liquids suddenly become dangerous weapons when dropped or spilled on the machine. Because static electricity can have adverse effects on VDU equipment, employers may attempt to locate machines in anti-static rooms and restrict entry of other employees. According to a report on the experience in Bradford Council's word processor installation:

'The machines are in constant operation and are programmed by the rate material comes in. The workers have one ten-minute break in the morning and afternoon, and otherwise have no contact with other workers during office time.
All new work comes in through a special anti-static glass box, and no non-section workers enter the room.'
(Counter Information Services report, *The New Technology*, p.12)

Make sure your protection comes before a machine's! Steps taken to protect VDUs must not be at the expense of unacceptable isolation and segregation of office workers.
A full record of repairs for each machine should be kept and workers should have access to it.
Where machines are provided with a service contract, this should include *regular* servicing and not just a 'call out' procedure when something goes wrong. It's not only the office workers who suffer. According to one Finnish study:

'The installation and repair of these machines necessitates many difficult and painful work positions and movements. It appears that insufficient attention was given to these aspects during machine design. Lighting levels and cleaning fluids are emphasised as hazardous.'[11]

The health risks from the long-term use of VDUs are totally unknown. Long-term risks of new technologies must not be ignored: look at the recent discoveries of cancer-causing properties in substances used at work, such as vinyl chloride and glass fibre, which have gone undetected for years while hailed as progressive, scientific discoveries.

Steps can be taken to improve the safety of VDUs and to improve the office environment where they are used. But the burden must be on the manufacturers to prove that equipment is safe and healthy, not on you to prove it is dangerous.

Where does new technology come from: silicon's ugly secret

Young women in South East Asia are employed (by the microprocessor multinationals like Hewlitt-Packard) to test the silicon chips – around 3,500 chips a day each. Caustic chemicals, all poisonous and many suspected of causing cancer, sit in open containers, giving off fumes. Eye ailments is another serious hazard. Most workers suffer at some time from conjunctivitis or 'red eye'. "After some time we can't see very clearly; it's blurred. We'll be looking into the microscope for over seven hours. We have to work with these gold wires, very thin like our hair…" Virtually anyone who stays on the job more than three years must eventually wear glasses.[15]

Microelectronics are being heralded as a triumph for world progress. Progress for whom? For you? For me? For the woman in the electronics plants in South East Asia on a dollar a day? Or for the multinationals and the businessman laughing all the way to the bank?

Social costs

'Where the computer does not eliminate the need for a human operator altogether, it has been associated with an increase in the intensity of work, whether this be for a design engineer or a typist. Automation has been observed to make jobs short-cycled and repetitive. The room for decision-making is reduced, the pace of work and attitude to work becomes determined by the machine. Work performance can be recorded and monitored. All this creates feelings of frustration, alienation and stress, and this affects the workers' health.' (*Women's Report*, April 1979)

The International Labour Office was saying in the 1950s that the long-term result of the development of mechanisation in offices in many cases 'has been a downgrading of clerical jobs, as the work formerly performed by experienced semi-skilled workers is now entrusted to young, unskilled machine operators'.

The new technology means *deskilling*. Traditionally office workers have exercised a whole range of skills, from shorthand to devising filing systems. As more and more jobs are reduced to pushing

142

buttons, these skills are no longer needed because the vast experience and skills which office workers have accumulated are being transferred to computers. The new technology carries on the old tradition, deskilling some jobs and eradicating others. Increased productivity through progressive deskilling is the objective.

> *All the natural breaks you get using a typewriter − when you change paper, shift the margin, move from one job to another − disappear, since the word processor does all these things for you at a very high speed. You still have to pay the same mental effort to each part of the task that remains to you, putting words together to make a grammatically sound sentence, and sentences together to make a complete piece of work. But you have to do more such tasks because of the speed of the word processor, with fewer gaps between tasks. The mental effort is more repetitive and more continuous. You get the feeling you are being forced to exert yourself ever more by the pace of the machine.*
> *(Fleet Street clerical worker quoted in* Is a Machine After Your Job? *by Chris Harman, Socialist Workers Party, 1979)*

Job satisfaction disappears when you lose control of the work process, and the loss of skills leads to the loss of promotion pro-spects, where these existed, and the loss of mobility. When new machinery is introduced it is claimed that it will only do the humdrum jobs, that such automation will free workers from soul-destroying jobs for more creative things. Well, one former secre-tary who now trains people to operate word processing machines said: 'All we do is chain the secretary to a machine. We only freed one secretary, and that was me...'

Word processor systems are sometimes described as 'master' (controller) stations and 'slave' (terminal) stations. The master is generally to be found in the manager's office, the slave at the typist's desk! Lanier have introduced a centralised dictating system with a management control unit. At the press of a button, the unit flashes on the screen a complete record of a secretary's activities, and the boss can pinpoint workers whose output has fallen beneath the required level.

We have regular rotation of jobs every 45 minutes

The reality is having to work at the machine's speed, and no longer being able to make decisions about what order to do things in, what wording to use in a letter, or the other little things that used to make some office work less boring. The VDU operator can spend her entire day a slave at the keyboard, with no opportunity for a walk, a chat or an extended lunch break. The intensity of the work is greatly increased. Word processors *make you work harder.*

> 'One survey of typing productivity has shown that the average secretary produces barely 76 lines of type in a day. With a centralised dictating unit, however, a typist can average at least 600 lines a day and show an improvement in production of more than 600 per cent.' (*The Times*, 2 October 1978)

Even if this is true, will her wage packet show an improvement of 'more than 600 per cent'? With the introduction of word processors at the Halifax Building Society, there has been a trebling of the workload and no new staff. Bonus systems are being introduced in many offices with VDUs and operators are paid according to the number of key depressions per hour.

Traditionally, few office workers have been paid on piece rates or with bonus schemes (although key punch operators were the exception) because there was no easy way to measure their productivity. All this has changed. Measurements can be taken undetected within the machines to see who is doing how much work, and when, with how many errors. Master Mind system is advertised as having a display terminal which 'provides complete information on the status of up to 200 active dictation and transcription jobs in the centre. A disc memory offers a permanent, unlimited archive of the completed work. A companion report printed provides detailed daily, weekly or monthly summaries of input and output activity.' Needless to say, such technology threatens the jobs of a whole layer of supervisory staff. Built-in supervision is a major selling point:

> 'A built-in reporting system helps you monitor your work flow. It automatically gives the author's and typist's names, the document number, the date and time of origin and last revision, the required editing time, and the length of the document.' (Wang, manufacturer of word processors)

If you suspect this kind of monitoring system, you could always try ringing the manufacturer to check. It might be best to bluff your way as prospective buyer. AUEW/TASS and TGWU/ACTSS won an agreement from the Ford Motor Company which stated that: 'All information acquired specifically or incidentally by computer systems shall not be used for individual or collective work performance measures.'

Management may deny that this information exists and never use it openly against individuals (although they might!), but they can still use it to reorganise the work, keep the pressure up and minimise the number of jobs. In one Danish store, cashiers went on strike until such surveillance programmes were wiped off the computerised cash registers. VDU operators in Leeds subvert this policing mechanism in their word processors. They sit pushing the space button so that they are recorded as working while they have a chat and a cup of tea!

Trade unions are now taking up the fight for control of the new technology. The NUJ, state that:

'We are sceptical of the benefits of new technology as proposed by managements here and elsewhere...but we recognise the rationale behind their plans. It is a rationale trade unionists should not adopt when faced with technical innovations likely to speed up the pace of work for those who remain and to add to the dole queues those who do not.'

ASTMS recommends:

'There should be no agreement on workloads before a six-month trial period is completed by the operator. Agreements fixing rigid targets should be avoided. All agreements should attempt to maximise the control of the operator over the output.'

Who controls the new technology is indeed a fundamental question, and the fight for jobs and for better working conditions is part of the struggle to control it.

'Information technology is basically a technology of co-ordination and *control of the labour force,* the white-collar workers which Taylorian organisation does not cover.' [author's emphasis.] (F. de Benedetti, managing director of Olivetti, in the *Financial Times,* 23 October 1979)

Technology that has been *specifically developed* to cut jobs and other clerical costs, to break down each task into its simplest component parts, to measure and control workers' performances-this kind of technology does not serve our needs. It is inherently bound up with the values of the society that produced it — a society based on power and production for profit. A different sort of society would evolve a different sort of technology. We need to question the very *nature* of technology. That goes for all of it. In health care, for example, at first glance technology seems progressive, its aim being to cure disease. But is it? Conventional 'high technology' medicine reinforces the interests of the medical profession and the drug companies, is developed for profit and prestige, and concentrates on cure rather than prevention, eg cancer therapy and organ transplants. Technology, whether military, medical or in business, is never neutral. It always serves the interests of those who own, develop and control it.

Workers' response to new technology — 'when my chip comes in'

Microprocessors affect jobs and health, and have far-reaching social and political implications. Your jobs and future school-leavers' jobs are threatened by this technology. *That is why you should consider saying 'no' to its introduction.*

Freeze it

The ACTU (the Australian TUC) has passed a motion in support of a freeze on the introduction of new technology for five years. At the very least you should call a halt to the introduction of new technology. Refuse to work on this equipment until you have carried out your own investigations.

It's a good idea to set up a trade union working party. Camden NALGO did this and brought out a report with their own recommendations. Try contacting office workers at other sites of the company you work for and find out how they feel. After investigations you may decide to accept some new technology *on your own conditions.*

The introduction of new equipment is bound to involve a period of disruption, with some jobs being redesigned and new job definitions arising. So good trade union representation is essential. It's crucial that agreements are negotiated before machines are installed so that you are not forced to bargain from a defensive position. If your employer attempts to introduce microelectronics by saying they will make your job easier, try demanding that they prove it by guaranteeing in advance and *in writing* that there will be no reduction in the total workforce and that working conditions will be improved by cutting your working week — for a start.

It took ASTMS and ACTSS members at CPC (UK) Ltd in Trafford Park two years to obtain acceptable conditions for the introduction of computerisation. They now have one of the few new technology agreements. Sam Darby explains:

From the start of our negotiations we involved rank and file members and stewards through a liaison committee which the management agreed to consult with on all aspects of the introduction of VDUs.

We took a dual approach to the health problems involved with VDU operation. In the first place we insisted that the management prove to us that the equipment was physically safe as far as radiation, implosion, character legibility, etc. were concerned.

Secondly, noting that constant operation could escalate general feelings of frustration, anxiety, stress into various physical symptoms such as headaches and backaches, we aimed to safeguard health and save jobs by trying to gain some reduction in the working day and by restricting the periods of constant VDU operation.

Although we did not achieve a reduction in working hours, our agreement now specifies:

1   *the maximum session of constant operation;*
2   *any session of constant operation must be followed by*
    30 minutes off VDUs (possibly on other types of work);
3   a total *of no more than three hours' operation in one day/*
    shift (6 x 30-minute sessions in our seven-hour working
    day).

It seems possible to us that as more and more work is
computerised, we will only have thirty minutes work in
every hour, as there will only be VDU work to do. (From
Red Collar, *September 1979)*

Making demands

1 Security of employment

Agreements should emphasise that no worker will be declared
redundant following the introduction of microprocessors, VDUs
or any other equipment. Natural wastage and voluntary redundancies are also dangerous: these are simply ways of running down
the workforce and selling future jobs for money, and depriving
school-leavers of work. The job is not yours to sell.

2 Prior consultation

Trade union representatives (shop stewards and safety reps) must
be involved in the decisions on purchasing of VDUs, their
location and use. Thus the criterion of health and safety can be
built into the new work situation being created. The type of
VDU should also be your decision, eg. colour and size of characters, screen thickness, keyboard design and layout. The report
for Air France stated:

> 'One is beginning to see on the market cheap versions of
> this type of unit which show most of the faults which we
> have tried to eliminate. These units will almost certainly
> cause adverse reactions in their operators and could present
> more serious problems than those we have shown.'

If you are to be expected to work with VDUs and other new
office technologies, given their manifold disadvantages, you have
the right to demand that the *very best* equipment be bought.
Expensive, safer versions are on the market, but who is going to
buy them? Your employer? Only if *you* put on the pressure.
Prior consultation is crucial on changes in staffing levels and work
methods, and changes in the workload. The training and re-
training of workers and the grading of everyone involved must
also be matters of consultation. Safety reps potentially have considerable powers (see chapter 11) which include the right to
consultation on any changes in the work process.

3 Health and safety

All measurements, technical information and results of tests
should be readily available: this is the legal right of safety reps
(see chapter 11). The number and length of rest breaks, and time
on the machine, as well as the basis of any medical checks with

guaranteed safeguards should be the subject of agreement. There should be written guarantees for no victimisation: no loss of earnings or position, and no sackings for anyone whose health prevents them from working on a VDU or whose health is impaired by the job. Workers involved should have the right to veto work on equipment they think unsafe or causes too much mental stress. Given the health risks, there should be no increase in shift work. The GMWU recommends that world-wide research on health effects of VDUs be monitored and new findings supplied by employers to safety reps. TASS recommends that the employer must provide a policy document giving guidance on the health hazards of VDUs. NALGO members in the Southern District working for the Gas Board have blacked the introduction of VDUs until they are satisfied that they meet their health and safety requirements.

4 No increased workload

Hours must be cut, not jobs. A shorter working week with increased holidays and rest breaks and fewer hours would guarantee better working conditions. Instead of part-time workers, who are highly exploited women with few rights and paid peanuts, ideally everyone should work 'part-time' with guaranteed full-time conditions of employment. This would avoid the misery of unemployment for millions on the one hand, and the misery of overwork on the other for those left. If a word processor can do eight hours work in four hours, then the VDU operator should only do four hours a day and then go home. If, as we're told, the new technology is more efficient and results in increased productivity, then it is our right to share the gains of that higher productivity without crippling ourselves.

The London Clerical branch of NATSOPA produced a petition and pamphlet with a programme for action to save jobs. They stated:

> 'The employers tell us of the benefits that will come from new technology. But it's always "jam tomorrow". We want our jam today.'

5 Variety in work

Jobs should be rotated so that VDU operation becomes merely part of the worker's more varied work tasks. Operators should be able to choose their own work rate. Be very wary of any proposed specialisation and centralisation of clerical workers' jobs which will deskill, routinise, lower status or isolate the affected staff. Why can't more office workers engage in the creative and design part of work — instead of always working on the production end of someone else's ideas?

6 Control

Demand written guarantees that management will not use the new machines to get information on the work speed. An agreement will only be the first step. Use the demands as the basis for draft resolutions to launch a debate at your union's national conference and to go on to mount a campaign around new technology. Link up with other union representatives in your workplace – this technology will affect everyone.

7 Saying no New technology usually represents a massive productivity deal in disguise. If you are well organised and decide that microelectronics on any terms will be against you and your co-workers' interests, it may be possible to oppose it altogether.

In 1979, 250 conference typists and translators at the United Nations walked out from their jobs in protest over the operation of word processing equipment. The walkout occurred when their management refused to agree to their demand that the cathode ray tubes presently in use by the typists should be shut down until a health study had been carried out. They further demanded that *alternative technology* be developed, technology that does not endanger health or jobs.

Broader implications of new technology

Some people, including the government, say that we must embrace the new technology whole-heartedly because it is 'progress' and Britain must be competitive in the world economy. The trouble with this approach is that it sees British employers' interests coming before the interests of working people. Workers in other countries are also fighting for their jobs. And when the 1975-79 Labour government committed £400 million to developing the use of new technology, it took no step towards protecting jobs in Britain.

This argument also equates Britain's interests with the interests of multinational corporations. What's good for ICI is assumed to be good for you and me. Yet big business increasingly moves capital and production outside Britain, pays little or no tax, and swallows millions of pounds of public money while creating mass redundancies. Whilst IBM and GEC make profits out of microelectronics the unemployment they cause costs us all massive amounts, not to mention the personal degradation, the effects on families and the medical costs of unemployment-induced stress.

Competition – 'if we don't use word processors, our competitors will, and we'll be out of business' – what kind of system is it that gives us this choice? New machinery and higher unemployment, or old machinery and higher unemployment? What kind of system is it that tries to blind us with a 'tomorrow's world' of technology which is supposed to be so progressive but which in reality makes working people's lives worse instead of better?

Microelectronics will get rid of a lot of boring jobs, but even boring jobs are preferable when the alternative is inadequate unemployment and social security benefits.

'People are not being "freed" to do more interesting work because there aren't interesting (or any) jobs available. In our society, unemployment means poverty (unless you have a private income) and lack of status. And cuts in the public sector are decreasing educational, childcare and leisure facilities.' (*Spare Rib*, June 1979)

As for more leisure — ask any pensioner or unemployed person what more leisure means to them in this society. If you argue that new technology means more leisure, *you are talking people into unemployment*. The overall effect of new technology could be to increase the difficulties faced by the poorest people who won't have access to all this stuff in their homes and have no jobs. Employers want fewer employees. They don't want a shorter week or union control. Their aim is to maximise their profits, Like other developments in automation, this new technology looks as though it will continue the trend to concentrate even more power in fewer hands, diminishing workers' control over how and what they produce — unless there is a concerted effort to oppose that trend.

Opposition is and has been in a variety of forms. Groups have formed to develop ideas about alternative technology, such as alternatives to nuclear power. Organisations linking trade unions, community and student groups are flourishing — SERA, the Socialist Environment and Resources Association, for example. And various left-wing political groups have taken up the questions of science and technology and include them as part of the struggle for change, part of the struggle for a new, more equal society. More specifically, shop stewards 'combine committees' in Lucas Aerospace and Vickers have recognised the need for socially useful technologies which serve our needs and don't replace workers or their skills. They have drafted 'alternative plans' in which they propose that the company develops useful products. They question not only the nature of technologies which deskill and dehumanise but also management's right to control technology and decision-making. This is part of the struggle to halt redundancies and secure better pay and conditions. Their battles are difficult and some have been victimised, but debate about this strategy and support among trade unionists is growing.

The British Society for Social Responsibility in Science (BSSRS) has formed a microelectronic working group to help trade unionists find out information about the implications of introducing new technology at their place of work, and to raise awareness of the possibilities of different sorts of technology in a society based on people's needs rather than profits and competition. The aim of all these groups is to launch an offensive against this 'white heat of technological revolution' that burns up jobs, increases economic and social inequality and degrades work.

Footnotes

1 Ostberg, Dr. O., 'CRTs pose health hazards for their operators' in *International Journal of Occupational Health and Safety,* November/December 1975, pp. 24-26, 46, 50 and 52.

2 Gunnarsson, E. and Ostberg, Dr. O., 'Physical and psychological working environment within a terminal based computer storage and retrieval system' in *Undersokningsrapport,* Stockholm, 1977.

3 Air France study cited in *Finance News,* journal of the Association of Scientific, Technical and Managerial Staffs (ASTMS). Article entitled 'VDUs: can they damage your eyes?' Undated.

4 Kovalenko, I.G., 'Occupational hygiene requirements regarding the conditions under which microfilms are read' in *Gigiena i sanitarija,* Vol. 35 No. 3, Moscow, March 1970, pp. 24-27.

5 'Hazards of Microfiche Viewers: Prevention of Occupational Eye-strain' in *ASTMS Health and Safety Monitor,* No. 3, April 1980.

6 Stansaab Elektroni AB, *Work Stations with Data Terminals,* 1974.

7 Quoted in *Ms London,* 14 January 1980, p. 76.

8 Hanzberg, 'Fatigue at the computer terminal workplace', MD thesis, Universite de Paris, medicine faculty, 1976.

9 Air France study (see footnote No. 3).

10 Rohmert, W., 'Ergonomic study of part-time shift work and rest periods in data processing work' in *International Archives of Occupational Health,* Vol. 31 No. 3, July 1973, pp. 171-191.

11 Jarvinen, T. et al, 'Ergonomic survey of office and data processing machine repair work', *Institute of Occupational Health,* Helsinki.

12 *Computerworld,* USA, 1 August 1978.

13 *Computer Talk,* 19 November 1980.

14 As above, footnote 13.

15 Grossman, R., 'Women's places in the integrated circuit' in *South-east Asia Chronicle,* No. 66/*Pacific Research,* Vol. 9 No. 5-6 (joint issue).

CHECK LIST

VDUs

1 Is the new technology being introduced without job loss?
2 Has a maximum working period of operating a VDU been agreed?
3 Are rest breaks plentiful and adequate?

General
4 Is the work varied?
5 Can jobs be rotated and shared?
6 Is good training available for operators, in the use of the system and in the recognition of health hazards?
7 Are there regular eye tests for operators, with safeguards against discrimination?
8 Is the new technology being used to monitor work levels, control or supervise those working with it?
9 Do operators suffer from any stress symptoms, body fatigue or eyestrain?
10 Have operators been prescribed drugs which might affect eye movements and cause increased stress and eyestrain?

Lighting	1	Is there adequate light for source documents?
	2	Is the room lighting comfortable and subdued?
	3	Is the user free from reflection and glare?
	4	Does the lighting have dimmer switches?
	5	Is fluorescent lighting worsening flicker problems?
Screen	1	Is the screen regularly cleaned?
	2	Are the symbols well focused and readable?
	3	Is there adjustable brightness?
	4	Is the screen uncluttered at all times?
	5	Are screen colours comfortable to the eyes? (eg. yellow/green on a dark green background)
	6	Is the screen angle adjustable?
	7	Has flicker been reduced to a technical minimum?
Workstation	1	Are adjustable footrests provided?
	2	Are chair and table heights adjustable and stable?
	3	Is there an adjustable backrest?
	4	Is the work surface large enough and non-reflective?
	5	Is the keyboard as low as possible on the desk?
	6	Is the console moveable, with screen and keyboard separate?
	7	Is there a document stand?
	8	Are special function keys on the right for right-handed, and on the left for left-handed, operators?
	9	Can the user reach and operate all controls?
	10	Is there plenty of leg and knee room?
	11	Is there enough accessible storage space for personal belongings and documents?
	12	Is the user safe from electrical hazards?
	13	Are any potentially hazardous chemicals used with the machine?
	14	Does the VDU generate excessive heat?
	15	Is all the equipment regularly maintained and radiation emissions monitored?
	16	Does the layout enable easy communication between operators?
Environment	1	Are windows screened?
	2	Are walls too light?
	3	Is the temperature comfortable and adjustable?
	4	Is the user's environment noisy?
	5	Is the VDU at right angles to, or away from a window?

Note   This is a very short basic checklist for VDUs. A comprehensive one has been published as Appendix 1 of *VDT Manual* by Cakir, Hart and Stewart (IFRA, INCA-FIEJ Research Association, Washington Platz, D-6100 Darmstadt, W. Germany).

5 What you can do

---

10 Using the law

How the law developed

In theory, health and safety legislation now exists to protect
everyone who works, but it doesn't automatically benefit you.
Some bits of the law give you basic rights, set minimum standards
from which you can negotiate, but there are still many loopholes.
Health and safety legislation is for the most part vague and
weakly enforced. It gives guidelines. If the law is broken, employers are rarely prosecuted, and even then the penalties are
small. Even where good legislation exists, when it is broken and
tested in court it is interpreted by judges, who fine huge companies tiny amounts for breaking health and safety laws. In 1970
Babcock and Wilcox were fined £600 for the death of a welder in
its Baglan Bay chemical plant. In the same year that firm made a
profit of over £3 million! It is important to see the difference
between the spirit of the law and the letter of the law: there is
always a danger of weakening through interpretation.

> *There is no doubt that those responsible for office health
> and safety have been overcomplacent in the past, not fully
> aware of their legal obligations, or have deliberately ignored
> them, or were perhaps too busy with other duties to give
> health and safety questions adequate attention. (*The Times,
> *14 September 1977)*

Many Bills to control office working conditions were introduced
into the House of Commons but failed miserably. One spectacular
failure was the Offices Regulation Bill, introduced in 1928 and
still being debated in 1936. Opposition came from a majority of
MPs − many of them the employers of clerical workers. Mr
Williams, MP, was a typical opponent, suggesting in 1936 that 'if
offices are dirty, agitators should get a pail of water and scrub
them'. Meanwhile, medical officers of health as well as male and

female clerks continued to press for an end to 'slum offices' where 'dustiness, mustiness and fustiness are the enemies of happiness and efficiency in clerical work'.[1]

The Gowers Report was set up to inquire into office conditions and reported after the war recommending state provision for health, welfare and safety in non-industrial employment. Factories had been covered by legislation since the late nineteenth century, but it was not until 1963, after over fifty years of agitation by the clerks' unions, that the government saw fit to pass the necessary legislation.

The Offices, Shops and Railway Premises Act (OSRPA) included requirements for cleanliness, avoidance of overcrowding, maintenance of a 'reasonable temperature', provision of 'adequate ventilation and guarding and adequate lighting', and provision of sanitary and washing and first aid facilities. The Act is on the one hand specific — it lists particular requirements — and on the other vague. It employs words like 'adequate' and 'reasonable' to define required standards. Nevertheless, bits of the Act are very useful and sometimes strongly worded, for example, the section on ventilation.

The Factories Act 1961, which brought together all the hundreds of bits and pieces of legislation, is worth dipping into. You may find you can 'borrow' a section and apply it to your situation. Borrowing from the Factories Act and using Codes of Practice and Guidance Notes (see below) are useful for backing up a case, but don't have the force of law. Push your employer to supply you with a copy of *Redgrave's Guides* to the Factories Act and to the Offices, Shops and Railway Premises Act. Redgrave's Guides give details of these Acts and all the regulations made under them, together with interpretations based on legal cases, and there are helpful indexes.

All health and safety legislation now comes under the umbrella of the *Health and Safety at Work Act 1974* (HASAWA). The Act is based on the philosophy and recommendations of the Robens Committee who considered that there was too much law around and that this was responsible for the 'apathy' about health issues at work. The conclusion was that simpler law was required and that results could only be achieved by co-operation between employer and employee. This approach was preferred to greater legal coercion.

The Health and Safety at Work Act reorganised all the legislation, and applies to people, not places. Everyone who works is now covered. This Act places on employers a *statutory duty* to ensure, so far as is reasonably practicable, the safety and health and welfare of their employees at work. The qualifying phrase 'as far as is reasonably practicable' is a loophole. It means that in court employers can argue that they cannot afford to make the required improvement, eg. to make your office quieter. Economic criteria are thus legally acceptable. Risks are balanced: profit versus health. Where a bit of law is not weakened by such a phrase as in the following section from the Offices, Shops and Railway Premises Act, you are on very strong ground:

> 'Effective and suitable provision *shall be made* for securing and maintaining, by the circulation of adequate supplies of fresh or artificially purified air, the ventilation of every room...' (Section 7(1))

What the Health and Safety at Work Act says:

Some sections of the *Health and Safety at Work Act* are of particular interest here and are briefly summarised below.

Section 1 states the aims of the Act:

(a) maintaining or improving standards of health, safety and welfare of people at work;

(b) protecting other people against risks to health and safety arising out of work activities;

(c) controlling the storage and use of dangerous substances;

(d) controlling certain emissions into the air from certain premises.

Section 2 puts a general duty on employers to ensure the safety, health and welfare at work of their employees; to consult them concerning arrangements for joint action on health and safety matters; and in certain circumstances, at the request of duly appointed or elected trade union safety representatives, to establish safety committees; and to prepare and publicise a written statement of their safety policy and arrangements. *Section 2(2) is at the heart of this Act, and its requirements potentially cover all hazards and risks to health. It covers the following aspects:*

(a) Plant and systems of work must be provided and maintained so as to be safe and without risk to health.

(b) Articles and substances must be used, handled, stored and transported in a safe and healthy way.

(c) Employees must be provided with information, instruction, training and supervision.

(d) A place of work must be safe, with safe access and egress.

(e) The working environment must be safe and healthy, and adequate welfare arrangements are required.

Section 6 places duties on anyone who designs, manufactures, imports or supplies an article or substance for use at work to ensure, so far as it is under their control, that the article or substance is safe when used in accordance with information supplied by them. The duty extends to the provision of necessary information and the carrying out of necessary testing, inspection and research. Those who install plant are also to have a duty to ensure that it is safely installed.

Section 7 places duties on employees to take reasonable care to ensure that they do not endanger themselves or anyone else who may be affected by their work activities; and to co-operate with employers and others in meeting statutory requirements. *This is a favourite section with employers, usually emphasised at the top of their policy statement, the implication being that* you *cause accidents and disease. This section can also be interpreted to mean that you have a right to refuse to do a job that could potentially damage your health, eg. not operate a VDU that's hurting your eyes.*

Section 9 provides that no employer may charge his employees for anything done or equipment provided for health or safety purposes under a statutory requirement.

Section 79 lays down that in their annual reports to shareholders, directors will be required to give information about what their companies are doing in safety and health matters. *Note that the Companies Act has not yet been amended to take account of health and safety in annual reports (1979).*

The regulations on safety representatives and safety committees

Regulations are made under the Acts and add more detailed requirements. These may cover particular hazards (eg. first aid) or industries (eg. foundries). They have the same force as the law under which they are made. The Health and Safety at Work Act, Offices, Shops and Railway Premises Act and Factories Act, together with the regulations made under them, are *criminal law,* and breaches by employers are punishable by fines or prison. These were made under Section 2 of the Health and Safety at Work Act and came into force in October 1978. The regulations make provisions for workers' inspectors to be elected by trade unionists in every workplace. They give workers unprecedented legal rights and powers in the sphere of health and safety at work. Safety representatives have the right to investigate complaints and hazards, causes of illnesses and accidents; the right to inspect the workplace; the right to know, by obtaining information on substances, processes, surveys and measurements; the right to take up problems with management. They have a right to time off, training and facilities to do the job. Safety reps are not legally liable for accidents or ill-health or if the law is broken. The regulations also make provisions for the setting up of safety committees where union and management agree they are desirable. (Chapter 11 goes into the regulations in more detail as part of the strategy for getting organised)

Codes of Practice (eg. on noise)

These are produced under the Acts. These do not have the force of law but are used by health and safety inspectors in their efforts to *persuade* employers to comply.

Guidance Notes

These are issued on various processes and substances. Like the old series of Technical Data Notes, they offer guidance and advice. They provide standards but do not have the force of law.

Codes of Practice and Guidance Notes, although not legally binding, can be useful ammunition in negotiations. Similarly, you can 'borrow' bits from different Acts to back up your case. (For example, if you have a problem with dust or fumes the wording in the Factories Act is stronger than in OSRPA.) All of these can be a starting point for a workplace agreement (see next chapter). The idea is to build your case based on the general duties under Section 2 of the Health and Safety at Work Act, combining these with arguments based on more specific laws and standards.

Other relevant legislation

Some pregnant workers are entitled to maternity rights under the *Employment Protection Act*. There are no legal provisions for paternity leave. Your trade union may have negotiated better conditions, or you may be able to do so. (See p. 166 for more on agreements)

The Employment Protection Act provides some minimum protection for part-time workers (note that you are a full-time worker if your hours are over 16 per week and you've been employed there for two years, or eight hours a week for five years). The Equal Pay Act, Sex Discrimination Act and Racial Discrimination Act also give some rights to workers. (See *National Council for Civil Liberties* handbooks or *Rights at Work* by Jeremy McMullen, for more information)

Enforcement of health and safety legislation

Only about nine hundred Health and Safety Executive (HSE) inspectors, together with about four hundred local authority environmental health inspectors are employed to police Britain's workplaces. If your workplace is a private office block or an office that's part of a shop, your inspector will probably be from the local authority. You can contact them through the local town hall. If your office is in a factory or in local government or Crown property, the inspector will probably be from the Health and Safety Executive.

The Health and Safety Executive is the collective name given to the inspectors, scientists and administrative staff. The HSE is now divided into 21 area offices. The HSE inspectors used to be known as factory inspectors before the Health and Safety at Work Act.

Inspectors may enter premises, inspect and investigate, take samples, examine documents, seize and destroy articles or substances that may cause serious injury. They must give information to union reps, such as on hazards or tests and details of what he or she has asked the employer to do. Inspectors can issue *Improvement Notices* warning employers that they have 21 days or more to comply with the law. (These notices can be ignored during appeal.) *Prohibition Notices* are much stronger and require an immediate halt to the work activity if the inspector believes there to be imminent danger.

It is the job of inspectors to enforce health and safety law, but in spite of their reorganisation and 'new powers' the inspectorate is still tiny, overworked and very weak. Their supposed expansion since the Health and Safety at Work Act has resulted in increasing layers of bureaucracy without increasing the number of inspectors in the field. It has been estimated than on average they only inspect a workplace every nine years! While they can't regularly inspect every workplace, *safety reps can*.

Inspectors don't prosecute very often — they tend to go more for persuasion and guidance. Even when they do prosecute, they may

A short lived advertising campaign by Colt

Four industrial workers die every day in this country. 3000 are injured seriously enough to lose three or more days from work.

Every responsible manager of Industry can have no greater concern than the health and safety of his workforce, and the reduction of these frightening statistics.

CAPTAIN OF INDUSTRY? OR MASS MURDERER?

Colt can help Industry in many ways.

By ensuring the safest working temperature.

By providing safer access to awkwardly placed plant and machinery.

be made a fool of in court, where the employer might get off or be fined a pitiful amount. Average fines are still only around £100. Although fines of up to £1,000 can be levied, and managers could be imprisoned for up to two years, it hasn't happened here yet (but it has in Italy and France).

> 'Four steelworkers were burned to death in November 1975: fifteen other workers were taken to hospital and seven later died. The British Steel Corporation was prosecuted under the Health and Safety at Work Act and was found to be responsible for the accident — they had provided defective equipment. They were fined £700. This was the price of eleven lives — £63 for every worker's life.'[2]

Few if any inspectors have experienced working on the shop or office floor. They are usually academics or managers and most of them are men. They have a disgraceful record on asbestos and many other hazards. However, it is important to use the Health and Safety Executive where you can. Some of them are sympathetic to trade unionists but are severely hampered by a stifling bureaucracy and government cutbacks.

> *The Health and Safety Executive is coming under discreet but growing pressure from Whitehall to cut back staff and expenditure, and adopt a more flexible attitude towards companies which are not observing recommended and even statutory, standards. (*Guardian, *28 January 1980)*

Office workers in the Social Service Department in Birmingham's Handsworth were seriously overcrowded. Those who were in NUPE formed an 'accommodation pressure group' to get something done. Things were really bad with filing cabinets blocking fire exits, no fire drills for years. They called in the health and safety inspector and the local authority environmental health inspector, who insisted that fire hazards be removed. The Health and Safety Inspector eventually issued an Improvement Notice and she warned the authorities that they would be fined £1,000 if better accommodation was not found within three months. £100 extra per day would be levied after that if nothing happened.

Management, under this pressure, agreed to install a Portacabin in the car park and move workers to a new building as soon as possible. The Health and Safety Inspector told NUPE Branch Chairperson John Hammerton that inspectors rarely get round to local authority premises *unless safety representatives* call them in. Every worker has the right to call in inspectors. Use them for advice on hazards, and remember that they should communicate with the safety rep when they come to inspect. You could try getting your local inspector along to talk at a union branch meeting. You'll find them in the telephone directory under Health and Safety Executive.

If you work on *Crown property,* i.e. in the Civil Service or in the Health Service, the inspectors cannot enforce the health and safety legislation. This is because 'the Crown cannot prosecute the Crown'. There are things called Crown Improvement and Prohibition Notices which may be served, but nothing happens if they are not complied with! Inspectors are in the farcical situation of being empowered only to threaten 'pressure' from other government departments where the law is broken. The TUC and the Health and Safety Commission are currently pressing for all this to be changed.

The *Health and Safety Commission* is at the head of government administration on health and safety. It is made up of representatives from the TUC, CBI and local authorities. This 'tripartite' body is responsible for research, information, setting up inquiries, proposing regulations and approving codes of practice. It makes decisions on things like the levels of dangerous substances that will be permissible for you and I to breathe at work — 'as far as is reasonably practicable'.

The *Employment Medical Advisory Service* (EMAS) is the medical wing of the HSE. One of its functions is to give workers 'information and advice on health in relation to employment'. EMAS employ doctors and have regional offices. You can try calling them in for occupational health problems. But beware, some are part-time company doctors.

Compensation, benefits and tribunals

The legal machine is very complicated — it almost looks as if it was constructed to make things difficult. If you have an accident or are exposed to a dangerous substance, report it. Make sure it is recorded in the accident book. This protects you later.

If you are injured at work or become ill as a result of inadequate safety precautions, you can sue your employer for *damages.* You will need legal help for this and should ask your trade union to provide you with a lawyer. Your local Citizens' Advice Bureau or Law Centre will also help. Widows and other relatives of people killed at work can also claim damages. It can take several years for this kind of action to be finalised. Only 20 per cent of cases are successful, and most cases are settled out of court. (See Kinnersley's *The Hazards of Work,* Chapter 11, 'Winning damages' for further guidance.)
Take a copy of every relevant scrap of paper. If applying, you will need full support from your fellow workers to follow the labyrinth of forms and tribunals. Your union should help too.

At the time of writing the government is reviewing an Industrial Injuries Scheme. If you are off work because of an accident at work or because of industrial illness you can claim National Insurance Benefit if you have paid enough National Insurance Contributions. Currently (December 1980) the government is proposing that employers pay £30 a week for up to eight weeks. State Sickness Benefit would be abolished except for long term illness; employers would be reimbursed by the State; the £30 would be taxed. It is crucial that trade unionists negotiate a more acceptable sick pay scheme (see p. 167).

The government's record in dealing with occupational health is not much better than management's, and its approach is virtually the same. The law mainly deals with the individual, not groups. It is only the lowest common denominator — a bottom level of legally protected rights. It is there to prevent the worst abuses.

> 'In a unionised workplace the union normally succeeds in negotiating much more favourable conditions for the workers than the law provides. In cases of dispute between workers and employers — for instance, involving discipline, dismissal or redundancy — the law is only a last resort where the normal industrial relations machinery fails to provide a satisfactory outcome.' (Pat Hewitt, National Council for Civil Liberties, *Know Your Rights,* No. 2, p.6)

Where you do have basic rights, as in the realm of health and safety, it is essential to know what those rights are and fight to get more. If you know what the law says, the boss will find it difficult to confuse you by telling you that you don't have the legal right to certain things. Law is often used by employers to mystify their employees. Knowing your rights can help you feel stronger when arguing with the boss. But it is also necessary to demand things the law doesn't mention: to extend your rights.

Footnotes

1   Association of Women Clerks and Secretaries, monthly newsletter, April 1936.
2   *Health and Safety at Work: A Basic Guide,* p.10, North-West District Workers' Educational Association (WEA), Manchester, undated.

11 Organising for safety

Health and safety, like wages, has to be negotiated between union and employer, so you need to build a strong union. *A strong, effective union is your best protection.*

Joining a union

If you are not yet a member of a trade union and don't know which one to join you should contact your local Trades Council (they're in the phone book). There is also a list of 'white-collar' trade union in Appendix 2 with addresses. You can contact them directly and obtain a local contact address.

If your firm isn't unionised, discuss the matter with other people at work and perhaps arrange a meeting (outside working hours) at which an official from the local office of a union could speak. It might be a good idea to get some leaflets from the union office and distribute these to your co-workers.

Union recognition

Your trade union should be recognised by the employer for the purposes of negotiating pay and other conditions, protecting health and safety, negotiating disciplinary procedures, negotiating pension schemes, and so on. If your workplace is newly organised, the union will have to apply for recognition. This will be done by the shop steward elected by the union members in the workplace, with the help of the full-time union official.

Time off

Members of a recognised union are entitled to time off for union activities, eg. to vote or to attend a meeting of an outside body as a union representative, or to attend an executive committee meeting or annual conference of the union as a branch delegate. Time off does not have to be given for normal branch meetings except where the matter to be discussed is urgent. The employer is not obliged to pay workers for time off for union activities – although the union can negotiate for payment to be made. Lay officials of a recognised union – shop stewards, branch secretaries, safety representatives, etc. are entitled to paid time off for union activities and for relevant training approved by the TUC or union.

Victimisation

Historically, unions have had to struggle hard just to gain decent wages and the right to organise at all. Many clerks, female and male, have been victimised in the past, and there are still attempts to victimise office workers who try to improve working conditions and to organise in their offices. In the early part of the century clerks were automatically sacked if they tried to claim overtime pay. Trade unionists are still victimised everywhere.

It is unlawful for an employer to victimise any worker for trying to join a trade union. If you think your employer may do so, or if you are threatened with dismissal, you should join a trade union immediately and discuss the position with the local official. But be very careful not to let the employer know. If you are sacked before other workers have joined the union, you have very little chance of getting your job back because there will be no workplace organisation to help you. Any meetings with the union must be outside working hours, or the employer will complain that you are spending time on an unauthorised activity. Make a complaint of victimisation to the industrial tribunal. This must be done within seven days, and you will need a certificate from the union's full-time official. All workers are protected against victimisation for joining or trying to join a union, including people who have only just started working for the firm and including part-time workers.

Organising within your union

A lot more could be done. More unions need research departments where members' inquiries can be efficiently answered and where handbooks like this one can be produced at a low cost for distribution to the membership. Unions can publicise health and safety issues in the press and campaign on national and local issues, like ASTMS does, for example. Unions can push for development of medical screening programmes to monitor health hazards, or push for an occupational health service to do this kind of work. What is your union doing?

For unions which represent office workers, the issue of health hazards and working conditions has not assumed a prominent position in recent years. But more people are becoming aware of the potential hazards of technology and shiftwork, for example. And the election and training of safety reps in offices all over the country has led to a new awareness and demand for information and improvements in conditions of work. People are also challenging the tradition of only dealing with formal 'union business' at branch meetings. There should also be a time when people can bring up problems about their work, talk about how they feel and get support; for example, you can mention a health and safety problem, discuss childcare provision, press for maternity and paternity leave.

Some white-collar workers have formed groups to agitate for change. They feel the unions are too slow and bureaucratic. Some bring out regular bulletins, like *Red Collar, Redder Tape,* and *Typists' Charter.* (See Appendix for contacts)

Because you are exposed to conditions in your office every day, you are in a good position to know when something is wrong. Talk with other women in your office about the working conditions, and see if you can do something about conditions as a group. Perhaps you'd consider standing for election as the safety representative in your department.

Safety
representatives

After a long struggle and many delays, in 1978 recognised trade unions in all industries and services won the legal right to elect their own workers as inspectors or safety reps. These representatives must be clearly distinguished from the safety officer, who is paid by the employer and is part of management. Safety reps are elected by the trade union membership. In some unions they are appointed, eg. in AUEW it is recommended that a safety rep is also a shop steward. The union branch decides how many and which areas they represent. At Williams and Glyn's Bank, for example, in 1979 BIFU had 80 safety reps covering 300 branches. They are office reps, like shop stewards, and now include safety in their brief.

Safety reps have certain basic rights under HASAWA, in the form of the *Regulations for Safety Representatives and Safety Committees.* An employer who does not give these rights to safety representatives is committing a criminal offence and can be prosecuted.

Following these regulations, safety reps have the right to

1   *Investigate* members' complaints, potential hazards, dangerous occurrences or near misses, causes of accidents and health problems. One very useful way of carrying out investigations is to draw up a short questionnaire and to do your own health survey in the office. (See Appendix 1 for a sample survey)

2   *Inspect* the workplace. Following the regulations these inspections should be made as and when necessary. Inspection should be carried out after an accident or near miss, and after the publication of any relevant Health and Safety Executive documents or trade union information. To help carry out inspections, it is useful to have checklists like the ones at the end of each chapter in this book. You can get plans to help you work out areas for inspection from the fire certificate of which management must give you a copy.

Rachel Squire is a NUPE rep and works in Birmingham's Aston Social Services Department. She was told she could not inspect the offices during paid work time. She promptly ignored this and put it in writing to management that it was her legal right, whereupon there was no comeback.

3   *Right to Information.* The information safety reps can legally demand is very widely defined and includes information concerning:
(a) plans, performance and any proposed changes concerning the organisation of the workplace;
(b) technical information concerning the hazards and precautions of machinery, equipment, processes and substances in use at work;
(c) accident and health/sickness records;
(d) results of measurements and surveys.
This right to information includes communication from employers, manufacturers and inspectors.

4   *Facilities.* To do the job of safety rep you'll need some facilities. The regulations don't specify what these are, but the

164

TUC recommends a room and desk, filing cabinet, access to telephone and internal mailing system, typing and duplication facilities, use of a notice board. You will also need a library (see Appendix 3 for a list of books and pamphlets). You may also want to negotiate things like the provision of a room for meetings of safety reps and other union reps.

5 *Training.* If your employer puts on health and safety courses you can go on these, but they are no substitute for TUC courses. Your regional TUC Education Office will send you a form. Employers must give reps time off with pay to go on TUC/union courses. These are usually ten-week courses, one day a week, organised by the TUC, but some unions do internal courses, eg. ASTMS, GMWU and NALGO, which are useful in addition to the basic course.

London's Barnet branch of NALGO runs one-day schools for new safety reps and safety committee members. During one school they went out in pairs to inspect ten offices and found heaps of hazards. On return the school discussed the inspections and what to do.

You could also try to negotiate health and safety training for all members in addition to union representatives. And where possible negotiate cover for when someone is away on a course so they don't have twice the work to come back to!

6 *Representations to management* on behalf of your members. If you make a complaint, make sure you insist on a time limit for a rectification of the fault so that some action can follow. Employers' safety policies should be clear on who to complain to.

Management safety committees

The Regulations for Safety Representatives and Safety Committees lays down guidelines for these committees which have both management and union representation, but there is nothing in the regulations that says you must have one. NALGO safety reps at the Greater London Council's County Hall withdrew from the committee and formed their own union one.

Management safety committees are the traditional way of dealing with health and safety – the issue is shelved and then wheeled out once every six months to be discussed in a dreary way over tea and biscuits. Health and safety are trivialised and treated as a consensus issue when left to this approach.

Now there is much more recognition in trade unions that health and safety is a conflict issue that needs to be bargained over. How much you will win depends on how strong you are. You can't begin to *negotiate* better conditions in tired committees. But in your situation you may feel you could use a committee in some way. You may wish to push for a new committee or reorganise the old one. If so, make sure there are equal numbers of management and union reps on it, and that there is someone on it from mangement who can *take decisions* there and then, especially regarding finances. Otherwise it will be forever a talking shop. The employer must set up a committee if two or more safety reps ask for one, and he must consult the reps about setting one up.

Union safety committees

Many workplaces have traditionally had joint shop stewards committees, which is a way of breaking down differences between unions and building unity and strength. Now, with the election of safety reps, health and safety is increasingly becoming a subject of joint negotiation. This is especially important for office workers, since manual workers are often better organised and can share experience. Skills can be shared, eg. scientific workers could help on technical points. Linking up with other unions is also crucial in the case of cleaners who work every day or night in your office too, although you may never see them. If there are dangerous substances about and you're getting something done, the cleaners should be in on it too.

It's always a good idea to 'caucus' or meet with other union reps before going in to meet management — be it on a safety committee or in any other kind of meeting. As one safety rep put it, 'Then you'll speak with one voice on the union side'.

Agreements

Safety reps are the first workers' representatives with statutory rights to challenge the employers' claim to sole control of plant, machinery and methods of work. The regulations give trade unionists a huge new power: workers' representatives should be consulted and advised *prior to any change* in working conditions. This power is crucial now, with 'new technologies' being brought in everywhere. You may want to have this right spelled out in detail in a *safety agreement.* A safety agreement can be negotiated with management to reinforce or extend your rights under the safety reps' regulations.

CHECK LIST

The TUC recommends the following checklist to help you negotiate:

Preparing your case
decide on negotiating objectives
collect relevant facts
decide on your key argument
note down possible counter-arguments
plan union tactics

Teamwork
make sure the union team is fully briefed
choose union spokesperson
make sure proper notes are taken

Tactics
never disagree in front of management
use adjournment where necessary
steer discussion towards your strong points and away from weak ones
look for management offers
encourage management to offer a compromise
make sure there is an agreed written record

Reporting back
keep members in touch during negotiations, and prepare full report-back at the end.

(From *Skills for Safety Reps: A COURSE FOR UNION REPRESENTA-TIVES*, Health and Safety at Work 4, TUC Education, 1979)

Many unions have negotiated national agreements, for example for longer holidays. But it's essential to get local or workplace agreements too, if you can — this can be on anything from reduction of overtime to paid educational leave. NATSOPA have got an agreement with International Publishing Corporation reducing working hours to 32½ per week by April 1982. The TUC recommends unions to negotiate sick pay schemes where full earnings are paid during sickness absence.

Agreements can be negotiated for just about everything at work regarding health, pay and general conditions. If you are pregnant or planning to have a baby, you should find out whether your union has negotiated a national agreement to provide paid maternity leave, and whether your job will be kept open for you after the birth of your baby. If there is no national agreement, it may be worth trying to negotiate maternity *and* paternity leave agreements at branch level — whether or not you plan to be a parent. ASTMS members at Islington and Hackney Health Authority have negotiated a maternity agreement with six weeks leave on full pay, and 12 weeks on half pay in addition to maternity benefits from the state. The job must be kept open for 15 months.

The health and safety legislation sets out basic minimum rights, which need to be improved and extended through negotiations in the form of agreements. The crucial thing to remember when drawing up an agreement is — think ahead; for example, negotiate the right to vet new machinery *before* it comes in.

ASTMS safety reps at the Design Council negotiated an agreement which outlines rights and facilities to be provided. This includes:

1   an office containing a lockable filing cabinet, a telephone to contact the Health and Safety Inspector, ASTMS or any other source of advice or expertise, and a bookcase to encourage the development of the safety reps' library;
2   a notice board in each department;
3   typing and duplicating facilities as required;
4   access to any monitoring equipment, for example, a camera, etc. where appropriate;
5   the right to a complete breakdown of all substances used at work, with the nature of them and the possible effects on workers;
6   the right to evacuate staff from any area where he or she feels there is a risk of danger or a breach of the regulations which might be dangerous.

Other safety reps have managed to negotiate the following in their agreement:

1   The right to stop the job: this is conspicuously absent from the legislation, but note that it is a *legal right* for Swedish safety reps.

2   The right to have outside advisers of the reps' choice on the office or shop floor, to take samples, make recommendations, etc.

3   Internal prohibition and improvement notices to be issued in the way the Health and Safety Inspectors issue them (see p. 158). If a process or product is held to be unsafe, the reps issue a notice saying that specific improvements must be made by a given date, or that the use of a given unsafe process is prohibited until further notice. The notices are signed by both union and management sides.

Direct action

If you can, get a good safety agreement, and where possible pursue the strategy of identify-measure-assess-control to keep health hazards to a minimum (see p. 169). But when management doesn't keep to the agreement or where you feel action is necessary for some other reason, strikes, slow-downs or the threat of them may be the fastest way to get what you want. This could be an all-out strike if things were serious enough. But the 1979 Civil Service dispute showed how much power could be concentrated in the hands of very few workers. Out of a total membership of several thousand CPSA and SCPS members, only a couple of hundred on strike was necessary to cause severe disruption.

Office workers can black telephone lines, have lightning stoppages, black a dangerous product (and put a red tag on it for danger). An on the spot meeting of all those affected can have the immediate effect of stopping services. NALGO universities staff, when pursuing a pay claim withdrew 'goodwill' — which meant anything from not making tea for the professors to not typing letters ringing their wives or ordering flowers. This is similar to working to rule and is a very effective strategy. NATSOPA secretaries at *The Times*, pressing for better wages and conditions, in 1977 pursued a vigorous campaign to publicise their cause. They stuck up posters and wrote slogans on outgoing letters.

Local area groups

Some local area groups are an extension of joint union committees, like the trade union area committee active on health and safety. Others have been organised by health and safety tutors or law centre workers. Groups are springing up all over the country, from Glasgow to Portsmouth, and there is probably one in your area. They comprise delegates from different workplaces in an area holding regular public meetings, working on local campaigns and building up resources to share. Many also publish safety material and hold regular 'surgeries' or advice sessions where they give help and advice on health and safety problems. (See Appendix 2 for your nearest group)

what we need here is better facilities...

A strategy for dealing with health hazards at work

Prevention is better than cure. A well organised office with active, trained safety reps and a good safety agreement will go a long way to prevent work hazards. But what do you do about health hazards that do arise? Each hazard will have its specific problems, issues and dangers, but there are some simple general rules to follow. As well as setting out the rules below we will look at how they applied when safety reps at North East London Polytechnic (NELP) took up the fight against ozone fumes from photo-copiers.

1 Investigate and identify

Do a careful inspection of your office and talk to the other people who work there. Use the checklists and questionnaires in this book to find out which health hazards exist in your work-place.

> 'At North East London Polytechnic the problem arose at the end of 1977 when a member of the Chemistry Depart-ment smelled ozone coming from a photocopying machine and informed his union safety rep.'

2 Measure

If you want to know exactly what risks you're being exposed to, it's best to get measurements taken — be it for noise, air pollution or a substance to be analysed.

It is management's responsibility to pay for the analysis or to get details from manufacturers. Get the results, and where necessary get your own survey done so you can check them. Some unions may be able to help you get air sampling etc. so always contact your union full-time officer. You could also try contacting the TUC Centenary Institute which is sponsored by the TUC to pro-vide a free advice service to all trade unionists. But you must go through your union head office, and this is a slow business.

Call in the Health and Safety Inspector. It is his or her job to do measurements — but they are overworked, and their equipment often doesn't measure very small quantities accurately. Some local colleges and universities have environmental science or

169

occupational health departments and are worth contacting for help. Local area trade union health and safety groups may have sampling equipment you can borrow (see Appendix 2 for addresses).

'After the unions had given a lot of publicity to the health hazards of ozone (see section 5 below), NELP management asked their safety officer to conduct a survey. Here are some of the results':

Room	C208	no detectable level*
	246	no detectable level*
	DPR	no detectable level*
	WFL	no detectable level*
	C & T	less than 0.01 ppm (parts of ozone per million parts of air)
	MFO	0.05 ppm (Rank Xerox 9200 photocopier)

* No detectable level does *not* mean zero. It means that the measuring machine did not register a reading.

3. Assess

You may have to assess measurements, eg. chemical levels in the air. To interpret figures and decide whether levels are safe you will need a standard or yardstick for guidance. For example, how much benzene is safe to breathe — is there a safe level?

There are standards for many hazards. Some are in precise arithmetical form, like the ones for dusts, chemicals and gases which have been given Threshold Limit Values. Certain others are vague as laid down in the Offices, Shops and Railway Premises Act, eg. lighting must be 'suitable'. A standard is what is considered to be acceptable. Somebody, somewhere (parliament, judges, scientists, inspectors) has decided what is an acceptable amount of noise, chemical, fumes or dust for you to be exposed to. But the only standard you should accept is *what you and your members consider acceptable.* Ideally you should set your own standards — after all, it's your health that is being affected. Official standards are set mainly by industry, taking their own interests into account. (See the section on Threshold Limit Values, p. 54). When trying to decide on the level of exposure you are prepared to accept, go for levels of comfort. If a substance is irritating it is probably doing you damage — whether the official 'safe level' is reached or not. Don't wait for a substance to be proved harmful — let management prove it's safe. Don't haggle over 'reasonably practicable' and 'practicable' with substances you know to be very dangerous and which are causing concern. Go for 'zero exposure'. Get your own standards written into agreements and collective bargaining. Reassess them regularly.

See Appendix 3 for sources which give official standards here and abroad. Often standards are much higher elsewhere and you can use these as your yardstick. Your union officer or local trade union health and safety group may be able to help here too.

'The Threshold Limit Value (TLV) for ozone is 0.1 ppm (ie. one part of ozone in every ten million parts of air). But even at a quarter of this level ozone can irritate the eyes, nose, throat and lungs. There is also a possibility that ozone may cause cancer and genetic defects in foetuses and young children. The union safety rep at North East London Polytechnic asked for machines which gave off ozone to an extent above one-tenth of the TLV to be withdrawn from service.'

4   Control

Go for control of a health hazard at source, ie. the elimination of the hazard. But the best way to control is prevention. Safety reps should vet new products and machinery before they are brought in. Where possible, *substitute* a safer process or product for a suspected one. Otherwise it may be possible to *enclose* the process, which may mean putting it in a separate room (eg. duplicating machine). Where fumes or dust are emitted, good ventilation is essential. Lastly, personal protection *may* help. But don't be fobbed off with a pair of rubber gloves if you are working with dangerous chemicals, or with special glasses if you're working with a visual display unit. This ploy of personal protection is a favourite management tactic. Covering up workers is no substitute for *cleaning up the workplace.*

If your union organisation is strong enough and the hazard is feared to be an immediate danger to health, black the process. Refuse to work with it, whether it's a solvent cleaning fluid or a faulty piece of equipment. There are lots of other kinds of direct action you can take — see p. 168 for some ideas.

'The safety rep at NELP pushed for the withdrawal of dangerous photocopying machines. If you look at the results of the survey (p.170 above) you will see that some machines emit much less ozone than others. In fact what happened at NELP was that efficient exhaust ventilation was installed to stop the fumes reaching the operator.'

5   Inform others

If you get some information on workplace hazards, make sure other workers get to know about it. You could try using the local press, and informing your union branch and health and safety officer. This is where a local health and safety group is very important too (see p. 168).

A union safety rep at North East London Polytechnic put together the following leaflet which was widely distributed throughout the workplace:

The hazards of photocopying

In many offices in NELP there is a photocopying machine: in some places, especially reprographic units, there is more than one. Photocopiers that use ultra-violet light produce a gas called ozone. Already one such machine has been used in the Chemistry Department.

The image most people have of ozone is of the substance that makes air 'fresh' and sea air good for us. This is false. The reality is that ozone is a sweet-smelling, very highly toxic gas. The 'official' maximum level to which the 'average' worker should be exposed is one part in ten million parts of air. If you can smell it, the level is too high!

Ozone is irritating to the eyes and the lining tissues of the throat, air passages and lungs. The irritation can arise at about one-quarter of the official Threshold Limit Value (TLV), ie. 0.1 ppm. Higher doses can cause chronic lung diseases.

Most important, ozone affects the genetic structure of cells in a manner similar to X-rays. No exposure is really safe. There is a good possibility that ozone may cause cancer and deformities in foetuses and young children. Older people may suffer from premature ageing and life-shortening. As one authority put it, writing in a Royal Society of Health publication: 'Special concern must exist about the long-term effects of even very low ozone concentrations, about which only a little investigation has been undertaken.' All photocopiers within the Polytechnic should be immediately monitored for ozone production, and any producing a detectable level of ozone (ie. greater than one part in one hundred million*) should be withdrawn from service.*

For further information about this or any other hazard, contact your union safety rep.

1   Stellmann, J.M. and Daum, S., *A Handbook of Health Hazards in the Workplace.*
2   American Conference of Government and Industrial Hygienists, *Documentation of TLVs.*

Photocopying machines

Immediately, the Polytechnic management issued a bulletin which read (safety rep's comments are in brackets):

A document recently circulated may have caused members of staff to believe that photocopying machines within the Polytechnic constitute a health hazard. I wish to confirm that to the best of my knowledge all our equipment is safe. (At least one machine was shown to be dangerous later.) *As a precaution, the majority of the manufacturers of photocopying equipment used in the Polytechnic have been contacted and verbal assurances obtained that their equipment does not present a health hazard.* (Why wasn't this done before purchase?)

Any member of staff who wishes to receive technical advice regarding their equipment is requested to contact the Reprographics Department.

If you have any reason to believe that the equipment in your charge is in any way dangerous, please report this immediately to the Polytechnic Safety Officer, who will then initiate the necessary enquiries and provide advice. (Why is this necessary if the equipment is supposed to be safe?) *I understand from the Chemistry Department that the exhaust gases from the machine referred to have been tested and the amount of ozone present did not exceed current safety standards.* (But the union leaflet shows why these standards are too low.)

During the investigations, other problems came to light:

(a)   Other people in the Polytechnic were exposed to ozone, eg. technicians using argon welding in a workshop.
(b)   In the past several staff working with photocopiers had complained of sore throats and nose irritation, but no action had been taken.
(c)   Other workers in the area had encountered similar problems at their place of work.

Script: Reynard/Drawings and © Shannon-Smith 1981.

One thing you'll be up against time and again will be the argument that there is no money for what you are demanding. Arguments about the cutbacks in public expenditure or the firm going to the wall are wheeled out every time. It is important to challenge management on their priorities about the health of their employees, profits or no profits. Try finding out whether the firm is part of a big company, and quote the last year's profits back at them. Or find out the salaries of the people you're negotiating with and quote these when poverty is pleaded! Approach the whole issue as you would a wages negotiation, where such arguments are only the beginning of the confrontation. At NELP, the victory of exhaust ventilation was worn in the face of vicious cuts in education.

Healthy and safe working conditions will not be won without a fight. They are not going to be given to you, despite all the management and government noises that 'we're concerned'. But some health problems run too deep for shop or office floor organisation. What can you do about the other hazards of a society which puts the profits of the few before the health of the majority? This society is organised in such a way that hazards to health are created and knowingly perpetuated daily in every work

In 1980 the arms bill cost £531 for each household in Britain. For the cost of one guided missile destroyer (£85 million) the government could provide three hospitals with 1000 beds (and have £10 million left over).

place. Yet they are preventable. So too are the hazards of unemployment, poverty, slums, overcrowded schools, polluted air, inadequate medical care. All of these, in our 'progressive', 'civilised' country are getting rapidly worse as public services are savagely cut back in order to 'economise'...

The fight for better working conditions must be part of a wider struggle to improve living conditions generally. Housing action groups, campaigns against public service cuts, women's groups, CND anti-nuclear groups — all are fighting for a better society. Perhaps local area health and safety groups, together with the other labour movement and socialist groups fighting for change, can turn the tide..

It's been a struggle

12 Improving working conditions in offices

Mary Williams went to work as a secretary at London University in 1977. Things were pretty bad:

'We had no facilities: no rest room, no tea breaks. We didn't even have proper lunch breaks because we were expected to staff the switchboard. The academics were always complaining about "bad service" and there was a strong resentment against them. Work just gets dumped on you at short notice.

Secretaries are expected to take responsibility for everything but aren't paid for it. Look at Muriel: she takes home £43 a week for a forty-hour week.

I started thinking about how the work is organised here and felt there was a need to get people involved, to take part in decision-making, to get better conditions. All office staff should be welcome at lectures. We'd be more involved and could get to know both staff and students better.

We've had one bit of militancy. The secretaries were working on the switchboard and one day they just stopped. We refuse to do it now because we were not even paid for it. Now it just shuts down for an hour. But there's a lot more to do. Secretaries and temps who work on Saturdays and Sundays must charge for overtime.

The last few weeks have been exhausing with NALGO branch meetings and staff meetings. Everything seems one hell of a struggle — but we're winning.'

There are extensive health hazards in offices. Workers on the 'office floor' operate under stress, often for long hours and often with little say in what's going on. The law, though sometimes helpful, is often not enforced. So what can be done? The answer is, things *can* be improved, and have been, where office workers have organised collectively. There is a bit of a myth that office workers are impossible to bring together into trade unions and that all progress has come through the goodwill of the employers.

Don't believe it. A strong effective union is your best protection. Historically, office workers have fought every inch of the way for decent wages and conditions. It is worth a brief look at our history. The first recorded reference to the word 'office' was in Chaucer's Friar's Tale in 1386. But the clerk existed from the beginning of recorded history: the scribe of ancient Egypt with his papyrus rolls and the clerk of medieval times in the monastery are the forebears of the Victorian clerk with his quill pen and ledgers. The counting house or office of the nineteenth century was small. The clerk stood or sat at a high desk. The job involved the meticulous keeping of ledgers, with male clerks responsible for correspondence, filing and copying. The ability to read and write, to balance figures and deal with correspondence were the basis of the clerk's craft, when education was still the privilege of a few. Clerkdom was for the middle classes. If the business was large enough to require employees, they could be recruited from among the dispossessed and younger sons of the literate classes. There was no danger of being required to rub shoulders with sweaty workers or endure the noise and dust of heavy machinery. The clerk identified with his employer, though few rose to this position themselves: in the small businesses of the time there was an almost feudal relationship between employer and clerk.

The expansion of empire meant more trade and more paper work. As industrial production and commerce increased, so management and government became more complex. More and more clerks were needed. In 1850 only one per cent of the working population worked in offices. By 1950 this was ten per cent. Then, between 1950 and 1975, it soared until office workers were 40 per cent of the total workforce. The vast majority of the new office workers were and are women.

The increase in education for women, together with the desperate need to earn a living, forced them into office work. The flow began in the 1850s and reached flood proportions in the 1870s with the introduction of the typewriter. Women were thought suited to this because of their so-called 'digital dexterity' (and

cheapness). At first only single women were employed. In 1874 the Post Office established a grade of 'lady typist' who was required to retire on marriage. Women began to be trained as 'typewriters' on a large scale. Men did not resist the 'lady clerks' much because this was a new area of work. The telephone, too, became a female monopoly.

Female secretaries, according to the early manuals, were to 'radiate the office with sunshine and sympathetic interest'. Women didn't aspire to promotion — clerical work was a dead end. They weren't a threat to men because they didn't compete with the boss, they serviced him. Men coped with the female flood by becoming managers and creating specialisms such as accountancy. 'Technical expertise' excluded women. Men no longer identified with the bosses: they *became* the bosses, for the most part. The sexual division of labour in offices, which if anything, is on the increase, is a division strengthened by the positions which men and women hold outside the office.

The division of labour in offices has been widening for a long time and is now polarised. On the one hand, an officer corps of male executives who satisfy the needs of top management for more control of information, and on the other an army of machine operatives, mainly women.

Just as in manufacturing processes, the work of the office has been analysed and divided up into minute simple tasks, and speeded up. The tapometer was developed in the 1930s to record the number of taps made by the typewriter, and in some instances a bonus system was introduced on this device: so much per week, and a bonus on the taps above a certain average.

In the 1930s clerical workers in retail, wholesale and warehousing were commonly working a sixty-hour week. Women were the 'clerical drudges' who worked in the first typing pools and used the first 'dictaphone' discs before the war. The twentieth century clerk became a cog in a huge machine. Bureaucracies grew. The 'clerical factory' had arrived.

The trend for the last hundred years has been to make offices the mirror image of the factories. Both are characterised by inhuman systems of work; both are stressful and hazardous. The same drive to increase productivity and cut costs has meant the same drive to automate, pollute and poison.

The office block itself has become a standardised product, an assembly of standard elements to be adapted by the company which rents the space, whether in Baghdad or Toronto, Tokyo or Budapest. Regardless of climate or use, there is often total air-conditioning and artificial light, which have repercussions for those who work in these blocks.

If this standardises our lives at work, it does so outside work too. The concentration of office blocks in town and city centres first uproots whole communities to clear the space, then turns the area into a desert outside worktime and condemns office workers to long, tiring journeys to and from work. 'Scientific management', which made jobs in offices heavily specialised, tries to ensure that the worker gets no understanding or control of the work process as a whole. Technological changes are carrying this ever further, as computers and microprocessor based equipment take over the flow of information, removing the need for skills such as shorthand and typing. To use office workers simply as cogs in this vast machine may make sense for the efficient management of an industrial society — it is never in the interest of those people who are used in this way.

One woman writing about her work, said:

> 'People who perform passionless routines among hostile machines (are) squashed flat by office pyramids and pecking orders…Most people don't seem to see that *office life* is a contradiction in terms. Office walls act as filters or transformers, dulling and dehumanising every aspect of human existence…Our offices gobble up our best hours and real energy, drained of which we return (at six, seven, eight) to the homes and relationships which are supposed to be the most important things in our lifes.'
> (Janet Watts, *The Observer*, 29 October 1978)

Trade unionism

'I DON'T NEED A UNION DEAH BOY; YOU SEE, I'VE GOT BWAINS'

Many nineteenth-century clerks were loath to join trade unions because that was what the labouring classes did. They felt superior. For the most part their grievances (nepotism, low pay, cramped conditions) were not articulated because clerks were socially isolated from one another and depended on the goodwill of their employer. The earliest attempts to start unions were in the large offices — Civil Service, railways, banking and insurance. At the beginning of this century the National Union of Clerks established a 'Clerks' Charter':

The Clerks' Charter.

1 A *Wage* that will enable them to live as educated citizens;
2 Healthy and comfortable *Offices* wherein they can work and keep sound minds in healthy bodies;
3 *Hours* that will not leave those minds and bodies exhausted at the end of the day, but will leave them *Leisure* to develop their faculties and their individuality.

Both the Association of Women Clerks and Secretaries and the National Union of Clerks campaigned for inspection and improvement of office conditions and for better pay. They worked closely together and finally merged into the Clerical and Administrative Workers' Union, now known as APEX. Other white-collar unions were formed later and have been growing ever since.

Clerks in the nineteenth century had a heavy mortality rate and stood lowest on the scale, with expectation of life only 75 per cent of the average (plumbers 81 per cent, miners 85 per cent). The main killer was tuberculosis and other respiratory diseases caused by ill-ventilated, damp and insanitary offices and crowded travel to and from work.

In 1911 the National Union of Clerks (NUC) began a campaign to fight tuberculosis and to get offices protected by legislation similar to the Factories Acts. Their Clerks' Charter stated:

> 'Clerks who do not help to get the NUC Inspection Bill through Parliament are by their *Apathy Helping in the Manslaughter of* thousands of their fellows. The death rate of clerks from lung disease is *twice* that of the ordinary population.'

In 1916 women clerks could expect the shortest lives of all occupations in the United States — again due to tuberculosis. In 1930 the International Labour Organisation recorded 'consumption' (tuberculosis) as still a major occupational disease for office workers.

> 'When you see a pale-faced multitude of clerks, victims of tubercular and nervous trouble, you may be sure that the impure air and unhealthy conditions of offices play a large part in the holocaust.' (National Federation of Professional Workers, *A Much Needed Measure,* 1926)

In a job which involved a great deal of copying, 'writer's cramp'

LONDON
WOMEN CLERKS' WEEK
OCTOBER 13th - 20th

AWKS

Join the Awks
The Association of Women Clerks
& Secretaries. 1 Churton St. S.W.

was common, and the clerks' unions succeeded in getting it recognised as an industrial disease. But pneumonia, heart disease, fatigue and digestive disorders were also the occupational diseases of office workers, and the latter three still are.

In the newly mechanised offices of the early twentieth century workers were exposed to the jangling of telephones and the clatter of typewriters, and to the danger of gas explosions. Eyestrain and nervous disorders continued to plague office workers. And until employers were forced to improve working conditions by law, in 1963, dirty, overcrowded rooms lacking ventilation and natural light, with insanitary toilet facilities, were common. The campaign to include offices in protective legislation was won only after fifty years of union campaigns. The Offices, Shops and Railway Premises Act of 1963 provided a basic minimum standard. In 1974, after more trade union pressure, all workplaces were included under the Health and Safety at Work Act. There is little documentation about the struggles of office workers and their successes in negotiating better conditions — but many have done so, and many more continue to struggle today. Some of their stories are told in this book.

Bernard Shaw said that the two groups most resistant to trade unionism were clerks and women. This may have been true in his day, but things are changing:

> 'The introduction of job evaluation into the white collar field has...caused great dissatisfaction, particularly in areas like banking where the 'grace and favour' system prevailed for many years, and merit awards were payable annually or biennially provided staff kept their noses clean.' (*Frank Dowling,* ASTMS organiser, City of London and banking)

Trade unionism in offices has more than doubled since even the late sixties. In 1967 only 18 per cent of office managements were negotiating with unions: in 1974 it was 40 per cent. Nonetheless, offices are still poorly organised, especially in the private sector: business offices, banks, insurance, the legal profession. It is difficult to organise where the pattern is small, widely spread workplaces. Office workers' history is like that of farmworkers — traditionally isolated and exploited. This is not such a problem in the public sector, in the civil service or local government, and office workers employed in factory offices also tend to be in trade unions.

Some employers still have 'house unions' or staff associations which operate against the long-term interests of workers: how many of these are campaigning for shorter hours, for example? They mostly offer fringe benefits to members, such as Barclay's offer insurance, and a lower membership fee than the equivalent trade union.

There is resistance among some office workers to the idea of trade unions. Some identify with their employer rather than with their co-workers. Their attitude is not surprising given the media's treatment of trade unions, whose members are pictured as mindless militants, unconcerned about other workers. And office workers often fear that protests against bad conditions or low pay will run them the risk of getting fired.

There have always been forms of resistance, however small. These range from staying away from work to paying many visits to the loo, refusal to get the boss's tea, protests about the rules for dress at work, complaints about overheating or tea breaks. It is possible to resist individually in this way, but it is more effective if office workers get together and decide that they will not, say, give in to management's demands for more work when one of the major causes of stress is speed-up. In this way, office workers together can organise a slowdown to improve working conditions.

Being in the union is particularly important where health and safety are concerned, because only where you are organised in a recognised trade union — one independent of management and recognised by them for negotiation — can you claim your legal right to elect a safety representative under the Health and Safety at Work Act. Safety reps can then claim rights to information, facilities and to hold inspections — all of which strengthen your ability to get safer and healthier working conditions from your employer.

If you are not a member of a trade union, you're on your own, you've no right to a safety rep and will have to rely on the goodwill of your employer.

Women and trade unions

Women are joining unions at a faster rate than ever before. In 1930, 468,090 women in Britain were in a union; by 1969 this had risen to 1,750,000 and by 1979 to 3,500,000. Now three out of every ten trade unionists are women. But some women don't. Why? Many women don't join the union because they see their work as temporary or part-time (even though they may do paid work for most of their lives). Temps don't tend to join unions. They work totally in isolation and are among the most exploited of office workers. The system of contract temps makes it harder for other workers to organise; they weaken the unions' negotiating position. Part-timers and temps often don't know how to go about joining a union or which one to join.

Most women are taught that their jobs aren't a very important part of their lives. Women's responsibilities have often taken them in and out of the labour market as they juggle jobs, home, husbands and children. Jobs seem temporary so it's hard to build permanent union organisation. Union meetings are often held at the wrong time for women.

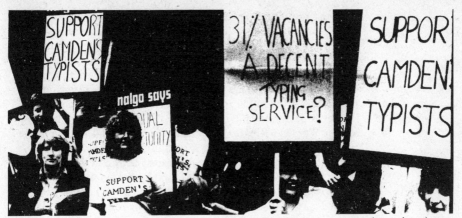

However, things seem to be changing, as women, through union
organisation and struggles for equal pay and job opportunity,
threaten to end employers' freedom to use them as a cheap labour
supply. Already in the public sector a higher proportion of women
than men are in unions.

Women who are reluctant to join unions often ask, 'What would
the union do for me?' With many unions still dominated by men,
even where the members are mostly women, the answer is often
'not much'. How far can trade unions be said to represent the
particular interests of women? It varies with the union, of course.
AUEW/TASS has a Rights for Women campaign. 'We believe in
positive discrimination, because unless special attention is paid to
the problems of women, their position is usually ignored.' (From
A New Deal for Office Staff, published by TASS)

The feeling of many women active in the labour movement is that
the time is ripe to push for a much shorter working week and a
shorter working year, for both men and women. This would break
down the distinction between part- and full-time and would mean
that 'part-time' workers all got full benefits. But we also feel we
have to change the nature of work. For too long we have just
been pressing for 'a woman's right to work'. We also want safe
work, interesting work. We need to change the way men do jobs,
the way men have organised work. We don't just want equal
access to the competitive male world. We need to challenge male
traditions of competition and specialisation. We have to fight
sexism in all its forms, both on the job and in the union. But
unionisation is the main tool for change, and so perhaps the most
urgent task facing those who want to change the servicing role
that women are given in offices is to become active in a union and
force it to serve women's needs.

There is a long tradition of women organising separately in trade
unions. The Association of Women Clerks and Secretaries, formed
in 1912, was for women only, but they worked closely with the
National Union of Clerks for better conditions and equal pay.

181

Women's groups inside trade unions have been springing up in recent years, both at branch and at national level. There are groups within ASTMS, NATFHE, NUPE and the NUT. Women who organised a women's group within their London polytechnic's branch of NALGO found that women who were previously resistant to the union are now pouring in. They are discussing such issues as the implication of microprocessors for women, and the need for nurseries. Women in the CPSA formed the Civil Service Women's Rights Group in 1978, open to all women in the civil service unions. The group is organising campaigns, eg. for creches, the right to abortion, and against sexism in the union. Typists in NALGO and NUPE, inspired by the typists' strike for better wages and prospects at Camden Council in London, have formed a Typists' Charter. They are fighting for the upgrading of typists and typing supervisors, an end to qualification bars, better training opportunities, and no word processors. (See Appendix 2 for addresses)

Some of our organised sisters in the United States have a Bill of Rights which takes some steps in this direction:

1   *The right to respect as women and as office workers.*
2   *The right to comprehensive, written job descriptions specifying the nature of all duties expected of the employee.*
3   *The right to defined and regular salary reviews and cost-of-living adjustments.*
4   *The right to detailed descriptions specifying compensation, terms, conditions and benefits of employment.*
5   *The right to compensation for overtime work and for work not included in our job descriptions.*
6   *The right to choose whether to do the personal work of employers (typing personal letters, serving coffee, running out for lunch).*
7   *The right to maternity benefits and to having pregnancy and other gynaecological conditions treated as temporary medical disabilities.*
8   *The right to benefits equal to those of men in similar job categories.*
9   *The right to equal access to promotion opportunities and on-the-job training programs.*
10   *The freedom to choose one's lifestyle and to participate in on-the-job organising or outside activities which do not detract from the execution of assigned tasks.*
11   *The right to written and systematic grievance procedures.*
12   *An end to discrimination on the basis of sex, age, race, creed, national origin, marital status, parenthood or disability as insured by the laws of the State of New York; and end to discrimination on the basis of affectional or sexual preference.*

A health survey is an excellent way of tracking down occupational illnesses – health problems that people share due to their jobs. Below is a sample questionnaire which you could adapt for use in your office. You may wish for example to follow up a particular problem, say eyestrain. You could ask the questions about eyes and also the ones on headaches. It might be useful to combine some of the questions with a checklist from a relevant chapter eg. lighting. Keep the list of questions as short as possible. When you get the questionnaire back you'll need to analyse the results. Make a list of the symptoms people are suffering and see if a lot of people are complaining about particular ones eg. sore eyes. The next step is to see if they coincide with suspected hazards in the office, eg. VDUs or lighting.

The conclusions you draw from your results should give you some guidance on the next steps to take. If a good percentage of people are suffering from eyestrain, and the lighting seems to be the problem, inform your members of the results of the survey and decide on what action to take. Check the sickness records too. The data you have collected will arm you with hard evidence to back up your case when you start negotiating to get something done about the problem. The individual answers should be strictly confidential.

The Questionnaire

1   Name (optional)

2   Department/Area

3   Age Group: Under 21   21-30   31-45   46-55   Over 55

4   Sex

5   Which of these categories describes your health
     Excellent   Good   Average   Bad

6   Do you suffer from any of the following while on the job:

	Often	Sometimes	Never
Digestive disorders			
Eyestrain			
Headaches			
Tension eg. digestive			
Tiredness			
Sore throat			
Sore eyes			
Stiff shoulders or neck			
Backache			
Nausea			
Skin rashes			
Varicose veins			
Bad chest			
Other			

Please give further details if you wish

7   Do you find you have more or fewer absences from work on account of transient illness eg. colds, headaches, flu, since starting this job?

More   Less   About the same

8   Do you visit your doctor more or less frequently since starting here

More   Less   About the same

9   Do you know what, if anything, your doctor has diagnosed?

Yes
No

Can you give details?

10 What are the health and safety problems that most affect you?

11 *Eyes and eyesight*
    Do your eyes bother you. What do you think the cause is?

12 Do you wear glasses or contact lenses?   Yes
                                                              No

    Did you wear them before you started here?   Yes
                                                              No

13 Do you feel there has been a deterioration in your eyesight   Yes
    since starting your present job?   No

14 If so, what do you think the cause(s) is?

15 *Headaches*
    Do your headaches occur mainly inside or outside working hours?

Outside   Inside   Both

16 Do they generally occur at a particular time?

Morning   Midday   Afternoon   Evening   No specific time

17 Do you think any of these factors contribute to your headaches?
    (Please tick)

                                        Yes   No   Perhaps

Stress
Lighting
Airconditioning
Smoke in atmosphere
Chemical fumes
Noise
Other (please specify)

18 *Fertility hazards*
    Have you ever suffered any of the following symptoms while at work
    here?   Yes   No

Irregular periods
Miscarriage
Other childbirth related problems
Sterility

Appendix 2 Help

Where to go for help to fight for better working conditions in offices.
Local Health and safety groups have all sorts of resources.
Find your nearest group from the list below:

Bedford – BASH
Bedford Association for Safety and Health
Secretary: David Lewis, 146 Spring Road, Kempston, Bedford.
Phone 0234 66755.

Birmingham – BRUSH
Birmingham Region Union Health and Safety Campaign
Secretary: Eric Shakespeare
160 Corisande Road, Birmingham 29.
Phone 021 471 1236.
Meetings: First Wednesday in the month, 7.30 pm, 164 Edmund St., Birmingham 3.

Bristol – BASH
Bristol Action on Safety and Health
Secretary: J. Halliday, 6 Keynes Road, Clevedon, Bristol.

Cannock – CHASE
Cannock Health and Safety Experiment
Secretary: Betty Dugmore
56 Grange Crescent, Penkridge, Staffs.

Cardiff
Contact: Jean Hare, 34 Maitland Street, Cardiff CF4 3J4

Coventry – CHASM
Coventry Health and Safety Movement
Secretary: Tony Hitchins, 229 Bredon Avenue, Binley, Coventry.
Phone 0203 456635.
Information Centre: Charterhouse, London Road, Coventry.
Meetings: Every Wednesday evening.

Derby – DASH
Derby Area Safety and Health
Secretary. Mick McLoughlin
Advice Sessions: Last Thursday in the month, RAOB Club, 34 Charnwood Street, Derby.

Doncaster – HASSARD
Secretary: John Dickenson, 29 High Street, Arksey, Doncaster DN5 0SE.
Phone 0302 874372.
Meetings: First Wednesday in the month, Trades Hall, Room 7.

Dunfermline – DASH
Dunfermline Area Safety and Health Group
Secretary: Mike Morris, Clackmannon House, Clackmannon.

Harlow – HTCHSG
Harlow Trades Council Health and Safety Group
Contact. Branch Chairperson, WEA.
Phone Harlow 416249.

Hull – HASH
Hull Action on Safety and Health
3 Ferens Avenue, Cottingham Road, Hull.

Isle of Wight – IWTUSG
Secretary: J. Lamb, 95 Sandcroft Avenue, Ryde, Isle of Wight.

Kent
North Kent Health and Safety Group
Secretary: K. Davenport
111 Twydall Lane, Gillingham, Kent.
Phone Medway 34125
Meetings: Third Thursday in the month, WEA Office, 4 Castle Hill, Rochester.

Leeds – LASH
Leeds Action on Safety and Health
Secretary: P. H. Thorpe, 6 Blenheim Terrace, Leeds 2. Phone 39633.

Leicestershire – LASSAM
Leicester Area Safety Action Movement
101 Hinkley Road, Leicester.
Phone Leicester 556614.

London North
North London Health and Safety Group
146 Kentish Town Road, London NW1 6QG.
Phone 01-485 6672.

London West
Middlesex – MASH
c/o 36 Blenheim Crescent, London W11. Phone 01-229 4714.

London South – SLASH
South London Action on Safety and Health, c/o 506 Brixton Road, London SW9 9EN.
Phone 01-733 4245.

London East
East London Health and Safety
Tony Fuller, 32 Roman Close, Rainham, Essex. Phone 01-592 3000 ext 2080 – daytime.

Tower Hamlets – THHUGS
Tower Hamlets and Hackney Union Group for Safety
Secretary: Jim Rogers
151 Bishopsfield, Harlow, Essex
home 0279 21561, work 980 1741

London South East – HASSEL
Health and Safety in South East London
Secretary: Doug McEwan,
6 Sedgebrook Road, Kidbrook, London SE3 8LP.
Advice Centre: Woolwich Adult Education Unit, 1a Burrage Road, Woolwich.
Meetings: Every Tuesday 7 - 9 pm.

Manchester – MASC
Secretary: Ken Green, 9 Dalston Drive, Didsbury, Manchester 20.
Phone 061 445 8795.

Merseyside – MHG
Merseyside Hazards Group
Secretary: Bob Isaac
10 Angus Road, Bromborough, Merseyside.
Meetings: Royal Institution, Colquitt Street, Liverpool L1, first Tuesday of the month
7 pm – 9 pm.

Middlesex
Middlesex Health and Safety Group
Contact: Ann Poyiadzis
45a Devonshire Road, Palmers Green, London N13.

Milton Keynes – MASH
Milton Keynes Association for Safety and Health
Chairperson: Ian Anderson
46 Blackdown, Fullers Slade, Milton Keynes, Bucks.
Phone 0908-564466.

Newcastle – TUSIU
Trade Union Studies Information Unit, Health and Safety Project, 'Southend' Fernwood Road, Jesmond, Newcastle.
Phone Newcastle 816087.

Norfolk – KLASH
King's Lynn Action on Safety and Health
Secretary: J. Wells, c/o TGWU, 16 Church Street, King's Lynn, Norfolk. Phone King's Lynn 65508/62080.

185

Nottingham – GNASH
Greater Nottingham Action on Safety and Health, 118 Mansfield Road, Nottingham. Phone 0602 582369

Rotherham – WISH
Workers in Safety and Health
Secretary: E.J. Hartley, WEA, Chantry Buildings, Corporation Street, Rotherham, Yorkshire. Phone 71016 74703.

Scotland West
West of Scotland Health and Safety Group
Alison West, Workers' Educational Association, 212 Bath Street, Glasgow G2 4HW
Meetings: Glasgow Trades Council, 83 Carlton Place, Glasgow

Sheffield – TUSC
Sheffield Trade Union Safety Committee
Secretary: Seb Schmoller, 312 Albert Road, Sheffield 8. STD 0742 584559.

Southampton – WHAC
Work Hazards Advisory Committee
Secretary: Graham Peterson, 27 Pointout Road, Bassett, Southampton.
Resource Centre: 4 Carlton Crescent, Southampton. Phone 0703 29810.
Meetings: Every Monday 6 – 9 pm.

Telford – TRASH
Telford and Region Action on Safety and Health
Secretary: Jim Bradford, 67 High Street, Dawley, Telford, Shropshire.

Walsall WASH
Trade Union WEA Branch
Secretary: George Mason, Schoolhouse, Teddesley Street, Walsall, West Midlands.

Worcester WASH
Worcester Action on Safety and Health
Secretary: Sylvie Pierce, c/o 95 Tudor Way, Dines Green, Worcester.
Meetings: Second Wednesday in the month, at Labour Club, New Street, Worcester.

Wolverhampton and West Bromwich
a new group is forming
Contact: J. Jones, TGWU Offices Berry Street, Wolverhampton.

Inspectors	You'll find the address of the local Health and Safety Executive in the phone book, or write to the Central Office at Baynards House, 1 Chepstow Place, Westbourne Grove, London W2 (01-229 3456). If you are covered by local government inspectors, ring the council for the Environmental Health Department.
TUC Centenary Institute of Occupational Health	Keppel Street, London WC1 (01-580 2386). Contact them through your own union's head office.
Employment and Medical Advisory Service	Contact them through the HSE or look in the phone book.
Stress	Local women's centres may give support. See phone book. *Women's Therapy Centre,* 19a Hartham Road, London N7.
Noise	Universities of Aston in Birmingham, Southampton and Salford in Manchester have noise assessment departments. Livingston – Hire, rents out noise meters. *Livingston Hire,* 27 Camden Road, London NW1 rent measuring equipment.
Lighting	*Illuminating Engineering Society, CIBS,* 222 High Road, London SW12 (01-675 5211). *British Standards Institute,* 2 Park Street, London W1. Will answer enquiries on their published standards.
Dangerous Substances	*TUC Centenary Institute of Occupational Health,* Keppel Street, London WC1 (01-580 2386). Contact them through your own union's head office. Local HSE offices have lists of consultants who will survey dusts etc. For measuring some substances, you'll need a Draegar tube, from Draegar Normalair, Blyth, Northumberland.

Temperature and Ventilation	*British Institute of Heating and Ventilation Engineers, CIBS.* (see Lighting) Humidity monitors for hire from Livingston Hire. (see Noise)
Basics	*British Standards Institute.* (see Seating) Nurseries: *Civil Service Creche Campaign* c/o 25 Villa Road, London SW9.
Safety	*British Standards Institute.* (see Seating) *ROSPA,* Cannon House, The Priory, Queensway, Birmingham 4. *British Safety Council,* 62 Chancellors Road, London W6.
New Technology	*BSSRS Microprocessors Group,* 9 Poland Street, London W1 (01-437 2728). *TUC Printing Industries Committee,* SOGAT House, 220 High Street North, Dunstable, Bedfordshire. *Trade Union Community and Resources Information Centre (TUCRIC),* 29 Blenheim Terrace, Leeds.
Law	Local law centres and citizens' advice bureaux addresses can be found in the phone book. *National Council for Civil Liberties,* 186 Kings Cross Road, London WC1.
Organising	Some 'white collar' unions' addresses: *Amalgamated Union of Engineering,* Workers Technical and Supervisory Section, Onslow Hall, Little Green, Richmond, Surrey. *Association of Scientific and Technical, Managerial Staff,* 10 Jamestown Road, London NW1. *Association of Professional, Clerical and Computer Staff,* 22 Worple Road, London SW19. *Civil and Public Servants Union,* 215 Balham High Road, London SW17. *Civil Service Union,* 17 Hatton Wall, London EC1. *General and Municipal Workers Union,* Thorne House, Ruxley Ridge, Esher, Surrey. *Inland Revenue Staff Federation,* 7 St George's Square, London SW1. *Institute of Professional Civil Servants,* 3 Northumberland Street, London WC2. *National Association of Local Government Officers,* 1 Mabledon Place, London WC1. *National Union of Journalists,* 314 Gray's Inn Road, London WC1. *National Union of Public Employees,* 8 Aberdeen Terrace, London SE3. *Transport and General Workers' Union/ Association of Clerical, Technical and Scientific Staff,* Transport House, Smith Square, London SW1.

Pressure Groups within the Unions	Usually produce a magazine and hold meetings: *Red Collar:* rank and file ASTMS members. 34 Cowley Road, Oxford. *Redder Tape:* rank and file civil servants. c/o 265 Seven Sisters Road, London N4. *Nalgo Action:* rank and file NALGO members. 81 Downs Park Road, London E5. *Typists' Charter:* mainly typists in NALGO and NUPE. 48 Forburg Road, London N16 (01-986 3266 Ext 438). *Civil Servants Women's Rights Group* c/o Ruth Harris, 1c Queens Avenue, London N10.
Miscellaneous	*LUCAS Aerospace Shop Stewards Combine Committee,* CAITS, North East London Polytechnic, Barking, Essex. *Working Women* (US National Association of Office Workers), 140 Clarendon Street, Boston, MA 02116 (produce excellent leaflets on a wide range of issues on which they campaign). *Labour Research Department,* 78 Blackfriars Road, London SE1. Excellent enquiry service for branches who affiliate. Lots of helpful publications too. *Socialist Medical Association,* 9 Poland Street, London W1 (01-439 3395). Can provide speakers. *Workers Educational Association,* 9 Upper Berkeley Street, London W1. The WEA organises trade union courses. See phone book for local addresses. *Films.* Most of the organisations listed will provide speakers to come to branch meetings. Another way of livening up meetings is to show a film or video. Here are some highly recommended ones: *Risky Business.* Ten minute colour cartoon film on general health and safety. Available for hire or 16mm film or video from Leeds Animation Workshop, 20 Westminster Buildings, 31 New York Street, Leeds 2. *Working for Your Life.* One hour long colour American documentary film. Focuses on the health hazards facing working women. For hire from Women and Work Hazards Group. *When the Chips are Down.* 'Horizon' documentary on new technology. On hire from BBC TV, phone: 07333-52257

Ask your library to order any of the books below, which you feel would be useful. Your union branch may wish to purchase some and build up a members' library. Many of the books below are available from:

Trade Union Book Service, 265 Seven Sisters Road, London N4 (01-802 6145).
Sisterwrite, 190 Upper Street, London N1 (01-226 9782).
Your local library may be able to help you find the periodicals in the footnotes.

General Health and Safety
The Hazards of Work by P. Kinnersley, Photo Press, 1977.
Work is Dangerous to Your Health by J.M. Stellman and S.M. Daum, Pantheon, 1973.
International Labour Office, *Encyclopaedia of Occupational Health and Safety,* Geneva, 1972.
Hazards Bulletin, published 5 times a year by BSSRS. Aimed at trade unionists, and contains useful legal and technical information. A must for every safety representative.
Many unions have now produced pamphlets for safety representatives eg. TGWU, NUPE.

Below are some recommended publications under each chapter heading. These are in addition to books referred to in the footnotes.

Stress
Women's Work, Women's Health: Myths and Realities (Chapter 2) by J.M. Stellman, Pantheon, 1977.
Sexual Shakedown (on sexual harassment) by L. Farley, McGraw Hill, 1979.
Prevention of Stress at Work ASTMS Policy Document, 1981.
Shiftwork GMWU, 1980.
Stress at Work by Dr N. Donald and M. Doyal, WEA, 1980.

Noise
Noise and Office Work by S.T. Mackenzie, New York School of Industrial and Labour Relations, Cornell University, Ithica, New York.

Lighting
Lighting in Offices, Shops and Railway Premises Health and Safety at Work Booklet 39, HMSO.
Artificial Lighting CIS Information Sheet 11, International Labour Office, Geneva, 1966.
Essentials of Good Lighting — A Simple Guide for Industry by the Electricity Council.

Seating
Seats for Workers in Factories, Offices and Shops Health and Safety at Work Booklet 45, HMSO.
The Book of the Back by B. Inglis.
Workers' Handbook on Ergonomics forthcoming, Pluto Press.

Dangerous Substances	No one book has all the information on breakdown and composition of toxic substances. You'll need to compare information in one or two. See relevant sections in the general books by Kinnersley, and Stellman and Daum, above. *Dangerous Properties of Industrial Materials* by N.I. Sax Van Nostrand Reinhold, 1978. *Documentation of Threshold Limit Values* by American Conference of Governmental Industrial Hygienists, 1976. Gives background information on official standards. *Poisoning by Drugs and Chemicals* by Peter Cooper, Alchemist Publications, 1974. *The Prevention of Occupational Cancer* ASTMS Policy Document, 1980.
Temperature and Ventilation	*Ventilation and Airconditioning Requirements* by Chartered Institute of Building Services (CIBS), 1972. *Ventilation of Buildings: fresh air requirements,* HSE Guidance Note EG22, 1979, HMSO.
Basics	*Cloakroom Accommodation and Washing Facilities* Health and Safety at Work Booklet 5, HMSO. Redgraves Guide to OSPRA.
Nurseries	*TUC Charter of Facilities for the Under-Fives,* 1978. *Workplace Nurseries: A Negotiating Kit* NALGO, 1979, The Kingsway Children's Centre. For report on this Trade Union organised, employer provided nursery, send SAE to Kingsway Hall, Kingsway, London WC2.
Safety	*Is My Office Safe?* Civil Service Training Department, HMSO, 1978. *Guide to the Fire Precautions Act,* 1971 Health and Safety at Work Booklet 3, HMSO. *What to do if you have an Accident at Work* Coventry Health and Safety Movement Checklist No.1 (address see Appendix 2). *Safety Representatives Guide to Fire Precautions* WEA, 1978.
New Technology	*The VDT Manual* by A. Cakir and others, IFRA, Inca-Fiej Research Association, Washington Platz 1, D-6100 Darmstadt, Germany. *The Hazards of VDU's* TUCRIC, 29 Blenheim Terrace, Leeds 2 (excellent leaflet for distribution to all office staff). *VDU's, Eyestrain and Low Back Pain* Scottish Ergonomics Study Group, Napier College, Edinburgh, 1979 (papers also on microfiches). 'Eye Discomfort when reading microfilm in different enlargers' by G.V. Hulfgren in *Applied Ergonomics* Volume 5 No. 4, pp. 194-200, 1974. *Microchips: The New Technology* Counter Information Services, 1979.

Job Massacre in the Office — Word Processors
Womens Voice, 1978.
Many unions have now produced pamphlets. One
of the best is *Automation and the Office Worker*
APEX, 1980 (good on agreements).

Law
Rights at Work by J. McMullen, Pluto Press, 1978.
Law at the Workplace WEA, 1975.
(The HSE, the TUC and many unions produce
leaflets on health and safety and the law)

Organising on
Health and Safety
Sick Pay — A Negotiator's Guide Labour Research
Department, 1980.
*Safety Representatives: Shop Floor Organisation
for Health and Safety* by M. Cunningham, WEA,
1978.
Hazard Spotting — A Guide for Safety Reps
Labour Research Department, 1980.
Time Off for Union Activities TUC, Great Russell
Street, London W1, 1978.

Women and
Organising
Part-Time Workers Need Full-Time Rights NCCL,
1980.
Women's Rights Pack NCCL, 1980.
*No Turning Back: Writings from the Women's
Movement 1975-1980* The Womens Press, 1981.
Maternity Rights for Working Women NCCL, 1980.

Health
*Working for Your Life: A Woman's Guide to Job
Health Hazards* by A. Hricko and M. Brunt, LOHP,
California, 1976.
Our Bodies, Ourselves Boston Women's Collective,
Penguin, 1979.
Women and Migraine, from 7 St Marks Rise,
London E8, 1980.
*For Her Own Good — 150 Years of the Experts'
Advice to Women* by B. Ehrenreich and D. English,
Pluto Press, 1979.
The Political Economy of Health by L. Doyal,
Pluto Press, 1979.

Office Work
Pink Collar Worker by L.K. Howe, Avon, 1977.
Labour and Monopoly Capital by H. Braverman,
Monthly Review Press, 1974.

APEX	Association of Professional, Executive, Clerical and Computer Staff
ASTMS	Association of Scientific, Technical and Managerial Staff
AUEW-TASS	Amalgamated Union of Engineering Workers – Technical and Supervisory Section
BIFU	Banking, Insurance and Finance Union
BSSRS	British Society for Social Responsibility in Science
CBI	Confederation of British Industry
CIBS	Chartered Institute of Building Services
CSCC	Civil Service Creche Campaign
CND	Campaign for Nuclear Disarmament
CSD	Civil Service Department
CPSA	Civil and Public Servants Association
dB	Decibels
DHSS	Department of Health and Social Security
EMAS	Employment & Medical Advisory Service
GEC	General Electricity Council
GLC	Greater London Council
GMWU	General and Municipal Workers Union
GP	General Practitioner (Doctor)
GPO	General Post Office
HASAWA	Health and Safety at Work Act
HSE	Health and Safety Executive (Government Inspectors)
HMFI	Her Majesty's Factory Inspectorate (replaced by HSE)
HMSO	Her Majesty's Stationery Office (Government bookshop)
IBM	International Business Machines
ICI	Imperial Chemical Industries
IES	Illuminating Engineering Society (now in CIBS)
IRSF	Inland Revenue Staff Federation
mg/M3	micrograms per cubic metre (dust measurement)
mm	millimetre
NALGO	National Association of Local Government Officers
NATSOPA	National Society of Operative Printers, Graphic and Media Personnel
NCCL	National Council for Civil Liberties
NELP	North East London Polytechnic
NGA	National Graphical Association
NIOSH	National Institute for Occupational Safety and Health (USA)
SCPS	Society of Civil and Public Servants
SOGAT	Society of Graphical and Allied Trades
SRSC Regs	Safety Representatives and Safety Committees Regulations
TGWU/ACTSS	Transport and General Workers Union – Association of Clerical, Technical and Scientific Staff
TLV	Threshold Limit Value
TUC	Trades Union Congress
TUCRIC	Trade Union and Community Resources and Information Centre
VDT	Visual Display Terminals (VDU's in USA)
VDU	Visual Display Units
WEA	Workers Educational Association

Index

* NOTE: *Figures in brackets are Section Numbers*

* NOTE: *Figures in brackets are* section *Numbers*

194

DANGER
PEOPLE AT WORK

Whilst the above illustration is a lighthearted look at just a few of the dangers that await you in a normal office environment – It does illustrate that accidents can happen –and that usually they are not funny.

The N.G.A. is not just an organisation to win you better pay and working hours. – It is there to ensure better – and safer working conditions – to advise you of dangers you might not even know existed, and to ensure proper compensation for accidents that do occur. The N.G.A. is not designed just for people on the shop floor but for everybody working within the printing industry.

Send for more information to

National Graphical Association
Graphic House, 63-67 Bromham Road, Bedford.

AGRICAPITAL

HAZARDS BULLETIN

This bi-monthly bulletin is a national Hazards publication written by and for trade unionists. It has been going four years and has now reached nearly twenty issues. It provides a good source of recent shop-floor struggles over health and safety; easily readable technical and medical information; recent government publications; information on what the 25 or so TU health and safety groups are doing up and down the country and comments etc. There is an active letters page where safety reps exchange views, air problems and seek support for campaigns. There is a regular interview with safety reps.

Hazards Bulletin aims to be a living publication to help with TU struggles over health and safety issues at the shop-floor level. Not another health and safety magazine saying 'it's all your fault' and pushing more safety clothing so that you end up like somebody on a trip to the moon!

Subscribe now! £2.10 per year (or five issues) post free.
Much reduced prices on bulk orders of five or more. Please contact us for details.

ISSN 0140-0525

Other publications from BSSRS Work Hazards Group.

ASBESTOS, KILLER DUST
A worker/community guide: how to fight the hazards of asbestos and its substitutes

The book that sums up all that is known about the effects of asbestos on your health, why the excuses given by the asbestos industry just don't hold water. It examines the role of our 'protectors': government, industry, scientists and doctors. And it's a worker/community guide on how to deal with asbestos — what are its substitutes, how can it be removed safely, how those who remove it can be protected. And above all, how trade unionists, community groups and individuals can and do fight this hazard.

OIL
A workers' guide to the health hazards and how to fight them

Oil used in industrial processes gives rise to a large number of diseases, including skin cancer. One engineering factory with 30 toolmaking machines estimates it loses 1000 gallons of oil a year in oil mist — and a lot of that ends up in the workers' lungs, eyes, stomach and on their skin. This pamphlet not only sets out what damage oil can do, but how this can be prevented — and, more important, what is and isn't being done by government and unions — and what we can do ourselves.

NOISE
Fighting the most widespread industrial disease

If you have to raise your voice to be heard at work, whether because of the noise from heavy machinery in the factory or typewriters in the office, then your hearing is at risk. If you're an industrial worker the chances are it's already damaged. This pamphlet not only outlines the dangers, but also what you and your union can do about them; how to measure noise levels, what rights you have under the law, the technical aspects of noise reduction.

VIBRATION
A workers' guide to the health hazards and their prevention

Vibration can kill. In 1969 a 59-year-old road driller died as a result of gangrene of his fingers caused by the vibrations of a pneumatic drill. And it maims many more. Pneumatic drills are the worst. At risk too are tractor, lorry, bus drivers, those who work with a whole range of hand-held tools such as chainsaws. This pamphlet looks at the dangers, and what can be done.

Available from
TRADE UNION BOOKSERVICE
265 Seven Sisters Road   London N4 2DE